Collected Poems
of Henry Thoreau

COLLECTED POEMS

of

Henry Thoreau

Enlarged Edition

Edited by Carl Bode

The Johns Hopkins Press   Baltimore   1964

To Barbara, Janet, and Carolyn

INTRODUCTION

"The purest strain, and the loftiest, I think, that has yet pealed from this unpoetic American forest," Ralph Waldo Emerson declared after being shown an early poem of Thoreau's.

A week later he wrote across the ocean to Thomas Carlyle about this young poet named Thoreau, who was writing "the truest verses." To the surprise of Concord, Emerson proceeded to act as evangelist for the poetry of his shy and prickly neighbor. But by 1841, two years after the letter to Carlyle, his enthusiasm had begun to cool. At that time the *Dial* was already being published, with Emerson and Margaret Fuller in charge of selecting the material to go into it. There the evangelist yielded to the editor; and Thoreau's verse, far from sacred, was exposed to heavy editorial suggestion or to rejection. And then, a year or so later, we know that Thoreau destroyed many of the verses he had written—destroyed them at the instance of Emerson, "who did not praise them."

There, in forecast, is the history of Thoreau's reputation as a poet. A hundred years ago, great men—as they are now reckoned in American literature—talked about his poems. Not always esteemed, the verses were by no means ignored. Bronson Alcott applauded them; Lowell asserted their rawness; Hawthorne gave them a grudging approval. Yet by about 1847 Thoreau's prose was beginning its bid for recognition; and soon, in his own eyes and in the eyes of his circle, Thoreau began to be viewed as a writer whose destined medium was prose. By the time of his death he was known to the discerning as a man to be reckoned with in American letters. By the turn of the century, Thoreau, author of *Walden*, was world-renowned. And Thoreau the poet was forgotten.

The world thus repeated Emerson's change of attitude toward Thoreau's verse. But there was a difference. Emerson afterward achieved a balanced judgment. His early praise and his later criticism corrected one another, and his final verdict, prepared shortly after Thoreau died, gave the poetry measured praise. In Thoreau's work, pronounced Emerson, it was true that the gold did "not yet run pure," was "drossy and crude." But still, it was gold. Then too, although Thoreau lacked technical ease, he had the genius of the true poet. Moreover, Emerson added, in a comment that was often to be echoed, Thoreau's "biography is in his verses."

That the poetry Henry Thoreau scrawled and labored over, and later neglected, has its defects as well as its values, no one would deny. Yet almost every bit of the verse has a dry, oblique power. It has, moreover, the virtue of lighting up its creator's life. There is of course the biography of the heart and the biography of the mind. The poems can help us to understand both. On the one hand, for example, Thoreau's earnest love for Ellen Sewall is illuminated in the lyrics he wrote when she came into his life. On the other, his rigid principle of intellect is revealed in such a poem as "Wait not till slaves pronounce the word," where his searching advice to the abolitionists is to remember that there are more forms of slavery besides negro slavery, there are subtler masters enchaining us all.

A generation before Emerson's penetrating remark, Thoreau himself had spoken to the point, saying "Poetry is a piece of very private history, which unostentatiously lets us into the secret of a man's life." Indeed, though Thoreau came to see, as everyone still does, that prose was his medium, he by no means overlooked the importance of poetry. For several years after graduation from "Cambridge College" he considered himself a practicing poet. Much of the large amount of verse he mentions writing has not come down to us, but what is left still forms a far larger body than a glance through his collected works might lead anyone to think. Furthermore, Thoreau did not confine himself to the actual production of poems. He found time to develop and set forth a considerable poetics. His statements about poetry and the poet are scattered through both the books and essays, and the Journal. In synthesis they embody a theory that is shrewd as well as intuitive. Thoreau, as a matter of record, maintained his interest in the theory of poetry long after he abandoned the practice. Jottings about the function of the poet appear in the Journal almost to the end. True, by then Thoreau had widened the definition of his important terms, *poet* and *poetry*, but his final comments still showed no basic conflict with his earliest pronouncements. So Thoreau theorized for nearly three decades but composed poems, with zeal, for only a handful of years. In that fact lies one of the main causes for the long-continued neglect of his verse by others. Thoreau's own loss of interest was duplicated by that of the rest of the world.

There are, on analysis, three major reasons why most persons have ignored Thoreau's poetry. The first in importance, perhaps, is its uneven quality. The second, and related, reason is the fact that he himself lost enthusiasm for the poetic medium; the quantity of his production quickly dwindled. The third is the mistaken belief that the verses are mere fragments woven into the prose, especially in the *Week*, and inseparable from it.

The quality and quantity of Thoreau's verse marched side by side during his literary career. When he wrote the most poetry, he was writing the best poetry—with one nearly inevitable qualification. Thoreau did improve, for a while, in his craft as he practiced it. He first paid distinct attention to verse writing in his final college years. His attempts at that time and up to about 1839 were uneven and mainly derivative. Among the best were "I am a parcel of vain strivings tied" and the 1838 "Friendship"; the worst included such an effusion as "My Boots." Soon he began to find his own style and approach, and, with a lapse in 1840, the years from 1839 through 1842 were his most skillful and productive. The readers of that radical publication, the *Dial*, were privileged to see some of the finest—in part despite editorial pressure and in part perhaps because of it—among Thoreau's poems. But the *Dial* did not live long, and by the time of its demise the output and quality of Thoreau's poetry had sagged. The most remarkable poems that he inserted in the 1849 *Week* were the very ones he had published in the *Dial* seven and eight years earlier. By February, 1852, Thoreau noted dryly but sadly:

> The strains from my muse are as rare nowadays,
> or of late years, as the notes of birds in the winter,—
> the faintest occasional tinkling sound, and mostly of

the woodpecker kind or the harsh jay or crow. It never melts into a song.

The verse used in *Walden,* except for the reprinted "Light-winged Smoke, Icarian bird," was negligible. The last few pieces set down in the Journal, aside from one final lyric of 1857, slid into prose. Then, aside from a line or so, Thoreau was done.

The third reason for the general neglect of his verse was given its fullest expression in the preface to the little volume of Thoreau's poetry, *Poems of Nature,* published in 1895. Explaining that it included only two-thirds (actually much less) of the available material, the editors, H. S. Salt and F. B. Sanborn, apologized for not printing more. Many lyrics, they argued, were nothing but pendants to Thoreau's prose; were little bits of verse, so interwoven that it would have been unjust, artistically, to wrench them from their context. The editors had the prose of the *Week* particularly in mind. It does have a great deal of verse apparently imbedded in it. Because the view put forth by Salt and Sanborn must be faced by anyone compiling a fuller edition of the poems, it ought at this point briefly to be examined. Was their stand well taken?

A study of the *Week* will tell. Close to a dozen of the fullest and most important poems in it had already been published, as separate poems, elsewhere. Most of them had appeared in the *Dial,* and all Thoreau did when he put them into the *Week* was to cut off their titles. In three cases he did not even do that. Besides these poems, there was a considerable number of others which Thoreau had composed, again separately, in his Journal. Later these were polished and inserted in the *Week.* A third group consists of fragments. They, it is true, are hard to separate from their prose context. On the other hand, these fragments are often parts of longer poems Thoreau had written, and can be collated against the full versions from which he took them. For example, Thoreau used half a dozen snatches of "The Assabet" and "Inspiration" in the *Week*. Yet they all exist as parts of these long full poems. There are also a few poems which are actually so interwoven in the prose that they contain references to the prose surrounding them. In those cases, a synopsis of the context has been added in the notes to the Critical Edition. There remain, finally, three or four poems that are fragmentary not through any fault of Thoreau's but because their opening pages have been cut out of the Journal in which he wrote them. To sum up, the great number of his poems can stand as entities and by themselves.

Here, then, is every available piece of original verse that Henry Thoreau composed. With only about half a dozen exceptions, it has the authority either of publication during his own life or else of his own autograph. In general, the posthumous verse is for the first time presented exactly—allowing for editorial error—as he wrote it. The glowing lines and the quiet, the prosaic and the Transcendental—they are all here. Almost all have at the very least the large, astringent force of young genius. Thoreau himself, let it be said, was pleased when his poetry won someone's commendation; but all, surely, that Thoreau would have needed to ask of the reader then or now, a century ago or today, is what his admired Wordsworth asked:

> One request I must make of my Reader, which is, that in judging these Poems, he would decide by his own feelings genuinely.

ACKNOWLEDGMENTS

For permission to use manuscripts of Thoreau's verse I am indebted to the Abernethy Library of American Literature, Middlebury College; the Harvard College Library; the Henry E. Huntington Library and Art Gallery; Mr. Albert Edgar Lownes; the Pierpont Morgan Library; the New York Public Library; Mr. W. Stephen Thomas; and the Yale University Library. The Houghton Mifflin Company has allowed me to quote from material by Thoreau, in particular, the published Journal and *Poems of Nature*, for which it holds the copyright.

I wish also to acknowledge the helpfulness of Professors Elsie F. Brickett and Gay W. Allen, who lent photostats and microfilms respectively. Dr. Viola White, besides preparing typescripts of the verse in the Abernethy Library, answered numerous questions connected with the edition; Miss Edythe N. Backus was responsible for the important Huntington Library transcriptions; and Mr. John Colwell recollated the poetry in the Harvard College Library. The painstaking secretarial help of Mrs. John W. Rau, Jr. and of Miss Dorothy Garrett has been invaluable. Nor should I want to take for granted the thorough coöperation afforded me by the librarians of Northwestern University and Keuka College. Henry Seidel Canby's careful and comprehensive biography has, for our generation, made any additional life of Thoreau unnecessary; and I have often drawn on his book for my notes, in the Critical Edition of the *Collected Poems*, on the content of the verse. Both Dr. Canby and Dr. Arthur Christy furthered the progress of my edition with information at their disposal; Mr. Walter Harding, secretary of the Thoreau Society, kindly checked the references about the Thoreau country in the notes to the

Critical Edition; and Professor Walter Hendricks was responsible for directing the book through the press.

This edition was first suggested to me by Professor Leon Howard of Northwestern University, and it owes much to his learning and common sense. My debt, finally, to my wife is great—how great, only someone who has undertaken a project like mine could appreciate.

C. B.

January 4, 1943

ENLARGED EDITION

In some ways Thoreau is now the most timely of our classic writers. As a matter of fact, interest has constantly mounted in every side of his work, including his poetry. Because both the Critical and Trade Editions of the *Collected Poems* are long out of print, indeed have become "rare books," it was felt that the time had come for a new printing, incorporating in it the miscellaneous poems to appear since the *Collected Poems* came out. For permission to add them to the others in the book, I am grateful to Professor Kenneth Cameron, Mr. George Davenport, Jr., and Mr. Charles Feinberg; to the librarians of the Harvard College Library, the New York Public Library, the Pierpont Morgan Library, and the Ridgley Library of Washington University; and to the Ralph Waldo Emerson Memorial Association. In addition, Professor Walter Harding should be thanked for bringing two of the poems to my attention.

Those are new debts I have incurred. I also want to acknowledge, again, one of long standing: to Leon Howard for first proposing that I study Thoreau.

C. B.

September 9, 1963

xiv

CONTENTS

---

* Titles of the poems are those drawn from the basic texts. If Thoreau omitted the title from the final version of a poem, the first line is used here, even though he may have given a title to earlier versions. Earlier titles, however, as well as those assigned by prior editors, are placed immediately below the title given. See also the Index of Titles and First Lines.

xvii

xix

xxii

Collected Poems
of Henry Thoreau

NOTE ON THE ORDER OF THE POEMS

Of the poems published mainly while Thoreau was still living those on pages 3-22 made their final appearance, during his lifetime, in the *Dial* and other periodicals. The only posthumously printed verses in this section, aside from "Carpe Diem," appeared in articles for which Thoreau had at least partly corrected the proofs and which came out in the *Atlantic Monthly* shortly after his death. The periodical verse is arranged in the order of publication; the couplets, however, are grouped together at the end of this section as are the couplets in succeeding sections. The quatrain on page 23 Thoreau printed in the 1849 edition of *A Week on the Concord and Merrimack Rivers* but dropped from the revised edition. The poems on pages 24-27 are the ones to be found in *Walden,* and the quatrain on page 28 first appeared in the 1864 edition of *The Maine Woods.* The poetry on pages 29-85 comes from the 1868 edition of the *Week.* When Thoreau revised the *Week* for this second edition, it should be noted, he made very few changes in the text of the poems; and he added only one quatrain and a couplet.

Of the poems unpublished during Thoreau's lifetime those on pages 86-187 have a date of composition determined, with the final date, if there are two or more, dictating where the poem is placed. The verse in this section is arranged chronologically. The poems without a known date of composition are divided into those having manuscript authority and those lacking it. Verse with manuscript authority, pages 188-229, is drawn from the noted Thoreau collections and is grouped according to those sources. This order is less arbitrary than it may first seem, since each major manuscript holding happens to have some homogeneity. The order of the poems within each manuscript holding, aside from that of the Huntington Library, is determined by a variety of external and internal factors. The succession of the Huntington Library poems is based on the Library's own tentative chronology. Verse without manuscript authority either entirely or for the basic text here in the *Collected Poems* is arranged according to the order of publication of its printed sources, and is to be found on pages 230-243. Finally, poems of doubtful authenticity, as well as miscellanea, are given on pages 244-247.

2

Within the circuit of this plodding life
There enter moments of an azure hue,
Untarnished fair as is the violet
Or anemone, when the spring strews them
By some meandering rivulet, which make
The best philosophy untrue that aims
But to console man for his grievances.
I have remembered when the winter came,
High in my chamber in the frosty nights,
When in the still light of the cheerful moon,
On every twig and rail and jutting spout,
The icy spears were adding to their length
Against the arrows of the coming sun,
How in the shimmering noon of summer past
Some unrecorded beam slanted across
The upland pastures where the Johnswort grew;
Or heard, amid the verdure of my mind,
The bee's long smothered hum, on the blue flag
Loitering amidst the mead; or busy rill,
Which now through all its course stands still and dumb
Its own memorial,—purling at its play
Along the slopes, and through the meadows next,
Until its youthful sound was hushed at last
In the staid current of the lowland stream;
Or seen the furrows shine but late upturned,
And where the fieldfare followed in the rear,
When all the fields around lay bound and hoar
Beneath a thick integument of snow.
So by God's cheap economy made rich
To go upon my winter's task again.

His steady sails he never furls
At any time o' year,
And perching now on Winter's curls,
He whistles in his ear.

Sometimes I hear the veery's clarion,
Or brazen trump of the impatient jay,
And in secluded woods the chicadee
Doles out her scanty notes, which sing the praise
Of heroes, and set forth the loveliness
Of virtue evermore.

Upon the lofty elm tree sprays
The vireo rings the changes sweet,
During the trivial summer days,
Striving to lift our thoughts above the street.

Thou dusky spirit of the wood,
Bird of an ancient brood,
Flitting thy lonely way,
A meteor in the summer's day,
From wood to wood, from hill to hill,
Low over forest, field and rill,
What wouldst thou say?
Why shouldst thou haunt the day?
What makes thy melancholy float?
What bravery inspires thy throat,
And bears thee up above the clouds,
Over desponding human crowds,
Which far below
Lay thy haunts low?

The river swelleth more and more,
Like some sweet influence stealing o'er
The passive town; and for a while
Each tussuck makes a tiny isle,
Where, on some friendly Ararat,
Resteth the weary water-rat.

No ripple shows Musketaquid,
Her very current e'en is hid,
As deepest souls do calmest rest,
When thoughts are swelling in the breast,
And she that in the summer's drought
Doth make a rippling and a rout,
Sleeps from Nahshawtuck to the Cliff,
Unruffled by a single skiff.
But by a thousand distant hills
The louder roar a thousand rills,
And many a spring which now is dumb,
And many a stream with smothered hum,
Doth swifter well and faster glide,
Though buried deep beneath the tide.

Our village shows a rural Venice,
Its broad lagoons where yonder fen is;
As lovely as the Bay of Naples
Yon placid cove amid the maples;
And in my neighbor's field of corn
I recognise the Golden Horn.

Here Nature taught from year to year,
When only red men came to hear,
Methinks 'twas in this school of art
Venice and Naples learned their part,
But still their mistress, to my mind,
Her young disciples leaves behind.

Great God, I ask thee for no meaner pelf
Than that I may not disappoint myself,
That in my action I may soar as high,
As I can now discern with this clear eye.

And next in value, which thy kindness lends,
That I may greatly disappoint my friends,
Howe'er they think or hope that it may be,
They may not dream how thou'st distinguished me.

That my weak hand may equal my firm faith,
And my life practice more than my tongue saith;
That my low conduct may not show,
Nor my relenting lines,
That I thy purpose did not know,
Or overrated thy designs.

> Time wears her not; she doth his chariot guide;
> Mortality below her orb is placed.
>
> *—Raleigh.*

The full-orbed moon with unchanged ray
  Mounts up the eastern sky,
Not doomed to these short nights for aye,
  But shining steadily.

She does not wane, but my fortune,
  Which her rays do not bless,
My wayward path declineth soon,
  But she shines not the less.

And if she faintly glimmers here,
  And paled is her light,
Yet alway in her proper sphere
  She's mistress of the night.

Poor bird! destined to lead thy life
    Far in the adventurous west,
And here to be debarred to-night
    From thy accustomed nest;
Must thou fall back upon old instinct now—
Well nigh extinct under man's fickle care?
Did heaven bestow its quenchless inner light
So long ago, for thy small want to-night?
Why stand'st upon thy toes to crow so late?
The moon is deaf to thy low feathered fate;
Or dost thou think so to possess the night,
And people the drear dark with thy brave sprite?
And now with anxious eye thou look'st about,
While the relentless shade draws on its veil,
For some sure shelter from approaching dews,
And the insidious steps of nightly foes.
I fear imprisonment has dulled thy wit,
Or ingrained servitude extinguished it.
But no—dim memory of the days of yore,
By Brahmapootra and the Jumna's shore,
Where thy proud race flew swiftly o'er the heath,
And sought its food the jungle's shade beneath,
Has taught thy wings to seek yon friendly trees,
As erst by Indus' banks and far Ganges.

The sluggish smoke curls up from some deep dell,
The stiffened air exploring in the dawn,
And making slow acquaintance with the day;
Delaying now upon its heavenward course,
In wreathed loiterings dallying with itself,
With as uncertain purpose and slow deed,
As its half-wakened master by the hearth,
Whose mind still slumbering and sluggish thoughts
Have not yet swept into the onward current
Of the new day;—and now it streams afar,
The while the chopper goes with step direct,
And mind intent to swing the early axe.
  First in the dusky dawn he sends abroad
His early scout, his emissary, smoke,
The earliest, latest pilgrim from the roof,
To feel the frosty air, inform the day;
And while he crouches still beside the hearth,
Nor musters courage to unbar the door,
It has gone down the glen with the light wind,
And o'er the plain unfurled its venturous wreath,
Draped the tree tops, loitered upon the hill,
And warmed the pinions of the early bird;
And now, perchance, high in the crispy air,
Has caught sight of the day o'er the earth's edge,
And greets its master's eye at his low door,
As some refulgent cloud in the upper sky.

When Winter fringes every bough
  With his fantastic wreath,
And puts the seal of silence now
  Upon the leaves beneath;

When every stream in its pent-house
  Goes gurgling on its way,
And in his gallery the mouse
  Nibbleth the meadow hay;

Methinks the summer still is nigh,
  And lurketh underneath,
As that same meadow mouse doth lie
  Snug in the last year's heath.

And if perchance the chicadee
  Lisp a faint note anon,
The snow in summer's canopy,
  Which she herself put on.

Fair blossoms deck the cheerful trees,
  And dazzling fruits depend,
The north wind sighs a summer breeze,
  The nipping frosts to fend,

Bringing glad tidings unto me,
  The while I stand all ear,
Of a serene eternity,
  Which need not winter fear.

Out on the silent pond straightway
 The restless ice doth crack,
And pond sprites merry gambols play
 Amid the deafening rack.

Eager I hasten to the vale,
 As if I heard brave news,
How nature held high festival,
 Which it were hard to lose.

I gambol with my neighbor ice,
 And sympathizing quake,
As each new crack darts in a trice
 Across the gladsome lake.

One with the cricket in the ground,
 And faggot on the hearth,
Resounds the rare domestic sound
 Along the forest path.

Not unconcerned Wachusett rears his head
Above the field, so late from nature won,
With patient brow reserved, as one who read
New annals in the history of man.

Where they once dug for money,
But never found any;
Where sometimes Martial Miles
Singly files,
And Elijah Wood,
I fear for no good:
No other man,
Save Elisha Dugan,—
O man of wild habits,
Partridges and rabbits,
Who hast no cares
Only to set snares,
Who liv'st all alone,
Close to the bone,
And where life is sweetest
Constantly eatest.
When the spring stirs my blood
With the instinct to travel,
I can get enough gravel
On the Old Marlborough Road.
Nobody repairs it,
For nobody wears it;
It is a living way,
As the Christians say.
Not many there be
Who enter therein,
Only the guests of the
Irishman Quin.

What is it, what is it,
But a direction out there,
And the bare possibility
Of going somewhere?
Great guide-boards of stone,
But travellers none;
Cenotaphs of the towns
Named on their crowns.
It is worth going to see
Where you *might* be.
What king
Did the thing,
I am still wondering;
Set up how or when,
By what selectmen,
Gourgas or Lee,
Clark or Darby?
They're a great endeavor
To be something forever;
Blank tablets of stone,
Where a traveller might groan,
And in one sentence
Grave all that it known;
Which another might read,
In his extreme need.
I know one or two
Lines that would do,
Literature that might stand
All over the land,
Which a man could remember
Till next December,

And read again in the spring,
　After the thawing.
If with fancy unfurled
　You leave your abode,
You may go round the world
　By the Old Marlborough Road.

In two years' time 't had thus
   Reached the level of the rocks,
Admired the stretching world,
   Nor feared the wandering flocks.

But at this tender age
   Its sufferings began:
There came a browsing ox
   And cut it down a span.

CARPE DIEM

Build not on to-morrow,
But seize on to-day!
From no future borrow,
The present to pay.

Wait not any longer
Thy work to begin;
The worker grows stronger,—
Be steadfast and win!

Forbode not new sorrow—
Bear that of to-day,
And trust that the morrow
Shall chase it away.

The task of the present
Be sure to fulfil;
If sad, or if pleasant,
Be true to it still.

God sendeth us sorrow
And cloudeth our day;
His sun on the morrow
Shines bright on our way.

EACH SUMMER SOUND

Each summer sound
Is a summer round.

THE NEEDLES OF THE PINE

The needles of the pine,
All to the west incline.

IN THE EAST FAMES ARE WON

In the East fames are won,
In the West deeds are done.

Love equals swift and slow,
   And high and low,
Racer and lame,
   The hunter and his game.

Men say they know many things;
But lo! they have taken wings,—
The arts and sciences,
And a thousand appliances;
The wind that blows
Is all that any body knows.

What's the railroad to me?
I never go to see
Where it ends.
It fills a few hollows,
And makes banks for the swallows,
It sets the sand a-blowing,
And the blackberries a-growing,

It is no dream of mine,
To ornament a line;
I cannot come nearer to God and Heaven
Than I live to Walden even.
I am its stony shore,
And the breeze that passes o'er;
In the hollow of my hand
Are its water and its sand,
And its deepest resort
Lies high in my thought.

Light-winged Smoke, Icarian bird,
Melting thy pinions in thy upward flight,
Lark without song, and messenger of dawn,
Circling above the hamlets as thy nest;
Or else, departing dream, and shadowy form
Of midnight vision, gathering up thy skirts;
By night star-veiling, and by day
Darkening the light and blotting out the sun;
Go thou my incense upward from this hearth,
And ask the gods to pardon this clear flame.

Die and be buried who will,
I mean to live here still;
My nature grows ever more young
The primitive pines among.

Where'er thou sail'st who sailed with me,
Though now thou climbest loftier mounts,
And fairer rivers dost ascend,
Be thou my Muse, my Brother—.

I AM BOUND, I AM BOUND, FOR A DISTANT SHORE

I am bound, I am bound, for a distant shore,
By a lonely isle, by a far Azore,
There it is, there it is, the treasure I seek,
On the barren sands of a desolate creek.

I sailed up a river with a pleasant wind,
New lands, new people, and new thoughts to find;
Many fair reaches and headlands appeared,
And many dangers were there to be feared;
But when I remember where I have been,
And the fair landscapes that I have seen,
THOU seemest the only permanent shore,
The cape never rounded, nor wandered o'er.

The respectable folks,—
Where dwell they?
They whisper in the oaks,
And they sigh in the hay;
Summer and winter, night and day,
Out on the meadow, there dwell they.
They never die,
Nor snivel, nor cry,
Nor ask our pity
With a wet eye.
A sound estate they ever mend,
To every asker readily lend;
To the ocean wealth,
To the meadow health,
To Time his length,
To the rocks strength,
To the stars light,
To the weary night,
To the busy day,
To the idle play;
And so their good cheer never ends,
For all are their debtors, and all their friends.

Ah, 'tis in vain the peaceful din
  That wakes the ignoble town,
Not thus did braver spirits win
  A patriot's renown.

There is one field beside this stream,
  Wherein no foot does fall,
But yet it beareth in my dream
  A richer crop than all.

Let me believe a dream so dear,
  Some heart beat high that day,
Above the petty Province here,
  And Britain far away;

Some hero of the ancient mould,
  Some arm of knightly worth,
Of strength unbought, and faith unsold,
  Honored this spot of earth;

Who sought the prize his heart described,
  And did not ask release,
Whose free-born valor was not bribed
  By prospect of a peace.

The men who stood on yonder height
  That day are long since gone;
Not the same hand directs the fight
  And monumental stone.

Ye were the Grecian cities then,
　The Romes of modern birth,
Where the New England husbandmen
　Have shown a Roman worth.

In vain I search a foreign land
　To find our Bunker Hill,
And Lexington and Concord stand
　By no Laconian rill.

But since we sailed
Some things have failed,
And many a dream
Gone down the stream.

Here then an aged shepherd dwelt,
Who to his flock his substance dealt,
And ruled them with a vigorous crook,
By precept of the sacred Book;
But he the pierless bridge passed o'er,
And solitary left the shore.

Anon a youthful pastor came,
Whose crook was not unknown to fame,
His lambs he viewed with gentle glance,
Spread o'er the country's wide expanse,
And fed with "Mosses from the Manse."
Here was our Hawthorne in the dale,
And here the shepherd told his tale.

On Ponkawtasset, since, we took our way,
Down this still stream to far Billericay,
A poet wise has settled, whose fine ray
Doth often shine on Concord's twilight day.

Like those first stars, whose silver beams on high,
Shining more brightly as the day goes by,
Most travellers cannot at first descry,
But eyes that wont to range the evening sky,

And know celestial lights, do plainly see,
And gladly hail them, numbering two or three;
For lore that's deep must deeply studied be,
As from deep wells men read star-poetry.

These stars are never paled, though out of sight,
But like the sun they shine forever bright;
Ay, *they* are suns, though earth must in its flight
Put out its eyes that it may see their light.

Who would neglect the least celestial sound,
Or faintest light that falls on earthly ground,
If he could know it one day would be found
That star in Cygnus whither we are bound,
And pale our sun with heavenly radiance round?

An early unconverted Saint,
Free from noontide or evening taint,
Heathen without reproach,
That did upon the civil day encroach,
And ever since its birth
Had trod the outskirts of the earth.

Low in the eastern sky
Is set thy glancing eye;
And though its gracious light
Ne'er riseth to my sight,
Yet every star that climbs
Above the gnarled limbs
   Of yonder hill,
Conveys thy gentle will.

Believe I knew thy thought,
And that the zephyrs brought
Thy kindest wishes through,
As mine they bear to you,
That some attentive cloud
Did pause amid the crowd
   Over my head,
While gentle things were said.

Believe the thrushes sung,
And that the flower-bells rung,
That herbs exhaled their scent,
And beasts knew what was meant,
The trees a welcome waved,
And lakes their margins laved,
   When thy free mind
To my retreat did wind.

It was a summer eve,
The air did gently heave
While yet a low-hung cloud
Thy eastern skies did shroud;
The lightning's silent gleam,
Startling my drowsy dream,
   Seemed like the flash
Under thy dark eyelash.

Still will I strive to be
As if thou wert with me;
Whatever path I take,
It shall be for thy sake,
Of gentle slope and wide,
As thou wert by my side,
   Without a root
To trip thy gentle foot.

I'll walk with gentle pace,
And choose the smoothest place,
And careful dip the oar,
And shun the winding shore,
And gently steer my boat
Where water-lilies float,
   And cardinal flowers
Stand in their sylvan bowers.

Dong, sounds the brass in the east,
As if to a funeral feast,
But I like that sound the best
Out of the fluttering west.

The steeple ringeth a knell,
But the fairies' silvery bell
Is the voice of that gentle folk,
Or else the horizon that spoke.

Its metal is not of brass,
But air, and water, and glass,
And under a cloud it is swung,
And by the wind it is rung.

When the steeple tolleth the noon,
It soundeth not so soon,
Yet it rings a far earlier hour,
And the sun has not reached its tower.

I make ye an offer,
Ye gods, hear the scoffer,
The scheme will not hurt you,
If ye will find goodness, I will find virtue.
Though I am your creature,
And child of your nature,
I have pride still unbended,
And blood undescended,
Some free independence,
And my own descendants.
I cannot toil blindly,
Though ye behave kindly,
And I swear by the rood,
I'll be slave to no God.
If ye will deal plainly,
I will strive mainly,
If ye will discover,
Great plans to your lover,
And give him a sphere
Somewhat larger than here.

Conscience is instinct bred in the house,
Feeling and Thinking propagate the sin
By an unnatural breeding in and in.
I say, Turn it out doors,
Into the moors.
I love a life whose plot is simple,
And does not thicken with every pimple,
A soul so sound no sickly conscience binds it,
That makes the universe no worse than 't finds it.
I love an earnest soul,
Whose mighty joy and sorrow
Are not drowned in a bowl,
And brought to life to-morrow;
That lives one tragedy,
And not seventy;
A conscience worth keeping,
Laughing not weeping;
A conscience wise and steady,
And forever ready;
Not changing with events,
Dealing in compliments;
A conscience exercised about
Large things, where one *may* doubt.
I love a soul not all of wood,
Predestinated to be good,
But true to the backbone
Unto itself alone,
And false to none;

Born to its own affairs,
Its own joys and own cares;
By whom the work which God begun
Is finished, and not undone;
Taken up where he left off,
Whether to worship or to scoff;
If not good, why then evil,
If not good god, good devil.
Goodness! you hypocrite, come out of that,
Live your life, do your work, then take your hat.
I have no patience towards
Such conscientious cowards.
Give me simple laboring folk,
Who love their work,
Whose virtue is a song
To cheer God along.

Such water do the gods distil,
And pour down every hill
    For their New England men;
A draught of this wild nectar bring,
And I'll not taste the spring
    Of Helicon again.

THAT PHAETON OF OUR DAY

That Phaeton of our day,
Who'd make another milky way,
And burn the world up with his ray;

By us an undisputed seer,—
Who'd drive his flaming car so near
Unto our shuddering mortal sphere,

Disgracing all our slender worth,
And scorching up the living earth,
To prove his heavenly birth.

The silver spokes, the golden tire,
Are glowing with unwonted fire,
And ever nigher roll and nigher;

The pins and axle melted are,
The silver radii fly afar,
Ah, he will spoil his Father's car!

Who let him have the steeds he cannot steer?
Henceforth the sun will not shine for a year;
And we shall Ethiops all appear.

Though all the fates should prove unkind,
Leave not your native land behind.
The ship, becalmed, at length stands still;
The steed must rest beneath the hill;
But swiftly still our fortunes pace
To find us out in every place.

The vessel, though her masts be firm,
Beneath her copper bears a worm;
Around the cape, across the line,
Till fields of ice her course confine;
It matters not how smooth the breeze,
How shallow or how deep the seas,
Whether she bears Manilla twine,
Or in her hold Madeira wine,
Or China teas, or Spanish hides,
In port or quarantine she rides;
Far from New England's blustering shore,
New England's worm her hulk shall bore,
And sink her in the Indian seas,
Twine, wine, and hides, and China teas.

WITH FRONTIER STRENGTH YE STAND YOUR GROUND

With frontier strength ye stand your ground,
With grand content ye circle round,
Tumultuous silence for all sound,
Ye distant nursery of rills,
Monadnock and the Peterborough Hills;—
Firm argument that never stirs,
Outcircling the philosophers,—
Like some vast fleet,
Sailing through rain and sleet,
Through winter's cold and summer's heat;
Still holding on upon your high emprise,
Until ye find a shore amid the skies;
Not skulking close to land,
With cargo contraband,
For they who sent a venture out by ye
Have set the Sun to see
Their honesty.
Ships of the line, each one,
Ye westward run,
Convoying clouds,
Which cluster in your shrouds,
Always before the gale,
Under a press of sail,
With weight of metal all untold,—
I seem to feel ye in my firm seat here,
Immeasurable depth of hold,
And breadth of beam, and length of running gear.

Methinks ye take luxurious pleasure
In your novel western leisure;
So cool your brows and freshly blue,
As Time had naught for ye to do;
For ye lie at your length,
An unappropriated strength,
Unhewn primeval timber,
For knees so stiff, for masts so limber;
The stock of which new earths are made,
One day to be our *western* trade,
Fit for the stanchions of a world
Which through the seas of space is hurled.

While we enjoy a lingering ray,
Ye still o'ertop the western day,
Reposing yonder on God's croft
Like solid stacks of hay;
So bold a line as ne'er was writ
On any page by human wit;
The forest glows as if
An enemy's camp-fires shone
Along the horizon,
Or the day's funeral pyre
Were lighted there;
Edged with silver and with gold,
The clouds hang o'er in damask fold,
And with such depth of amber light
The west is dight,
Where still a few rays slant,
That even Heaven seems extravagant.

Watatic Hill
Lies on the horizon's sill
Like a child's toy left overnight,
And other duds to left and right,
On the earth's edge, mountains and trees
Stand as they were on air graven,
Or as the vessels in a haven
Await the morning breeze.
I fancy even
Through your defiles windeth the way to heaven;
And yonder still, in spite of history's page,
Linger the golden and the silver age;
Upon the laboring gale
The news of future centuries is brought,
And of new dynasties of thought,
From your remotest vale.

But special I remember thee,
Wachusett, who like me
Standest alone without society.
Thy far blue eye,
A remnant of the sky,
Seen through the clearing or the gorge,
Or from the windows of the forge,
Doth leaven all it passes by.
Nothing is true
But stands 'tween me and you,
Thou western pioneer,
Who know'st not shame nor fear,
By venturous spirit driven
Under the eaves of heaven;

And canst expand thee there,
And breathe enough of air?
Even beyond the West
Thou migratest,
Into unclouded tracts,
Without a pilgrim's axe,
Cleaving thy road on high
With thy well-tempered brow,
And mak'st thyself a clearing in the sky.
Upholding heaven, holding down earth,
Thy pastime from thy birth;
Not steadied by the one, nor leaning on the other,
May I approve myself thy worthy brother!

Here lies an honest man,
Rear-Admiral Van.

———

Faith, then ye have
Two in one grave,
For in his favor,
Here too lies the Engraver.

The western wind came lumbering in,
Bearing a faint Pacific din,
Our evening mail, swift at the call
Of its Postmaster General;
Laden with news from Californ',
Whate'er transpired hath since morn,
How wags the world by brier and brake
From hence to Athabasca Lake;—

There is a vale which none hath seen,
Where foot of man has never been,
Such as here lives with toil and strife,
An anxious and a sinful life.

There every virtue has its birth,
Ere it descends upon the earth,
And thither every deed returns,
Which in the generous bosom burns.

There love is warm, and youth is young,
And poetry is yet unsung,
For Virtue still adventures there,
And freely breathes her native air.

And ever, if you hearken well,
You still may hear its vesper bell,
And tread of high-souled men go by,
Their thoughts conversing with the sky.

"Before each van
Prick forth the aery knights, and couch their spears
Till thickest legions close; with feats of arms
From either end of Heaven the welkin burns."

———————

Away! away! away! away!
 Ye have not kept your secret well,
I will abide that other day,
 Those other lands ye tell.

Has time no leisure left for these,
 The acts that ye rehearse?
Is not eternity a lease
 For better deeds than verse?

'Tis sweet to hear of heroes dead,
 To know them still alive,
But sweeter if we earn their bread,
 And in us they survive.

Our life should feed the springs of fame
 With a perennial wave,
As ocean feeds the babbling founts
 Which find in it their grave.

Ye skies drop gently round my breast,
 And be my corselet blue,
Ye earth receive my lance in rest,
 My faithful charger you;

Ye stars my spear-heads in the sky,
  My arrow-tips ye are;
I see the routed foemen fly,
  My bright spears fixed are.

Give me an angel for a foe,
  Fix now the place and time,
And straight to meet him I will go
  Above the starry chime.

And with our clashing bucklers' clang
  The heavenly spheres shall ring,
While bright the northern lights shall hang
  Beside our tourneying.

And if she lose her champion true,
  Tell Heaven not despair,
For I will be her champion new,
  Her fame I will repair.

Low-anchored cloud,
Newfoundland air,
Fountain-head and source of rivers,
Dew-cloth, dream drapery,
And napkin spread by fays;
Drifting meadow of the air,
Where bloom the daisied banks and violets,
And in whose fenny labyrinth
The bittern booms and heron wades;
Spirit of lakes and seas and rivers,
Bear only perfumes and the scent
Of healing herbs to just men's fields!

Man's little acts are grand,
Beheld from land to land,
There as they lie in time,
Within their native clime.
    Ships with the noontide weigh,
    And glide before its ray
    To some retired bay,
    Their haunt,
    Whence, under tropic sun,
    Again they run,
    Bearing gum Senegal and Tragicant.
For this was ocean meant,
For this the sun was sent,
And moon was lent,
And winds in distant caverns pent.

The waves slowly beat,
Just to keep the noon sweet,
And no sound is floated o'er,
Save the mallet on shore,
Which echoing on high
Seems a-calking the sky.

Woof of the sun, ethereal gauze,
Woven of Nature's richest stuffs,
Visible heat, air-water, and dry sea,
Last conquest of the eye;
Toil of the day displayed, sun-dust,
Aerial surf upon the shores of earth,
Ethereal estuary, frith of light,
Breakers of air, billows of heat,
Fine summer spray on inland seas;
Bird of the sun, transparent-winged
Owlet of noon, soft-pinioned,
From heath or stubble rising without song;
Establish thy serenity o'er the fields.

Where gleaming fields of haze
Meet the voyageur's gaze,
And above, the heated air
Seems to make a river there,
The pines stand up with pride
By the Souhegan's side,
And the hemlock and the larch
With their triumphal arch
Are waving o'er its march
   To the sea.
No wind stirs its waves,
But the spirits of the braves
   Hov'ring o'er,
Whose antiquated graves
Its still water laves
   On the shore.
With an Indian's stealthy tread,
It goes sleeping in its bed,
Without joy or grief,
Or the rustle of a leaf,
Without a ripple or a billow,
Or the sigh of a willow,
From the Lyndeboro' hills
To the Merrimack mills.
With a louder din
Did its current begin,

When melted the snow
On the far mountain's brow,
And the drops came together
In that rainy weather.
Experienced river,
Hast thou flowed forever?
Souhegan soundeth old,
But the half is not told,
What names hast thou borne,
In the ages far gone,
When the Xanthus and Meander
Commenced to wander,
Ere the black bear haunted
    Thy red forest-floor,
Or Nature had planted
    The pines by thy shore?

This is my Carnac, whose unmeasured dome
Shelters the measuring art and measurer's home.
Behold these flowers, let us be up with time,
Not dreaming of three thousand years ago,
Erect ourselves and let those columns lie,
Not stoop to raise a foil against the sky.
Where is the spirit of that time but in
This present day, perchance the present line?
Three thousand years ago are not agone,
They are still lingering in this summer morn,
And Memnon's Mother sprightly greets us now,
Wearing her youthful radiance on her brow.
If Carnac's columns still stand on the plain,
To enjoy our opportunities they remain.

True kindness is a pure divine affinity,
Not founded upon human consanguinity.
It is a spirit, not a blood relation,
Superior to family and station.

Lately, alas, I knew a gentle boy,
　　Whose features all were cast in Virtue's mould,
As one she had designed for Beauty's toy,
　　But after manned him for her own strong-hold.

On every side he open was as day,
　　That you might see no lack of strength within,
For walls and ports do only serve alway
　　For a pretence to feebleness and sin.

Say not that Caesar was victorious,
　　With toil and strife who stormed the House of Fame,
In other sense this youth was glorious,
　　Himself a kingdom wheresoe'er he came.

No strength went out to get him victory,
　　When all was income of its own accord;
For where he went none other was to see,
　　But all were parcel of their noble lord.

He forayed like the subtile haze of summer,
　　That stilly shows fresh landscapes to our eyes,
And revolutions works without a murmur,
　　Or rustling of a leaf beneath the skies.

So was I taken unawares by this,
　　I quite forgot my homage to confess;
Yet now am forced to know, though hard it is,
　　I might have loved him had I loved him less.

Each moment as we nearer drew to each,
  A stern respect withheld us farther yet,
So that we seemed beyond each other's reach,
  And less acquainted than when first we met.

We two were one while we did sympathize,
  So could we not the simplest bargain drive;
And what avails it now that we are wise,
  If absence doth this doubleness contrive?

Eternity may not the chance repeat,
  But I must tread my single way alone,
In sad remembrance that we once did meet,
  And know that bliss irrevocably gone.

The spheres henceforth my elegy shall sing,
  For elegy has other subject none;
Each strain of music in my ears shall ring
  Knell of departure from that other one.

Make haste and celebrate my tragedy;
  With fitting strain resound ye woods and fields;
Sorrow is dearer in such case to me
  Than all the joys other occasion yields.

———————

Is't then too late the damage to repair?
  Distance, forsooth, from my weak grasp hath reft
The empty husk, and clutched the useless tare,
  But in my hands the wheat and kernel left.

If I but love that virtue which he is,
  Though it be scented in the morning air,
Still shall we be truest acquaintances,
  Nor mortals know a sympathy more rare.

The smothered streams of love, which flow
More bright than Phlegethon, more low,
Island us ever, like the sea,
In an Atlantic mystery.
Our fabled shores none ever reach,
No mariner has found our beach,
Scarcely our mirage now is seen,
And neighboring waves with floating green,
Yet still the oldest charts contain
Some dotted outline of our main;
In ancient times midsummer days
Unto the western islands' gaze,
To Teneriffe and the Azores,
Have shown our faint and cloud-like shores.

But sink not yet, ye desolate isles,
Anon your coast with commerce smiles,
And richer freights ye'll furnish far
Than Africa or Malabar.
Be fair, be fertile evermore,
Ye rumored but untrodden shore,
Princes and monarchs will contend
Who first unto your land shall send,
And pawn the jewels of the crown
To call your distant soil their own.

My love must be as free
  As is the eagle's wing,
Hovering o'er land and sea
  And everything.

I must not dim my eye
  In thy saloon,
I must not leave my sky
  And nightly moon.

Be not the fowler's net
  Which stays my flight,
And craftily is set
  T' allure the sight.

But be the favoring gale
  That bears me on,
And still doth fill my sail
  When thou art gone.

I cannot leave my sky
  For thy caprice,
True love would soar as high
  As heaven is.

The eagle would not brook
  Her mate thus won,
Who trained his eye to look
  Beneath the sun.

The Good how can we trust?
Only the Wise are just.
The Good we use,
The Wise we cannot choose.
These there are none above;
The Good they know and love,
But are not known again
By those of lesser ken.
They do not charm us with their eyes,
But they transfix with their advice;
No partial sympathy they feel,
With private woe or private weal,
But with the universe joy and sigh,
Whose knowledge is their sympathy.

Nature doth have her dawn each day,
    But mine are far between;
Content, I cry, for sooth to say,
    Mine brightest are I ween.

For when my sun doth deign to rise,
    Though it be her noontide,
Her fairest field in shadow lies,
    Nor can my light abide.

Sometimes I bask me in her day,
    Conversing with my mate,
But if we interchange one ray,
    Forthwith her heats abate.

Through his discourse I climb and see,
    As from some eastern hill,
A brighter morrow rise to me
    Than lieth in her skill.

As 'twere two summer days in one,
    Two Sundays come together,
Our rays united make one sun,
    With fairest summer weather.

LET SUCH PURE HATE
STILL UNDERPROP

"Friends, Romans, Countrymen, and Lovers."

Let such pure hate still underprop
Our love, that we may be
Each other's conscience,
And have our sympathy
Mainly from thence.

We'll one another treat like gods,
And all the faith we have
In virtue and in truth, bestow
On either, and suspicion leave
To gods below.

Two solitary stars,—
Unmeasured systems far
Between us roll,
But by our conscious light we are
Determined to one pole.

What need confound the sphere,—
Love can afford to wait,
For it no hour's too late
That witnesseth one duty's end,
Or to another doth beginning lend.

It will subserve no use,
More than the tints of flowers,
Only the independent guest
Frequents its bowers,
Inherits its bequest.

No speech though kind has it,
But kinder silence doles
Unto its mates,
By night consoles,
By day congratulates.

What saith the tongue to tongue?
What heareth ear of ear?
By the decrees of fate
From year to year,
Does it communicate.

Pathless the gulf of feeling yawns,—
No trivial bridge of words,
Or arch of boldest span,
Can leap the moat that girds
The sincere man.

No show of bolts and bars
Can keep the foeman out,
Or 'scape his secret mine
Who entered with the doubt
That drew the line.

No warder at the gate
Can let the friendly in,
But, like the sun, o'er all
He will the castle win,
And shine along the wall.

There's nothing in the world I know
That can escape from love,
For every depth it goes below,
And every height above.
It waits as waits the sky,
Until the clouds go by,
Yet shines serenely on
With an eternal day,
Alike when they are gone,
And when they stay.

Implacable is Love,—
Foes may be bought or teased
From their hostile intent,
But he goes unappeased
Who is on kindness bent.

Packed in my mind lie all the clothes
   Which outward nature wears,
And in its fashion's hourly change
   It all things else repairs.

In vain I look for change abroad,
   And can no difference find,
Till some new ray of peace uncalled
   Illumes my inmost mind.

What is it gilds the trees and clouds,
   And paints the heavens so gay,
But yonder fast-abiding light
   With its unchanging ray?

Lo, when the sun streams through the wood,
   Upon a winter's morn,
Where'er his silent beams intrude
   The murky night is gone.

How could the patient pine have known
   The morning breeze would come,
Or humble flowers anticipate
   The insect's noonday hum,—

Till the new light with morning cheer
  From far streamed through the aisles,
And nimbly told the forest trees
  For many stretching miles?

I've heard within my inmost soul
  Such cheerful morning news,
In the horizon of my mind
  Have seen such orient hues,

As in the twilight of the dawn,
  When the first birds awake,
Are heard within some silent wood,
  Where they the small twigs break,

Or in the eastern skies are seen,
  Before the sun appears,
The harbingers of summer heats
  Which from afar he bears.

My books I'd fain cast off, I cannot read,
'Twixt every page my thoughts go stray at large
Down in the meadow, where is richer feed,
And will not mind to hit their proper targe.

Plutarch was good, and so was Homer too,
Our Shakespeare's life were rich to live again,
What Plutarch read, that was not good nor true,
Nor Shakespeare's books, unless his books were men.

Here while I lie beneath this walnut bough,
What care I for the Greeks or for Troy town,
If juster battles are enacted now
Between the ants upon this hummock's crown?

Bid Homer wait till I the issue learn,
If red or black the gods will favor most,
Or yonder Ajax will the phalanx turn,
Struggling to heave some rock against the host.

Tell Shakespeare to attend some leisure hour,
For now I've business with this drop of dew,
And see you not, the clouds prepare a shower,—
I'll meet him shortly when the sky is blue.

This bed of herd's-grass and wild oats was spread
Last year with nicer skill than monarchs use,
A clover tuft is pillow for my head,
And violets quite overtop my shoes.

And now the cordial clouds have shut all in,
And gently swells the wind to say all's well,
The scattered drops are falling fast and thin,
Some in the pool, some in the flower-bell.

I am well drenched upon my bed of oats;
But see that globe come rolling down its stem,
Now like a lonely planet there it floats,
And now it sinks into my garment's hem.

Drip drip the trees for all the country round,
And richness rare distils from every bough,
The wind alone it is makes every sound,
Shaking down crystals on the leaves below.

For shame the sun will never show himself,
Who could not with his beams e'er melt me so,
My dripping locks,—they would become an elf,
Who in a beaded coat does gayly go.

THE POET'S DELAY

In vain I see the morning rise,
    In vain observe the western blaze,
Who idly look to other skies,
    Expecting life by other ways.

Amidst such boundless wealth without,
    I only still am poor within,
The birds have sung their summer out,
    But still my spring does not begin.

Shall I then wait the autumn wind,
    Compelled to seek a milder day,
And leave no curious nest behind,
    No woods still echoing to my lay?

Salmon Brook,
Penichook,
Ye sweet waters of my brain,
When shall I look,
Or cast the hook,
In your waves again?

Silver eels,
Wooden creels,
These the baits that still allure,
And dragon-fly
That floated by,
May they still endure?

I am the autumnal sun,
With autumn gales my race is run;
When will the hazel put forth its flowers,
Or the grape ripen under my bowers?
When will the harvest or the hunter's moon,
Turn my midnight into mid-noon?
    I am all sere and yellow,
    And to my core mellow.
The mast is dropping within my woods,
The winter is lurking within my moods,
And the rustling of the withered leaf
Is the constant music of my grief.

I am a parcel of vain strivings tied
    By a chance bond together,
  Dangling this way and that, their links
    Were made so loose and wide,
        Methinks,
      For milder weather.

A bunch of violets without their roots,
    And sorrel intermixed,
  Encircled by a wisp of straw
    Once coiled about their shoots,
        The law
      By which I'm fixed.

A nosegay which Time clutched from out
    Those fair Elysian fields,
  With weeds and broken stems, in haste,
    Doth make the rabble rout
        That waste
      The day he yields.

And here I bloom for a short hour unseen,
    Drinking my juices up,
  With no root in the land
    To keep my branches green,
        But stand
      In a bare cup.

Some tender buds were left upon my stem
  In mimicry of life,
 But ah! the children will not know,
  Till time has withered them,
   The woe
  With which they're rife.

But now I see I was not plucked for naught,
  And after in life's vase
 Of glass set while I might survive,
  But by a kind hand brought
   Alive
  To a strange place.

That stock thus thinned will soon redeem its hours,
  And by another year,
 Such as God knows, with freer air,
  More fruits and fairer flowers
   Will bear,
  While I droop here.

All things are current found
On earthly ground,
Spirits and elements
Have their descents.

Night and day, year on year,
High and low, far and near,
These are our own aspects,
These are our own regrets.

Ye gods of the shore,
Who abide evermore,
I see your far headland,
Stretching on either hand;

I hear the sweet evening sounds
From your undecaying grounds;
Cheat me no more with time,
Take me to your clime.

WHO SLEEPS BY DAY AND WALKS BY NIGHT

Who sleeps by day and walks by night,
Will meet no spirit but some sprite.

WE SHOULD NOT MIND IF ON OUR EAR THERE FELL

We should not mind if on our ear there fell
Some less of cunning, more of oracle.

THEN SPEND AN AGE IN WHETTING THY DESIRE

Then spend an age in whetting thy desire,
Thou needs't not *hasten* if thou dost *stand fast*.

THEREFORE A TORRENT OF SADNESS DEEP

Therefore a torrent of sadness deep,
Through the strains of thy triumph is heard to sweep.

84

SUCH NEAR ASPECTS HAD WE

Such near aspects had we
Of our life's scenery.

MY LIFE HAS BEEN THE POEM I WOULD HAVE WRIT

My life has been the poem I would have writ,
But I could not both live and utter it.

WE SEE THE PLANET FALL

We see the *planet* fall,
And that is all.

The other couplets of the *Week* appear as collations in the poems of which they are a part. For "It doth expand my privacies" and "The work we choose should be our own" see "Inspiration"; for "Our uninquiring corpses lie more low" see "Travelling"; for "Men are by birth equal in this, that given" see "Poverty."

Gentle river, gentle river
Swift as glid[e]s thy stream along,
Many a bold Canadian voyageur,
Bravely swelled the gay chanson

Thus of old our valiant fathers,
Many a lagging year agone
Gliding oer the rippling waters,
Taught to banish care in song.

Now the sun's behind the willows,
Now he gleams along the lake,
Hark across the bounding billows
Liquid songs the echoes wake.

Rise Apollo up before us,
E'ne the lark's begun her lay
Let us all in deafning chorus
Praise the glorious king of day.

Thus we lead a life of pleasure,
Thus we while the hours away,
Thus we revel beyond measure,
Gaily live we while we may.

"Long life and success to you."
Ubique.

I love a careless streamlet,
That takes a mad-cap leap,
And like a sparkling beamlet
Goes dashing down the steep.

———

Like torrents of the mountain
We've coursed along the lea,
From many a crystal fountain
Toward the far-distant sea.

And now we've gained life's valley,
And through the lowlands roam,
No longer may'st thou dally,
No longer spout and foam.

May pleasant meads await thee,
Where thou may'st freely roll
Towards that bright heavenly sea,
Thy resting place and goal.

And when thou reach'st life's down-hill,
So gentle be thy stream,
As would not turn a grist-mill
Without the aid of steam.

87

My sincerity doth surpass
  The pretence of optic glass.

Say what are the highlands yonder
Which do keep the spheres asunder
The streams of light which centre in our sun
And those which from some other system run?

Distinguished stranger, system ranger,
Plenipotentiary to our sphere,
Dost thou know of any danger,
War or famine near?

Special envoy, foreign minister,
From the empire of the sky,
Dost thou threaten aught that's sinister
By thy course on high?

Runner of the firmament
On what errand wast thou sent,
Art thou some great general's scout
Come to spy our weakness out?
Sculling thy way without a sail,
Mid the stars and constellations,
The pioneer*er* of a tail
Through the stary nations.
  Thou celestial privateer
We entreat thee come not near.

I think awhile of Love, and while I think,
　　　Love is to me a world,
　　　Sole meat and sweetest drink,
　　　And close connecting link
　　　　Tween heaven and earth.

I only know it is, not how or why,
　　　My greatest happiness;
　　　However hard I try,
　　　Not if I were to die,
　　　　Can I explain.

I fain would ask my friend how it can be,
　　　But when the time arrives,
　　　Then Love is more lovely
　　　Than anything to me,
　　　　And so I'm dumb.

For if the truth were known, Love cannot speak,
　　　But only thinks and does;
　　　Though surely out 'twill leak
　　　Without the help of Greek,
　　　　Or any tongue.

A man may love the truth and practise it,
　　　Beauty he may admire,
　　　And goodness not omit,
　　　As much as may befit
　　　　To reverence.

But only when these three together meet,
        As they always incline,
        And make one soul the seat,
        And favorite retreat
            Of loveliness;

When under kindred shape, like loves and hates
        And a kindred nature,
        Proclaim us to be mates,
        Exposed to equal fates
            Eternally;

And each may other help, and service do,
        Drawing Love's bands more tight,
        Service he ne'er shall rue
        While one and one make two,
            And two are one;

In such case only doth man fully prove
        Fully as man can do,
        What power there is in Love
        His inmost soul to move
            Resistlessly.

————

Two sturdy oaks I mean, which side by side,
        Withstand the winter's storm,
        And spite of wind and tide,
        Grow up the meadow's pride,
            For both are strong

Above they barely touch, but undermined
    Down to their deepest source,
    Admiring you shall find
    Their roots are intertwined
    Insep'rably.

When breathless noon hath paused on hill and vale,
And now no more the woodman plies his axe,
Nor mower whets his scythe,
Somewhat it is, sole sojourner on earth,
To hear the veery on her oaken perch
Ringing her modest trill—
Sole sound of all the din that makes a world,
And I sole ear.
Fondly to nestle me in that sweet melody,
And own a kindred soul, speaking to me
From out the depths of universal being.
O'er birch and hazle, through the sultry air,
Comes that faint sound this way,
On Zephyr borne, straight to my ear.
No longer time or place, nor faintest trace
Of earth, the landscape's shimmer is my only space,
Sole remnant of a world.
Anon that throat has done, and familiar sounds
Swell strangely on the breeze, the low of cattle,
And the novel cries of sturdy swains
That plod the neighboring vale—
And I walk once more confounded a denizen of earth.

In the midst of the poplar that stands by our door,
We planted a bluebird box,
And we hoped before the summer was o'er
A transient pair to coax.

One warm summer's day the bluebirds came
And lighted on our tree,
But at first the wand'rers were not so tame
But they were afraid of me.

They seemed to come from the distant south,
Just over the Walden wood,
And they skimmed it along with open mouth
Close by where the bellows stood.

Warbling they swept round the distant cliff,
And they warbled it over the lea,
And over the blacksmith's shop in a jiff
Did they come warbling to me.

They came and sat on the box's top
Without looking into the hole,
And only from this side to that did they hop,
As 'twere a common well-pole.

Methinks I had never seen them before,
Nor indeed had they seen me,
Till I chanced to stand by our back door,
And they came to the poplar tree.

In course of time they built their nest
And reared a happy brood,
And every morn they piped their best
As they flew away to the wood.

Thus wore the summer hours away
To the bluebirds and to me,
And every hour was a summer's day,
So pleasantly lived we.

They were a world within themselves,
And I a world in me,
Up in the tree—the little elves—
With their callow family.

One morn the wind blowed cold and strong,
And the leaves when whirling away;
The birds prepared for their journey long
That raw and gusty day.

Boreas came blust'ring down from the north,
And ruffled their azure smocks,
So they launched them forth, though somewhat loth,
By way of the old Cliff rocks.

Meanwhile the earth jogged steadily on
In her mantle of purest white,
And anon another spring was born
When winter was vanished quite.

And I wandered forth o'er the steamy earth,
And gazed at the mellow sky,
But never before from the hour of my birth
Had I wandered so thoughtfully.

For never before was the earth so still,
And never so mild was the sky,
The river, the fields, the woods, and the hill,
Seemed to heave an audible sigh.

I felt that the heavens were all around,
And the earth was all below,
As when in the ears there rushes a sound
Which thrills you from top to toe.

I dreamed that I was an waking thought—
A something I hardly knew—
Not a solid piece, nor an empty nought,
But a drop of morning dew.

'Twas the world and I at a game of bo-peep,
As a man would dodge his shadow,
An idea becalmed in eternity's deep—
'Tween Lima and Segraddo.

Anon a faintly warbled note
From out the azure deep,
Into my ears did gently float
As is the approach of sleep.

.

It thrilled but startled not my soul;
Across my mind strange mem'ries gleamed,
As often distant scenes u[n]roll
When we have lately dreamed

The bluebird had come from the distant South
To his box in the poplar tree,
And he opened wide his slender mouth,
On purpose to sing to me.

The school boy loitered on his way to school,
Scorning to live so rare a day by rule.
So mild the air a pleasure 'twas to breathe,
For what seems heaven above was earth beneath.

Soured neighbors chatted by the garden pale,
Nor quarrelled who should drive the needed nail—
The most unsocial made new friends that day,
As when the sun shines husbandmen make hay

How long I slept I know not, but at last
I felt my consciousness returning fast,
For Zephyr rustled past with leafy tread,
And heedlessly with one heel grazed my head.

My eyelids opened on a field of blue,
For close above a nodding violet grew,
A part of heaven it seemed, which one could scent,
Its blue commingling with the firmament.

—True, our converse a stranger is to speech,
Only the practised ear can catch the surging words,
That break and die upon thy pebbled lips.
Thy flow of thought is noiseless as the lapse of thy
own waters,
Wafted as is the morning mist up from thy surface,
So that the passive Soul doth breathe it in,
And is infected with the truth thou wouldst express.

E'en the remotest stars have come in troops
And stooped low to catch the benediction
Of thy countenance. Oft as the day came round,
Impartial has the sun exhibited himself
Before thy narrow skylight—nor has the moon
For cycles failed to roll this way
As oft as elsewhither, and tell thee of the night.
No cloud so rare but hitherward it stalked,
And in thy face looked doubly beautiful.
O! tell me what the winds have writ within these
thousand years,
On the blue vault that spans thy flood—
Or sun transferred and delicately reprinted
For thy own private reading. Somewhat
Within these latter days I've read,
But surely there was much that would have thrilled
the Soul,

Which human eye saw not
I would give much to read that first bright page,
Wet from a virgin press, when Eurus—Boreas—
And the host of airy quill-drivers
First dipped their pens in mist.

Truth–Goodness–Beauty–those celestial thrins,
Continually are born; e'en now the Universe,
With thousand throats—and eke with greener smiles,
Its joy confesses at their recent birth.

In the busy streets, domains of trade,
Man is a surly porter, or a vain and hectoring bully,
Who can claim no nearer kindredship with me
Than brotherhood by law.

I knew a man by sight,
   A blameless wight,
Who, for a year or more,
Had daily passed my door,
Yet converse none had had with him.

I met him in a lane,
   Him and his cane,
About three miles from home,
Where I had chanced to roam,
And volumes stared at him, and he at me.

In a more distant place
   I glimpsed his face,
And bowed instinctively;
Starting he bowed to me,
Bowed simultaneously, and passed along.

Next, in a foreign land
   I grasped his hand,
And had a social chat,
About this thing and that,
As I had known him well a thousand years.

Late in a wilderness
   I shared his mess,
For he had hardships seen,
And I a wanderer been;
He was my bosom friend, and I was his.

And as, methinks, shall all,
   Both great and small,
That ever lived on earth,
Early or late their birth,
Stranger and foe, one day each other know.

The loudest sound that burdens here the breeze
Is the wood's whisper; 'tis when we choose to list
Audible sound, and when we list not,
It is calm profound. Tongues were provided
But to vex the ear with superficial thoughts.
When deeper thoughts upswell, the jarring discord
Of harsh speech is hushed, and senses seem
As little as may be to share the extacy.

Anon with gaping fearlessness they quaff
The dewy nectar with a natural thirst,
Or wet their leathern lungs where cranberries lurk,
With sweeter wine than Chian, Lesbian, or Falernian
                                     far.
Theirs was the inward lustre that bespeaks
An open sole—unknowing to exclude
The cheerful day—a worthier glory far
Than that which gilds the outmost rind with darkness
                                     visible—
Virtues that fast abide through lapse of years,
Rather rubbed in than off.

What time the bittern, solitary bird,
Hides now her head amid the whispering fern,
And not a paddock vexes all the shore—
Nor feather ruffles the incumbent air,
Save where the wagtail interrupts the noon.

THE THAW

I saw the civil sun drying earth's tears—
Her tears of joy that only faster flowed,

Fain would I stretch me by the hig[h]way side,
To thaw and trickle with the melting snow,
That mingled soul and body with the tide,
I too may through the pores of nature flow.

But I alas nor trickle can nor fume,
One jot to forward the great work of Time,
'Tis mine to hearken while these ply the loom,
So shall my silence with their music chime.

LAST NIGHT AS I LAY GAZING WITH SHUT EYES

Last night as I lay gazing with shut eyes
    Into the golden land of dreams,
I thought I gazed adown a quiet reach
    Of land and water prospect,
      Whose low beach
Was peopled with the now subsiding hum
Of happy industry—whose work is done.

And as I turned me on my pillow o'er,
I heard the lapse of waves upon the shore,
Distinct as it had been at broad noonday,
And I were wandering at Rockaway.

We two that planets erst had been
Are now a double star,
And in the heavens may be seen,
Where that we fixed are.

Yet whirled with subtle power along,
Into new space we enter,
And evermore with spheral song
Revolve about one centre.

'Twill soon appear if we but look
At evening into earth's day book,
Which way the great account doth stand
Between the heavens and the land.

When the world grows old by the chimney side,
Then forth to the youngling rocks I glide—
Where over the water, and over the land,
The bells are booming on either hand.

Now up they go ding, then down again dong,
And awhile they swing to the same old song,
And the metal goes round 't a single bound,
A-lulling the fields with i[t]s measured sound—
Till the tired tongue falls with a lengthened boom,
As solemn and loud as the crack of doom.
Then changed is their measure to tone upon tone,
And seldom it is that one sound comes alone,
For they ring out their peals in a mingled throng,
And the breezes waft the loud ding-dong along.

When the echo has reached me in this lone vale,
I am straightway a hero in coat of mail,
I tug at my belt and I march on my post,
And feel myself more than a match for a host.

I am on the alert for some wonderful Thing,
W[h]ich somewhere's a taking place,
'Tis perchance the salute which our planet doth ring
When it meeteth another in space.

—With cunning plates the polished leaves were decked,
Each one a window to the poet's world,
So rich a prospect that you might suspect
In that small space all paradise unfurled.
It was a right delightful road to go,
    marching through pastures of such fair herbage,
O'er hill and dale it lead, and to and fro,
From bard to bard, making an easy stage.

Where ever and anon I slaked my thirst
Like a tired traveller at some poet's well,
Which from the teeming ground did bubbling burst,
And tinkling thence adown the page it fell.
Still through the leaves its music you might hear,
Till other springs fell faintly on the ear.

Up this pleasant stream let's row
For the livelong summer's day,
Sprinkling foam where'er we go
In wreaths as white as driven snow—
Ply the oars, away! away!

Now we glide along the shore,
Chucking lillies as we go,
While the yellow-sanded floor
Doggedly resists the oar,
Like some turtle dull and slow.

Now we stem the middle tide
Ploughing through the deepest soil,
Ridges pile on either side,
While we through the furrow glide,
Reaping bubbles for our toil.

Dew before and drought behind,
Onward all doth seem to fly;
Nought contents the eager mind,
Only rapids now are kind,
Forward are the earth and sky.

Sudden music strikes the ear,
Leaking out from yonder bank,
Fit such voyagers to cheer—
Sure there must be naiads here,
Who have kindly played this prank.

There I know the cunning pack
Where yon self-sufficient rill
All its telltale hath kept back,
Through the meadows held its clack,
And now bubbleth its fill.

Silent flows the parent stream,
And if rocks do lie below
Smothers with her waves the din,
As it were a youthful sin,
Just as still and just as slow.

But this gleeful little rill,
Purling round its storied pebble,
Tinkles to the selfsame tune
From December until June,
Nor doth any drought enfeeble.

See the sun behind the willows,
Rising through the golden haze,
How he gleams along the billows—
Their white crests the easy pillows
Of his dew besprinkled rays.

Forward press we to the dawning,
For Aurora leads the way,
Sultry noon and twilight scorning,
In each dew drop of the morning
Lies the promise of a day.

Rivers from the sun do flow,
Springing with the dewy morn,
Voyageurs 'gainst time do row,
Idle noon nor sunset know,
Ever even with the dawn.

Since that first away! away!
Many a lengthy league we've rowed,
Still the sparrow on the spray,
Hastes to usher in the day
With her simple stanza'd ode.

Come let's roam the breezy pastures,
Where the freest zephyrs blow,
Batten on the oak tree's rustle,
And the pleasant insect bustle,
Dripping with the streamlet's flow.

What if I no wings do wear,
Thro' this solid seeming air
I can skim like any swallow
Who so dareth let her follow,
And we'll be a jovial pair.

Like two careless swifts let's sail,
Zephyrus shall think for me—
Over hill and over dale,
Riding on the easy gale,
We will scan the earth and sea.

Yonder see that willow tree
Winnowing the buxom air,
You a gnat and I a bee,
With our merry minstrelsy
We will make a concert there.

One green leaf shall be our screen,
Till the sun doth go to bed,
I the king and you the queen
Of that peaceful little green,
Without any subject's aid.

To our music Time will linger,
And earth open wide her ear,
Nor shall any need to tarry
To immortal verse to marry
Such sweet music as he'll hear.

Light hearted, careless, shall I take my way,
When I to thee this being have resigned,
Well knowing where upon a future day,
With usurer's craft, more than myself to find.

EACH MORE MELODIOUS NOTE
I HEAR

Each more melodious note I hear
Brings this reproach to me,
That I alone afford the ear,
Who would the music be.

I WAS BORN UPON THY
BANK RIVER

I was born upon thy bank river
My blood flows in thy stream
And thou meanderest forever
   At the bottom of my dream

I know the world where land and water meet,
By yonder hill abutting on the main,
One while I hear the waves incessant beat,
Then turning round survey the land again.

Within a humble cot that looks to sea
Daily I breathe this curious warm life,
Beneath a friendly haven's sheltering lea
My noiseless day with myst'ry still is rife.

'Tis here, they say, my simple life began,
And easy credit to the tale I lend,
For well I know 'tis here I am a man,
But who will simply tell me of the end?

These eyes fresh opened spied the far off Sea,
Which like a silent godfather did stand,
Nor uttered one explaining word to me,
But introduced straight godmother Sand.

And yonder still stretches that silent main,
With many glancing ships besprinkled o'er,
And earnest still I gaze and gaze again
Upon the self same waves and friendly shore

Till like a watery humor on the eye
It still appears whichever way I turn,
Its silent waste and mute oerarching sky
With close shut eyes I clearly still discern.

And yet with lingering doubt I haste each morn
To see if Ocean still my gaze will greet,
And with each day once more to life am born,
And tread the earth once more with tott'ring feet.

———

My years are like a stroll upon the beach,
As near the ocean's edge as I can go;
My tardy steps its waves sometimes o'erreach,
Sometimes I stay to let them overflow.

Infinite work my hands find there to do,
Gathering the relics which the waves up cast;
Each tempest scours the deep for something new,
And every time the strangest is the last.

My sole employment 'tis and scrupulous care,
To place my gains beyond the reach of tides,
Each smoother pebble and each shell more rare
Which ocean kindly to my hand confides.

I have but few companions on the shore,
They scorn the strand who sail upon the sea,
Yet oft I think the ocean they've sailed oer
Is deeper known upon the strand to me.

My neighbors sometimes come with lumb'ring carts,
As if they wished my pleasant toil to share,
But straightway go again to distant marts
For only weeds and ballast are their care.

———

'Tis by some strange coincidence if I
Make common cause with ocean when he storms
Who can so well support a separate sky,
And people it with multitude of forms.

Oft in the stillness of the night I hear
Some restless bird presage the coming din,
And distant murmurs faintly strike my ear
From some bold bluff projecting far within.

My stillest depths straightway do inly heave
More genially than rests the summer's calm,
The howling winds through my soul's cordage grieve,
Till every shelf and ledge gives the alarm.

Oft at some ruling star my tide has swelled,
The sea can scarcely brag more wrecks than I,
Ere other influence my waves has quelled
The staunchest bark that floats is high and dry.

I'm guided in the darkest night
By flashes of auroral light,
Which over dart thy eastern home
And teach me not in vain to roam.
Thy steady light on t'other side
Pales the sunset, makes day abide,
And after sunrise stays the dawn,
Forerunner of a brighter morn.

There is no being here to me
But staying here to be
When others laugh I am not glad,
When others cry I am not sad,
But be they grieved or be they merry
I'm supernumerary.
I am a miser without blame
Am conscience stricken without shame.
An idler am I without leisure,
A busy body without pleasure.
I did not think so bright a day
Would issue in so dark a night.
I did not think such sober play
Would leave me in so sad a plight,
And I should be most sorely spent
Where first I was most innocent.
I thought by loving all beside
To prove to you my love was wide,
And by the rites I soared above
To show you my peculiar love.

Now we are partners in such legal trade,
We'll look to the beginnings, not the ends,
Nor to pay day—knowing true wealth is made
For current stock and not for dividends.

Methinks all things have travelled since you shined,
But only Time, and clouds, Time's team, have moved;
Again foul weather shall not change my mind,
But In the shade I will believe what in the sun I loved.

They who prepare my evening meal below
Carelessly hit the kettle as they go
With tongs or shovel,
And ringing round and round,
Out of this hovel
It makes an eastern temple by the sound.

At first I thought a cow-bell right at hand
Mid birches sounded o'er the open land,
Where I plucked flowers
Many years ago,
Spending midsummer hours
With such secure delight they hardly seemed to flow.

My ground is high,
But 'tis not dry,
What you call dew
Comes filtering through;
Though in the sky,
It still is nigh;
Its soil is blue
And virgin too.

IF FROM YOUR PRICE YE
WILL NOT SWERVE

If from your price ye will not swerve,
Why then Ill think the gods reserve
A greater bargain there above,
Out of their sup'rabundant love,
Have meantime better for me cared,
And so will get my stock prepared,
Plows of new pattern, hoes the same,
Designed a different soil to tame,
And sow my seed broadcast in air,
Certain to reap my harvest there.

FRIENDSHIP'S STEADFASTNESS

True friendship is so firm a league
That's maintenance falls into the even tenor
Of our lives, and is no tie,
But the continuance of our lifes thread.

If I would safely keep this new got pelf,
I have no care henceforth but watch myself,
For lo! it goes untended from my sight,
Waxes and wanes secure with the safe star of night.

See with what liberal step it makes its way,
As we could well afford to let it stray
Throughout the universe, with the sun & moon,
Which would dissolve allegiance as soon.

Shall I concern myself for fickleness,
And undertake to make my friends more sure,
When the great gods out of sheer kindliness,
Gave me this office for a sinecure?

DEATH CANNOT COME TOO SOON

Death cannot come too soon
Where it can come at all,
But always is too late
Unless the fates it call.

My life more civil is and free
Than any civil polity.

Ye princes keep your realms
And circumscribed power,
Not wide as are my dreams,
Nor rich as is this hour.

What can ye give which I have not?
What can ye take which I have got?
Can ye defend the dangerless?
Can ye inherit nakedness?

To all true wants time's ear is deaf,
Penurious states lend no relief
Out of their pelf—
But a free soul—thank God—
Can help itself.

Be sure your fate
Doth keep apart its state—
Not linked with any band—
Even the nobles of the land

In tented fields with cloth of gold—
No place doth hold
But is more chivalrous than they are.
And sigheth for a nobler war.
A finer strain its trumpet rings—
A brighter gleam its armor flings.

The life that I aspire to live
No man proposeth me—
No trade upon the street
Wears its emblazonry.

It is a noble country where we dwell,
Fit for a stalwart race to summer in;
From Madawaska to Red River raft,
From Florid keys to the Missouri forks,
See what unwearied (and) copious streams
Come tumbling to the east and southern shore,
To find a man stand on their lowland banks:
Behold the innumerous rivers and the licks
Where he may drink to quench his summer's thirst,
And the broad corn and rice fields yonder, where
His hands may gather for his winter's store.

See the fair reaches of the northern lakes
To cool his summer with their inland breeze,
And the long slumbering Appalachian range
Offering its slopes to his unwearied knees!
See what a long-lipped sea doth clip the shores,
And noble strands where navies may find port;
See Boston, Baltimore, and New York stand
Fair in the sunshine on the eastern sea,
And yonder too the fair green prairie.

See the red race with sullen step retreat,
Emptying its graves, striking the wigwam tent,
And where the rude camps of its brethern stand,
Dotting the distant green, their herds around;
In serried ranks, and with a distant clang,
Their fowl fly o'er, bound to the northern lakes,
Whose plashing waves invite their webbéd feet.

Such the fair reach and prospect of the land,
The journeying summer creeps from south to north
With wearied feet, resting in many a vale;
Its length doth tire the seasons to o'ercome,
Its widening breadth doth make the sea-breeze pause
And spend its breath against the mountain's side:
Still serene Summer paints the southern fields,
While the stern Winter reigns on northern hills.

Look nearer,—know the lineaments of each face,—
Learn the far-travelled race, and find here met
The so long gathering congress of the world!
The Afric race brought here to curse its fate,
Erin to bless,—the patient German too,
Th' industrious Swiss, the fickle, sanguine Gaul,
And manly Saxon, leading all the rest.
All things invite this earth's inhabitants
To rear their lives to an unheard-of height,
And meet the expectation of the land;
To give at length the restless race of man
A pause in the long westering caravan.

The moon now rises to her absolute rule,
And the husbandman and hunter
Acknowledge her for their mistress.
Asters and golden reign in the fields
And the life everlasting withers not.
The fields are reaped and shorn of their pride
But [?] an inward verdure still crowns them
The thistle scatters its down on the pool
And yellow leaves clothe the river—
And nought disturbs the serious life of men.
But behind the sheaves and under the sod
There lurks a ripe fruit which the reapers have not
                      gathered
The true harvest of the year—the boreal[?] fruit
Which it bears forever.
With fondness annually watering and maturing it.
But man never severs the stalk
Which bears this palatable fruit.

My friends, why should we live?
Life is an idle war a toilsome peace;
   To-day I would not give
One small consent for its securest ease.

   Shall we out-wear the year
In our pavilions on its dusty plain
   And yet no signal hear
To strike our tents and take the road again?

   Or else drag up the slope
The heavy ordnance of nature's train?
   Useless but in the hope,
Some far remote and heavenward hill to gain.

I mark the summer's swift decline
The springing sward its grave clothes weaves
Whose rustling woods the gales confine
The aged year turns on its couch of leaves.

Oh could I catch the sounds remote
Could I but tell to human ear—
The strains which on the breezes float
And sing the requiem of the dying year.

METHINKS THAT BY A STRICT BEHAVIOR

Methinks that by a strict behavior
I could elicit back the brightest star
That lurks behind a cloud.

I HAVE ROLLED NEAR SOME
OTHER SPIRITS PATH

I have rolled near some other spirits path
And with a pleased anxiety have felt
Its purer influence on my opaque mass
But always was I doomed to learn, alas!
I had scarce changed its sidireal time.

How little curious is man
He has not searched his mystery a span
But dreams of mines of treasure
Which he neglects to measure.

For three score years and ten
Walks to and fro amid his fellow men
O'er this small tract of continental land
And never uses a divining wand.

Our uninquiring corpses lie more low
Than our life's curiosity doth go
Our ambitious steps ne'er climb so high
As in their daily sport the sparrows fly

And yonder cloud's borne farther in a day
Than our most vagrant steps may ever stray.
Surely, O Lord, he has not greatly erred,
Who has so little from his threshhold stirred.

He wanders through this low and shallow world
Scarcely his loftier thoughts and hopes unfurled,
Through this low walled world, where his huge sin
Has hardly room to rest and harbor in.

He wanders round until his end draws nigh
And then lays down his aged head to dye
And this is life, this is that famous strife.

ON FIELDS OER WHICH THE REAPER'S
HAND HAS PASS[E]D

On fields oer which the reaper's hand has pass[e]d,
Lit by the harvest moon and autumn sun,
My thoughts like stubble floating in the wind
And of such fineness as October airs,
There after harvest could I glean my life
A richer harvest reaping without toil,
And weaving gorgeous fancies at my will
In subtler webs than finest summer haze.

There is health in thy gray wing
Health of nature's furnishing.
Say thou modern-winged antique,
Was thy mistress ever sick?
In each heaving of thy wing
Thou dost health and leisure bring,
Thou dost waive disease & pain
And resume new life again.

I walk in nature still alone
   And know no one
Discern no lineament nor feature
   Of any creature.

Though all the firmament
   Is oer me bent,
Yet still I miss the grace
   Of an intelligent and kindred face.

I still must seek the friend
Who does with nature blend,
Who is the person in her mask,
He is the man I ask.

Who is the expression of her meaning,
Who is the uprightness of her leaning,
Who is the grown child of her weaning

The center of this world,
The face of nature,
The site of human life,
Some sure foundation
And nucleus of a nation—
At least a private station.

We twain would walk together
Through every weather,
And see this aged nature,
Go with a bending stature.

Yet let us Thank the purblind race,
  Who still have thought it good
With lasting stone to mark the place
  Where braver men have stood.

In concord, town of quiet name
  And quiet fame as well,

Ive seen ye, sisters, on the mountain-side
When your green mantles fluttered in the wind
Ive seen your foot-prints on the lakes smooth shore
Lesser than man's, a more ethereal trace,
I have heard of ye as some far-famed race—
Daughters of gods whom I should one day meet—
Or mothers I might say of all our race.
I reverence your natures so like mine
Yet strangely different, like but still unlike
Thou only stranger that hast crossed my path
Accept my hospitality—let me hear
The message which thou bring'st
    Made different from me
   Perchance thou't made to be
   The creature of a different destiny.
I know not who ye are that meekly stand
Thus side by side with man in every land.
When did ye form alliance with our race
Ye children of the moon who in placid nights
Vaulted upon the hills and sought this earth.
Reveal that which I fear ye can not tell
Wherein ye are not I, wherein ye dwell
Where I can never come.
What boots it that I do regard ye so
Does it make suns to shine or crops to grow?
What boots that I never should forget
Thee[?], I have sisters sitting for me yet

And what are sisters
The robust man who can so stoutly strive
In this bleak world is hardly kept alive.
And who is it protects *ye* smooths *your* way

Ye do command me to all virtue ever
And simple truth the law by which we live
Methinks that I can trust your clearer sense
And your immediate knowledge of the truth.
I would obey your influence—one with fate

On shoulders whirled in some eccentric orbit
Just by old Paestum's temples and the perch
Where Time doth plume his wings.

Dull water spirit—and Protean god
Descended cloud fast anchored to the earth
That drawest too much air for shallow coasts
Thou ocean branch that flowest to the sun
Incense of earth, perfumed with flowers—
Spirit of lakes and rivers, seas and rills
Come to revisit now thy native scenes
Night thoughts of earth—dream drapery
Dew cloth and fairy napkin
Thou wind-blown meadow of the air.

Brother where dost thou dwell?
    What sun shines for thee now?
Dost thou indeed farewell?
    As we wished here below.

What season didst thou find?
    'Twas winter here.
Are not the fates more kind
    Than they appear?

Is thy brow clear again
    As in thy youthful years?
And was that ugly pain
    The summit of thy fears?

Yet thou wast cheery still,
    They could not quench thy fire,
Thou dids't abide their will,
    And then retire.

Where chiefly shall I look
    To feel thy presence near?
Along the neighboring brook
    May I thy voice still hear?

Dost thou still haunt the brink
    Of yonder river's tide?
And may I ever think
    That thou art at my side?

What bird wilt thou employ
　　To bring me word of thee?
For it would give them joy,
　　'Twould give them liberty,
　　To serve their former lord
　　With wing and minstrelsy.

A sadder strain has mixed with their song,
　　They've slowlier built their nests,
Since thou art gone
　　Their lively labor rests.

Where is the finch—the thrush,
　　I used to hear?
Ah! they could well abide
　　The dying year.

Now they no more return,
　　I hear them not;
They have remained to mourn,
　　Or else forgot.

Traveller, this is no prison,
He is not dead, but risen.
    Then is there need,
    To fill his grave,
    And truth to save,
    That we should read,—
    In Pursy's favor
    Here lies the engraver.

Here lies the body of this world,
Whose soul alas to hell is hurled.
This golden youth long since was past,
Its silver manhood went as fast,
And iron age drew on at last;
'Tis vain its character to tell,
The several fates which it befell,
What year it died, when 'twill arise,
We only know that here it lies.

By death's favor
Here lies the engraver
And now I think o't
Where lies he not?
If the archangel look but where he lies
He ne'er will get translated to the skies.

A stately music rises on my ear,
Borne on the breeze from some adjacent vale;
A host of knights, my own true ancestors,
Tread to the lofty strains and pass away
In long procession; to this music's sound
The Just move onward in deep serried ranks,
With looks serene of hope, and gleaming brows,
As if they were the temples of the Day.

Gilt by an unseen sun's resplendent ray
They firmly move, sure as the lapse of Time;
Departed worth, leaving these trivial fields
Where sedate valor finds no worthy aim,
And still is Fame the noblest cause of all.

Forward they press and with exalted eye,
As if their road, which seems a level plain,
Did still ascend, and were again subdued
'Neath their proud feet. Forward they move, and leave
The sun and moon and stars alone behind:
And now, by the still fainter strains, I know
They surely pass; and soon their quivering harp,
And faintly clashing cymbal, will have ceased
To feed my ear.

It is the steadiest motion eye hath seen,
A Godlike progress; e'en the hills and rocks
Do forward come, so to congratulate
Their feet; the rivers eddy backward, and
The waves recurl to accompany their march.

Onward they move, like to the life of man,
Which cannot rest, but goes without delay
Right to the gates of Death, not losing time
In its majestic tread to Eternity,
As if Man's blood, a river, flowed right on
Far as the eye could reach, to the Heart of hearts,
Nor eddied round about these complex limbs.

'Tis the slow march of life,—I feel the feet
Of tiny drops go pattering through *my* veins;
Their arteries flow with an Assyrian pace,
And empires rise and fall beneath their stride.

Still, as they move, flees the horizon wall;
The low-roofed sky o'erarches their true path;
For they have caught at last the pace of Heaven,
Their great Commander's true and timely tread.

Lo! how the sky before them is cast up
Into an archèd road, like to the gallery
Of the small mouse that bores the meadow's turf:
Chapels of ease swift open o'er the path,
And domes continuous span the lengthening way.

Tell me ye wise ones if ye can
Whither and whence the race of man.
For I have seen his slender clan
Clinging to hoar hills with their feet
Threading the forest for their meat
Moss and lichens bark & grain
They rake together with might & main
And they digest them with anxiety & pain.
I meet them in their rags and unwashed hair
Instructed to eke out their scanty fare
Brave race—with a yet humbler prayer
Beggars they are aye on the largest scale
They beg their daily bread at heavens door
And if their this years crop alone shou[l]d fail
They neither bread nor begging would know more.
They are the titmans [?] of their race
And hug the vales with mincing pace
Like Troglodites. and fight with cranes.
We walk mid great relations feet
What they let fall alone we eat
We are only able
to catch the fragments from their table
These elder brothers of our race
By us unseen with larger pace
Walk oer our heads, and live our lives
embody our desires and dreams
Anticipate our hoped for gleams

We grub the earth for our food
We know not what is good
Where does the fragrance of our orchards go
Our vineyards while we toil below—
A finer race and finer fed
Feast and revel above our head.
The tints and fragrance of the flowers & fruits
Are but the crumbs from off their table
While we consume the pulp and roots
Some times we do assert our kin
And stand a moment where once they have been
We hear their sounds and see their sights
And we experience their delights—
But for the moment that we stand
Astonished on the Olympian land
We do discern no traveller's face
No elder brother of our race.
To lead us to the monarch's court
And represent our case.
But straightway we must journey back
retracing slow the arduous track,
Without the privilege to tell
Even, the sight we know so well.

The Earth

Which seems so barren once gave birth
To heroes—who oerran her plains,
Who plowed her seas and reaped her grains

What doth he ask?
Some worthy task.
Never to run
Till that be done,
that never done
Under the sun.
Here to begin
All things to win
By his endeavor
Forever and ever—
Happy and well
On this ground to dwell
This soil subdue
Plant and renew.
By might & main
Hea[l]th & strength gain
So to give nerve
To his slenderness
Yet Some mighty pain
He would sustain.
So to preserve
His tenderness.
Not be deceived
Of suffring bereaved
Not lose his life
By living too well
Nor escape strife
In his lonely cell

And so find out Heaven
By not knowing Hell.
Strength like the rock
To withstand any shock—
Yet some Aaron's rod
Some smiting by god
Occasion to gain
To shed human tears
And to entertain
Still divine fears.
Not once for all, forever, blest,
Still to be cheered out of the west
Not from his heart to banish all sighs
Still be encouraged by the sun rise
Forever to love and to love and to love
Within him, around him—beneath him above
To love is to know, is to feel, is to be
At once 'tis his birth & his destiny
For earthly pleasures
Celestial pains
Heavenly losses
For earthly gains.
Must we still eat
The bread we have spurned
Must we rekindle
The faggots we've burned—
Must we go out
By the poor man's gate
Die by degrees
Not by new fate.

Is then[?] no road
This way my friend
Is there no road
Without any end—
When I have slumbered
I have heard sounds
As travellers passing
Over my grounds—
'Twas a sweet music
Wafted them by
I could not tell
If far off or nigh.
Unless I dreamed it
This was of yore—
But I never told it
To mortal before—
Never remembered
But in my dreams
What to me waking
A miracle seems
If you will give of your pulse or your grain
We will rekindle those flames again
Here will we tarry it is without doubt
Till a miracle putteth that fire out.

At midnight's hour I raised my head
The owls were seeking for their bread
The foxes barked impatient still
At their wan[?] fate they bear so ill—
I thought me of eternities delayed
And of commands but half obeyed—
The night wind rustled through the glade
As if a force of men there staid
The word was whispered through the ranks
And every hero seized his lance
The word was whispered through the ranks
    Advance.

I seek the Present Time,
No other clime,
Life in to-day,
Not to sail another way,
To Paris or to Rome,
Or farther still from home.
That man, whoe'er he is,
Lives but a moral death,
Whose life is not coeval
With his breath.
What are deeds done
Away from home?
What the best essay
On the Ruins of Rome?
The dusty highways,
What Scripture says,
This pleasant weather
And all signs together—
The river's meander,
All things, in short,
Forbid me to wander
In deed or in thought.
In cold or in drouth,
seek Not the sunny South,
But make the whole tour
Of the sunny Present Hour.

For here if thou fail,
Where canst thou prevail?
If you love not
Your own land most,
You'll find nothing lovely
Upon a distant coast.
If you love not
The latest sunset,
What is there in pictures
Or old gems set?

If no man should travel
Till he had the means,
There'd be little travelling
For kings or for Queens.
The means, what are they!
They are the wherewithal
Great expenses to pay;—
Life got, and some to spare,
Great works on hand,
And freedom from care.
Plenty of time well spent,
To use,—
Clothes paid for, and no rent
In your shoes;—
Something to eat,
And something to burn,
And, above all, no need to return;—

For they who come back,
,have they not failed,
Wherever they've ridden
Or steamed it, or sailed?
All your grass hayed,—
All your debts paid,—
All your wills made?
Then you might as well have stayed,
For are you not dead,
Only not buried?

The way unto "Today",
The rail road to "Here,"
They never'll grade that way,
Nor shorten it, I fear.
There are plenty of depots
All the world o'er,
But not a single station
At a man's door;
If we would get near
To the secret of things,
We shall not have to hear
When the engine bell rings.

LOVES INVALIDES ARE NOT THOSE
OF COMMON WARS

Loves invalides are not those of common wars
   More than its scars—
They are not disabled for a higher love
   But taught to look above.

With erring men I have small affair
   Though they can do some harm & do not care.
It is a part of them which I can not commend
A part of them that never was my friend.

And once again
When I went a-maying—
& once or twice more I had seen thee before.
For there grow the May flowe[r]
  (Epigaea repens)
& the mt cranberry
  & the screech owl *strepens*

Old meeting-house bell
I love thy music well
It peals through the air
Sweetly full & fair
As in the early times
When I listened to its chimes.

Is consigned to the nine.
I to nature consign.
I am but the [word] of myself.
Without inlet it lies
without outlet it flows
From & to the skies
It comes & it goes
I am its source,
& my life is its course
I am its stoney shore
& the gale that passes oer

Among the worst of men that ever lived
However we did seriously attend
A little space we let our thoughts ascend
Experienced our religion & confessed
'Twas good for us to be there—be anywhere
Then to a heap of apples we addressed
& cleared the topmost rider *sine* care
But our Icarian thoughts returned to ground
And we went on to heaven the long way round.

Among the signs of autumn I perceive
The Roman wormwood (called by learned men
Ambrosia elatior, food for gods,—
For to impartial science the humblest weed
Is as immortal once[?] as the proudest flower—)
Sprinkles its yellow dust over my shoes
As I cross the now neglected garden
—We trample under foot the food of gods
& spill their nectar in each drop of dew—
My honest shoes Fast friends that never stray
far from my couch thus powdered countryfied
Bearing many a mile the marks of their adventure
At the post-house disgrace the Gallic gloss
Of those well dressed ones who no morning dew
Nor Roman wormwood ever have been through
Who never walk but are *transported* rather—
For what old crime of theirs I do not gather

TH' AMBROSIA OF THE GODS 'S
A WEED ON EARTH

Th' ambrosia of the Gods 's a weed on earth
Their nectar is the morning dew which on
'ly our shoes taste—For they are simple folks
'Tis very fit the ambrosia of the gods
Should be a weed on earth. As nectar is
The morning dew with which we wet our shoes
For the gods are simple folks and we should pine
                            upon their humble fare

I SAW A DELICATE FLOWER HAD GROWN UP 2 FEET HIGH

I saw a delicate flower had grown up 2 feet high
Between the horse's paths & the wheel track
Which Dakin's & Maynards wagons had
Passed over many a time
An inch more to right or left had sealed its fate
Or an inch higher. And yet it lived & flourish[e]d
As much as if it had a thousand acres
Of untrodden space around it—and never
Knew the danger it incurred.
It did not borrow trouble nor invite an
Evil fate by apprehending it.
For though the distant market-wagon
Every other day—inevitably rolled
This way—it just as inevitably rolled
In those ruts—And the same
Charioteer who steered the flower
Upward—guided the horse & cart aside from it.
There were other flowers which you would say
Incurred less danger grew more out of the way
Which no cart rattled near, no walker daily passed.
But at length one rambling deviously
For no rut restrained plucked them
And then it appeared that they stood
Directly in his way though he had come
From farther than the market wagon—

TO DAY I CLIMBED A HANDSOME ROUNDED HILL

To day I climbed a handsome rounded hill
Covered with hickory trees wishing to see
The country from its top—for low hills
show unexpected prospects—I looked
many miles over a woody low-land
Toward Marlborough Framingham & Sudbury
And as I sat amid the hickory trees

I am the little Irish boy
   That lives in the shanty
I am four years old today
   And shall soon be one and twenty
   I shall grow up
   And be a great man
   And shovel all day
   As hard as I can.

   Down in the deep cut
   Where the men lived
   Who made the Rail road.

for supper
   I have some potatoe
   And sometimes some bread
   And then if it's cold
     I go right to bed.

   I lie on some straw
   Under my fathers coat

   My mother does not cry
   And my father does not scold
   For I am a little Irish Boy
   And I'm four years old.

Every day I go to school
Along the Railroad
It was so cold it made me cry
The day that it snowed.

And if my feet ache
I do not mind the cold
For I am a little Irish boy
& I'm four years old.

I do not fear my thoughts will die
For never yet it was so dry
as to scorch the azure of the sky.
It knows no withering & no drought
Though all eyes crop it ne'er gives out
My eyes my flocks are
Mountains my crops are
I do not fear my flocks will stray
For they were made to roam the day
For they can wander with the latest light
Yet be at home at night.

Cans't thou love with thy mind,
  And reason with thy heart?
Cans't thou be kind,
  And from thy darling part?

Cans't thou range earth sea, & air,
And so meet me everywhere?
Through all events I will pursue thee,
Through all persons I will woo thee.

Indeed indeed, I cannot tell,
Though I ponder on it well,
Which were easier to state,
All my love or all my hate.
Surely, surely, thou wilt trust me
When I say thou dost disgust me.
O, I hate thee with a hate
That would fain annihilate;
Yet sometimes against my will,
My dear friend, I love thee still.
It were treason to our love,
And a sin to God above,
One iota to abate
Of a pure impartial hate.

THE VESSEL OF LOVE, THE
VESSEL OF STATE

The vessel of love, the vessel of state,
Each is ballasted with hate.
Every Congress that we hold
Means the union is dissolved.

But though the south is still enslaved,
By that oath the Union's saved,
For 'tis our love and not our hate
Interests us in their fate.

When the toads begin to ring,
Then thinner clothing bring
or Off your greatcoat fling

Forever in my dream & in my morning thought
 Eastward a mount ascends—
But when in the sunbeam its hard outline is sought—
 It all dissolves & ends.
The woods that way are gates—the pastures too slop[e] up
 To an unearthly ground—
But when I ask my mates, to take the staff & cup,
 It can no more be found—
Perchanc[e] I have no shoes fit for the lofty soil
 Where my thoughts graze—
No properly spun clues—nor well strained mid day oil
 Or—must I mend my ways?
It is a promised land which I have not yet earned,
 I have not made beginning
With consecrated hand—I have not even learned
 To lay the underpinning.
The mountain sinks by day—as do my lofty thoughts,
 Because I'm not highminded.
If I could think alway above these hills & warts
 I should see it, though blinded.
It is a spiral path within the pilgrim's soul
 Leads to this mountain's brow
Commencing at his hearth he reache[s] to this goal
 He knows not when nor how.

STRANGE THAT SO MANY FICKLE GODS, AS FICKLE AS THE WEATHER

Strange that so many fickle gods, as fickle as the weather,
Throughout Dame Natures provinces should always pull
   together.

THE DEEDS OF KING AND MEANEST HEDGER

The deeds of king and meanest hedger,
Stand side by side in heaven's ledger.

WAIT NOT TILL I INVITE THEE, BUT OBSERVE

Wait not till I invite thee, but observe
I'm glad to see thee when thou com'st.

GREATER IS THE DEPTH OF SADNESS

Greater is the depth of sadness
Than is any height of gladness.

WHERE I HAVE BEEN

Where I have been
There was none seen.

BETTER WAIT

Better wait
Than be too late.

ON A GOOD MAN

Here lies—the world
There rises one.

MAN MAN IS THE DEVIL

Man Man is the Devil
The source of all evil.

YOU MUST NOT ONLY AIM ARIGHT

You must not only aim aright,
But draw the bow with all your might.

THE CHICADEE

The chicadee
Hops near to me.

ANY FOOL CAN MAKE A RULE

Any fool can make a rule
And every fool will mind it.

ALL THINGS DECAY

All things decay
& so must our sleigh

EXPECTATION

No sound from my forge
Has been heard in the gorge,
But as a brittle cup
I've held the hammer up.

For though the caves were rabitted,
  And the well sweeps were slanted,
Each house seemed not inhabited
  But haunted.

The pensive traveller held his way,
  Silent & melancholy,
For every man an ideot was,
  And every house a folly.

My friends, my noble friends, know ye—
That in my waking hours I think of ye
  Ever[?] in godlike band uncompromised & free

NO EARNEST WORK THAT WILL
EXPAND THE FRAME

No earnest work that will expand the frame,
And give a soundness to the muscles to[o]?
How ye do waste your time!
Pray make it wor[th] the while to live,
Or worth the while to die.
Show us great actions piled on high,
Tasking our utmost strength touching the sky,
As if we lived in a mountainous country.
     Hell were not quite so hard to bear
  If one were honored with its hottest place.
And did ye fear ye should spoil Hell
By making it sublime?

The moon hung low o'er Provence vales,
   'Twas night upon the sea,
Fair France was woo'd by Afric gales
   And paid in minstrelsy.
Along the Rhone then moves a band,
   Their banner in the breeze,
Of mail-clad men with iron hand,
   And steel on breast and knees.
The herdsman following his droves
   Far in the night alone,
Read faintly through the olive groves,—
   'Twas Godfrey of Boulogne

The mist still slumbered on the heights
   The glaciers lay in shade,
The stars withdrew with faded lights,
   The moon went down the glade.
Proud Jura saw the day from far,
   And showed it to the plain;
She heard the din of coming war,
   But told it not again.
The goatherd seated on the rocks,
   Dreaming of battles none
Was wakened by his startled flocks,—
   'Twas Godfrey of Boulogne.

Night hung upon the Danube's stream,
  Deep midnight on the vales,
Along the shore no beacons gleam,
  No sound is on the gales.
The Turkish lord has banished care
  The harem sleeps profound,
Save one fair Georgian sitting there
  Upon the Moslem ground.
The lightning flashed a transient gleam,
  A glancing banner shone,
A host swept swiftly down the stream,—
  'Twas Godfrey of Boulogne.

'Twas noon upon Byzantium,
  On street and tower and sea,
On Europe's edge a warlike hum
  Of gathered chivalry.
A troop went boldly through the throng,
  Of Ethiops, Arabs, Huns,
Jews Greeks and Turk, to right their wrong
  Their swords flashed thousand suns.
Their banner cleaved Byzantium's dust,
  And like the sun it shone,
their armor had acquired no rust,—
  'Twas Godfrey of Boulogne.

Who equallest the coward's haste
And still inspires the faintest heart
Whose lofty fame is not disgraced
Though it assume the lowest part

Ive searched my faculties around
To learn why life to me was lent
I will attend his faintest sound
And then declare to man what God hath meant

Until at length the north winds blow,
And beating high mid ice and snow,
The sturdy goose brings up the rear,
Leaving behind the cold cold year.

I was made erect and lone
And within me is the bone
Still my vision will be clear
Still my life will not be drear
To the center all is near
Where I sit there is my throne
If age choose to sit apart
If age choose give me the start
Take the sap and leave the heart

Spes sibi quisque
Each one his own hope

Wait not till slaves pronounce the word
  To set the captive free,
Be free yourselves, be not deferred,
  And farewell slavery.

Ye are all slaves, ye have your price,
  And gang but cries to gang.
Then rise, the highest of ye rise,
  I hear your fetters clang.

Think not the tyrant sits afar
  In your own breasts ye have
The District of Columbia
  And power to free the Slave.

The warmest heart the north doth breed,
  Is still too cold and far,
The colored man's release must come
  From outcast Africa.

Make haste & set the captive free!—
  Are ye so free that cry?
The lowest depths of slavery
  Leave freedom for a sigh.

What is your whole republic worth?
   Ye hold out vulgar lures,
Why will ye be disparting earth
   When all of heaven is yours?

He's governéd well who rules himself,
   No despot vetoes him,
There's no defaulter steals his pelf,
   Nor revolution grim.

'Tis neither silver rags nor gold
   'S the better currency,
The only specie that will hold
   Is current honesty.

The minister of state hath cares,
   He cannot get release,
Administer his own affairs,
   Nor settle his own peace,

'Tis easier to treat with kings,
   And please our country's foes,
Than treat with conscience of the things
   Which only conscience knows.

There's but the party of the great,
   And party of the mean,
And if there is an Empire State
   'Tis the upright, I ween.

And when the sun puts out his lamp
We'll sleep serene within the camp,
Trusting to his invet'rate skill
Who leads the stars oer yonder hill,
Whose discipline doth never cease
To watch the slumberings of peace,
And from the virtuous hold afar
The melancholy din of war.—
For ye our sentries still outlie,
The earth your pallet and your screen the sky.

From steadfastness I will not swerve
Remembering my sweet reserve.

With all your kindness shown from year to year
Ye do but civil demons still appear,
Still to my mind
Ye are inhuman and unkind,
And bear an untamed aspect to my sight
After the "civil-suited" night
As if ye had lain out
Like to the Indian scout
Who lingers in the purlieus of the towns
With unexplored grace and savage frowns.

The great friend
Dwells at the land's end,
There lives he
Next to the Sea.
Fleets come and go,
Carrying commerce to and fro,
But still sits he on the sand
And maketh firm that headland.
Mariners steer them by his light
Safely in the darkest night,
He holds no visible communion
For his friendship is a union.
Many men dwell far inland,
But he alone sits on the strand,
Whether he ponders men or books
Ever still he seaward looks,
Feels the sea-breeze on his cheek,
At each word the landsmen speak;
From some distant port he hears
Of the ventures of past years
In this the sullen ocean's roar
Of wrecks upon a distant shore;
In every companions eye
A sailing vessel doth descry;
Marine news he ever reads
And the slightest glances heeds.

Near is India to him
Though his native shore is dim,
But the bark which long was due,
Never—never—heaves in view,
Which shall put an end to commerce
And bring back what it took from us,
(Which shall make Siberia free
Of the climes beyond the Sea)
Fetch the Indies in its hold,
All their spices and their gold,
And men sail the sea no more
The sea itself become a shore,
To a broader deeper sea,
A profounder mystery.

Upon the bank at early dawn
   I hear the cocks proclaim the day,
Though the moon shines securely on,
   As if her course they could not stay.

The stars withhold their shining not
Or singly or in scattered crowds,
But seem like Parthian arrows shot
   By yielding Night mid the advancing clouds.

Far in the east their larum rings,
   As if a wakeful host were there,
And now its early clarion sings
   To warn us sluggard knights beware.

One on more distant perch, more clear,
But fainter, brags him still,
But ah, he promises, I fear,
More than her master's household will fulfil.

The sound invades each silent wood,
   Awakes each slumbering bird,
Till every fowl leads forth her brood,
   Which on her nest the tuneful summons heard.

Methinks that Time has reached his prime,
   Eternity is in the flower,
And this the faint, confused chime
   That ushers in the sacred hour.

And has Time got so forward then?
    From what perennial fount of joy,
Dost thou inspire the hearts of men,
    And teach them how the daylight to employ?

From thy abundance pray impart,
    Who dost so freely spill,
Some bravery unto my heart,
    And let me taste of thy perennial rill.

There is such health and length of years
    In the elixir of thy note,
That God himself more young appears,
    From the rare bragging of thy throat.

BETWEEN THE TRAVELLER AND
THE SETTING SUN

Between the traveller and the setting sun,
Upon some drifting sand heap of the shore,
A hound stands o'er the carcass of a man.

Must we still eat
The bread we have spurned?
Must we re kindle
The faggots we've burned?

I'M CONTENTED YOU
SHOULD STAY

I'm contented you should stay
   For ever and aye
If you can take yourself away
   Any day.

He knows no change who knows the true,
   And on it keeps his eye,
Who always still the unseen doth view;
   Only the false & the apparent die.

Things change, but change not far
   From what they are not but to what they are,
Or rather 'tis our ignorance that dies;
   Forever lives the knowledge of the wise.

In this roadstead I have ridden
In this covert I have hidden
Friendly thoughts were cliffs to me
And I hid beneath their lea.

This true people took the stranger
And warm hearted housed the ranger
They received their roving guest,
And have fed him with the best

Whatsoe'er the land afforded
To the stranger's wish accorded,
Shook the olive, stripped the vine,
And expressed the strengthening wine.

And at night they did spread o'er him
What by day they spread before him,
That good-will which was repast
Was his covering at last.

The stranger moored him to their pier
Without anxiety or fear;
By day he walked the sloping land,
    By night the gentle heavens he scanned.

When first his bark stood inland
To the coast of this far Finland,
Sweet-watered brooks came tumbling to the shore
The weary mariner to restore.

And still he stayed from day to day
If he their kindness might repay
But more and more
The sullen waves came rolling to the shore.

And still the more the stranger waited
The less his argosy was freighted,
And still the more he stayed
The less his debt was paid.

So He unfurled his mast
To receive the fragrant blast,
And that same refreshing gale
Which had woo'd him to remain
  Again and again—
It was that filled his sail
  And drove him to the main.

All day the low hung clouds
  Dropt tears into the sea
And the wind amid the shrouds
  Sighed plaintively.

One more is gone
Out of the busy throng
That tread these paths;
The church bell tolls,
Its sad knell rolls
To many hearths.

    Flower bells toll not,
    Their echoes roll not
    Unto my ear;—
    There still perchance,
    That gentle spirit haunts
    A fragrant bier.

Low lies the pall,
Lowly the mourners all
Their passage grope;—
No sable hue
Mars the serene blue
Of heaven's cope.

    In distant dell
    Faint sounds the funeral bell,
    A heavenly chime;
    Some poet there
    Weaves the light burthened air
    Into sweet rhyme.

With her calm, aspiring eyes
She doth tempt the earth to rise,
With humility over all,
She doth tempt the sky to fall.

In her place she still doth stand
A pattern unto the firm land
While revolving spheres come round
To embrace her stable ground.

This life, O king, of men on earth,
Compared with that unknown,
Gave to a pleasant fancy birth,
    Close by thy throne.

———

 The hall is swept,
 The table set,
 And anxious guests are there,
 With shrinking forms,
 For wintry storms
 Go howling through the air.

Thy noble Ealderman and Thegnes
A cheerful blaze prepare,
And while without it snows and rains
    Are merry there.

And presently a sparrow comes
And flutters through the hall,
It barely picks the scattered crumbs,
    And that is all.

The while the hall it flies about,
It laughs the cold to scorn,
But soon it goes a window out,
    And summer's gone.

So is it with this life of men,
Thus do our moments fly,
We flutter round the hall, and then
          We pine, and die.

If this new lore can tell us where
We go when summer's gone,
Or how this soul of ours did fare
          Ere we were born,

If it do this, then should we try
To live as may befit,
So I, for one, gladly do cry,
          Welcome be it!

Whether we've far withdrawn
   Or come more near
Equally the outward form
   Doth no more appear.
Not thou by distance lost
No—for regret doth bind
Me faster to thee now
   Than neighborhood confined.
Where thy love followeth me
Is enough society. [?]
Thy indelible mild eye
   Is my sky.
Whether by land or sea
   I wander to and fro,
Oft as I think of thee
   The heavens hang more low
The pure glance of thy eye
Doth purge the summer's sky,
And thy breath so rare
Doth refine the winter's air.
my feet would weary be
Ere they travelled from thee.
I [discover] by thy face
That we are of one race
Flowed in one vein our blood
Ere the sea found its flood
The worm may [be] divided
And each part become a whole,
But the nobler creature man
May not separate a span.

O nature I do not aspire
To be the highest in thy quire,
To be a meteor in the sky
Or comet that may range on high,
Only a zephyr that may blow
Among the reeds by the river low.
Give me thy most privy place
Where to run my airy race.
In some withdrawn unpublic mead
Let me sigh upon a reed,
Or in the [?] woods with leafy din
Whisper the still evening in,
For I had rather be thy child
And pupil in the forest wild
Than be the king of men elsewhere
And most sovereign slave of care
To have one moment of thy dawn
Than share the city's year forlorn.
Some still work give me to do
Only be it near to you.

216

The God of day rolls his car up the slopes,
Reining his prancing steeds with steady hand,
The moon's pale orb through west°rn shadows gropes,
While morning sheds its light o'er sea and land.

Castles and cities by the sounding main
Resound with all the busy din of life,
The fisherman unfurls his sails again
And the recruited warrior bides the strife.

The early breeze ruffles the poplar leaves,
The curling waves reflect the washed [?] light,
The slumbering sea with the day's impulse heaves,
While o'er the western hills retires the drowsy night.

The sea birds dip their bills in ocean's foam,
Far circling out over the frothy waves—

———

GREECE

When life contracts into a vulgar span
And human nature tires to be a man,
I thank the gods for Greece
That permanent realm of peace,
For as the rising moon far in the night
Checquers the shade with her forerunning light,
So in my darkest hour my senses seem
To catch from her Acropolis a gleam.
Greece who am I that should remember thee?
Thy Marathon and thy Thermopylae
Is my life vulgar my fate mean
Which on such golden memories can lean?

POVERTY

If I am poor it is that I am proud,
If God has made me naked and a boor
He did not think it fit his work to shroud.

The poor man comes from heaven direct to earth
As stars drop down the sky and tropic beams.
The rich receives in our gross air his birth,
As from low suns are slanted golden gleams.

Men are by birth equal in this that given
Themselves and their condition they are even.
The less of inward essence is to leaven
The more of outward circumstance is given.

Yon sun is naked bare of satellite
Unless our earths and moons that office hold,
Though his perpetual day feareth no night
And his perennial summer dreads no cold.

Where are his gilded rays but in our sky?
His solid disk doth float far from us still,
The orb which through the central way doth fly
Shall naked seem [?] though proudly circumstanced.

Ill leave my mineral wealth hoarded in earth?
Buried in seas in mines and ocean caves
More safely kept than is the merchant's worth,
Which every storm committeth to the waves.

Man kind may delve but cannot my wealth spend,
If I no partial store appropriate
no armed ships into the Indies send
To rob me of my orient estate

The rich man's clothes keep out the genial sun
But scarce defend him from the piercing cold
If he did not his heavenly garment shun
He would not need to hide beneath a fold.

I'm not alone
If I stand by myself,
But more than one,
And not [?] in my own pelf.

I'm understood
If my intent is good,
For who obeys
The truth finds his own praise.

What sought th[e]y th[u]s afar
They sought a faith's pure shrine.

Seek! shall I seek! The Gods above should give,
They have enough & w[e] do poorly live.

"I ask today for no external thing
For sight of upland hill and waving tree,
I do not wish to see the glancing wing
Of bird nor hear with trembling heart her melody,
I ask for that which is our whole life's light,
for the perpetual, true, & clear insight."

Away! away! Thou speakest to me of things
which in all my endless life I have found
not and shall not find.
                              [Word] to Music
Thy lot, or portion of life, is seeking after
thee; therefore be at rest from seeking
after it. [Word?]

Far from this atmosphere that music sounds
Bursting some azure chink in the dull clouds
Of sense that overarch my recent years
And steal his freshness from the noonday sun.
Ah, I have wandered many ways and lost
The boyant step, the whole responsive life
That stood with joy to hear what seemed then
Its echo, its own harmony borne back
Upon its ear. This tells of better space,
Far far beyond the hills the woods the clouds
That bound my low and plodding valley life,
Far from my sin, remote from my distrust,
When first my healthy morning life perchance
Trod lightly as on clouds, and not as yet
My weary and faint hearted noon had sunk
Upon the clod while the bright day went by.
   Lately, I feared my life was empty, now
I know though a frail tenement that it still
Is worth repair, if yet its hollowness
Doth entertain so fine a guest within, and through
Its empty aisles there still doth ring
Though but the echo of so high a strain;
It shall be swept again and cleansed from sin
To be a thoroughfare for celestial airs;
Perchance the God who is proprietor
Will pity take on his poor tenant here
And countenance his efforts to improve
His property and make it worthy to revert,
At some late day Unto himself again.

I'M THANKFUL THAT MY LIFE
DOTH NOT DECEIVE

I'm thankful that my life doth not deceive
Itself with a low loftiness, half height,
And think it soars when still it dip its way
Beneath the clouds on noiseless pinion
Like the crow or owl, but it doth know
The full extent of all its trivialness,
Compared with the splendid heights above.
   See how it waits to watch the mail come in
While 'hind its back *the sun goes out perchance.*
And yet their lumbering cart brings me no word
Not one scrawled leaf such as my neighbors get
To cheer them with the slight events forsooth
Faint ups and downs of their far distant friends—
And now tis passed. What next? See the long train
Of teams wreathed in dust, their atmosphere;
Shall I attend until the last is passed?
Else why these ears that hear the leader's bells
Or eyes that link me in procession.
But hark! the drowsy day has done its task,
Far in yon hazy field where stands a barn
Unanxious hens improve the sultry hour
And with contented voice now brag their deed—
A new laid egg—Now let the day decline—
Th[e]y'll lay another by tomorrow's sun.

MANHOOD

I love to see the man, a long-lived child,
As yet uninjured by all worldly taint
As the fresh infant whose whole life is play.
'Tis a serene spectacle for a serene day;
But better still I love to contemplate
The mature soul of lesser innocence,
Who hath travelled far on life's dusty road
Far from the starting point of infancy
And proudly bears his small degen'racy
Blazon'd on his memorial standard high
Who from the sad experience of his fate
Since his bark struck on that unlucky rock
Has proudly steered his life with his own hands.
Though his face harbors less of innocence
Yet there do chiefly lurk within its depths
Furrowed by care, but yet all over spread
With the ripe bloom of a self-wrought content
Noble resolves which do reprove the gods
And it doth more assert man's eminence
Above the happy level of the brute
And more doth advertise me of the heights
To which no natural path doth ever lead
No natural light can ever light our steps,
—But the far-piercing ray that shines
From the recesses of a brave man's eye.

225

The moon moves up her smooth and sheeny path
Without impediment; and happily
The brook Glides by lulled by its tinkling;
Meteors drop down the sky without chagrin
And rise again; but my cares never rest.
No charitable laws alas cut me
An easy orbit round the sun, but I
Must make my way through rocks and seas and earth
my steep and devious way Uncertain still.
My current never rounds into a lake
In whose fair heart the heavens come to bathe
Nor does my life drop freely but a rod[?]
By its resistless course
As Meteors do.

My life is like a stately warrior horse,
That walks with fluent pace along the way,
And I the upright horseman that bestrides
His flexuous back, feeding my private thoughts.—
Alas, when will this rambling head and neck
Be welded to that firm and brawny breast?—
But still my steady steed goes proudly forth,
Mincing his stately steps along the road;
The sun may set, the silver moon may rise,
But my unresting steed holds on his way.
He is far gone ere this, you fain would say,
He is far going. Plants grow and rivers run;
You ne'er may look upon the ocean waves,
At morn or eventide, but you will see
Far in th' horizon with expanded sail,
Some solitary bark stand out to sea,
Far bound—well so my life sails far,
To double some far cape not yet explored.
A cloud ne'er standeth in the summer's sky,
The eagle sailing high, with outspread wings
Cleaving the silent air, resteth him not
A moment in his flight, the air is not his perch.
Nor doth my life fold its unwearied wings,
And hide its head within its downy breast,
But still it plows the shoreless seas of time,
Breasting the waves with an unsanded bow.

PRAY TO WHAT EARTH DOES THIS
SWEET COLD BELONG

Pray to what earth does this sweet cold belong,
Which asks no duties and no conscience?
The moon goes up by leaps her cheerful path
In some far summer stratum of the sky,
While stars with their cold shine bedot her way.
The fields gleam mildly back upon the sky,
And far and near upon the leafless shrubs
The snow dust still emits a silvery light.
Under the hedge, where drift banks are their screen,
The titmice now pursue their downy dreams,
As often in the sweltering summer nights
The bee doth drop asleep in the flower cup,
When evening overtakes him with his load.
By the brooksides, in the still genial night,
The more adventurous wanderer may hear
The crystals shoot and form, and winter slow
Increase his rule by gentlest summer means.

When the oaks are in the gray
Then Farmers plant away.

INSPIRATION

Whate'er we leave to God, God does,
    And blesses us;
The work we choose should be our own,
    God lets alone.

If with light head erect I sing,
    Though all the muses lend their force,
From my poor love of anything,
    The verse is weak and shallow as its source.

But if with bended neck I grope,
    Listening behind me for my wit,
With faith superior to hope,
    More anxious to keep back than forward it,

Making my soul accomplice there
    Unto the flame my heart hath lit,
Then will the verse forever wear,—
    Time cannot bend the line which God hath writ.

Always the general show of things
    Floats in review before my mind,
And such true love and reverence brings,
    That sometimes I forget that I am blind.

But now there comes unsought, unseen,
    Some clear, divine electuary,
And I who had but sensual been,
    Grow sensible, and as God is, am wary.

I hearing get who had but ears,
  And sight, who had but eyes before,
I moments live who lived but years,
  And truth discern who knew but learning's lore.

I hear beyond the range of sound,
  I see beyond the range of sight,
New earths and skies and seas around,
  And in my day the sun doth pale his light.

A clear and ancient harmony
  Pierces my soul through all its din,
As through its utmost melody,—
  Farther behind than they—farther within.

More swift its bolt than lightning is,
  Its voice than thunder is more loud,
It doth expand my privacies
  To all, and leave me single in the crowd.

It speaks with such authority,
  With so serene and lofty tone,
That idle Time runs gadding by,
  And leaves me with Eternity alone.

Then chiefly is my natal hour,
  And only then my prime of life,
Of manhood's strength it is the flower,
  'Tis peace's end and war's beginning strife.

'T 'hath come in summer's broadest noon,
    By a grey wall or some chance place,
Unseasoned time, insulted June,
    And vexed the day with its presuming face.

Such fragrance round my couch it makes,
    More rich than are Arabian drugs,
That my soul scents its life and wakes
    The body up beneath its perfumed rugs.

Such is the Muse—the heavenly maid,
    The star that guides our mortal course,
Which shows where life's true kernel's laid,
    Its wheat's fine flower, and its undying force.

She with one breath attunes the spheres,
    And also my poor human heart,
With one impulse propels the years
    Around, and gives my throbbing pulse its start.

I will not doubt forever more,
    Nor falter from a steadfast faith,
For though the system be turned o'er,
    God takes not back the word which once he saith.

I will then trust the love untold
    Which not my worth nor want has bought,
Which wooed me young and woos me old,
    And to this evening hath me brought.

My memory I'll educate
   To know the one historic truth,
Remembering to the latest date
   The only true and sole immortal youth.

Be but thy inspiration given,
   No matter through what danger sought,
I'll fathom hell or climb to heaven,
   And yet esteem that cheap which love has bought.

———

Fame cannot tempt the bard
   Who's famous with his God,
Nor laurel him reward
   Who hath his Maker's nod.

If thou wilt but stand by my ear,
When through the field thy anthem's rung,
When that is done I will not fear
But the same power will abet my tongue.

No generous action can delay
Or thwart our higher, steadier aims,
But if sincere and true are they,
It will arouse our sight and nerve our frames.

Thank God who seasons thus the year,
   And sometimes kindly slants his rays;
For in his winter he's most near
   And plainest seen upon the shortest days.

Who gently tempers now his heats,
   And then his harsher cold, lest we
Should surfeit on the summer's sweets,
   Or pine upon the winter's crudity.

A sober mind will walk alone,
   Apart from nature, if need be,
And only its own seasons own;
   For nature leaving its humanity.

Sometimes a late autumnal thought
   Has crossed my mind in green July,
And to its early freshness brought
   Late ripened fruits, and an autumnal sky.

.   .   .   .

The evening of the year draws on,
   The fields a later aspect wear;
Since Summer's garishness is gone,
   Some grains of night tincture the noontide air.

236

Behold! the shadows of the trees
  Now circle wider 'bout their stem,
Like sentries that by slow degrees
  Perform their rounds, gently protecting them.

And as the year doth decline,
  The sun allows a scantier light;
Behind each needle of the pine
  There lurks a small auxiliar to the night.

I hear the cricket's slumbrous lay
  Around, beneath me, and on high;
It rocks the night, it soothes the day,
  And everywhere is Nature's lullaby.

But most he chirps beneath the sod,
  When he has made his winter bed;
His creak grown fainter but more broad,
  A film of autumn o'er the summer spread.

Small birds, in fleets migrating by,
  Now beat across some meadow's bay,
And as they tack and veer on high,
  With faint and hurried click beguile the way.

Far in the woods, these golden days,
  Some leaf obeys its Maker's call;
And through their hollow aisles it plays
  With delicate touch the prelude of the Fall.

Gently withdrawing from its stem,
   It lightly lays itself along
Where the same hand hath pillowed them,
   Resigned to sleep upon the old year's throng.

The loneliest birch is brown and sere,
   The furthest pool is strewn with leaves,
Which float upon their watery bier,
   Where is no eye that sees, no heart that grieves.

The jay screams through the chestnut wood;
   The crisped and yellow leaves around
Are hue and texture of my mood—
   And these rough burrs my heirlooms on the ground.

The threadbare trees, so poor and thin—
   They are no wealthier than I;
But with as brave a core within
   They rear their boughs to the October sky.

Poor knights they are which bravely wait
   The charge of Winter's cavalry,
Keeping a simple Roman state,
   Discumbered of their Persian luxury.

The willows droop,
The alders stoop,
The pheasants group
   Beneath the snow;
The fishes glide
From side to side,
In the clear tide,
   The ice below.

The ferret weeps,
The marmot sleeps,
The owlet keeps
   In his snug nook.
The rabbit leaps,
The mouse out-creeps,
The flag out-peeps,
   Beside the brook.

The snow-dust falls,
The otter crawls,
The partridge calls
   Far in the wood;
The traveller dreams,
The tree-ice gleams,
The blue jay screams
   In angry mood.

The apples thaw,
The ravens caw,
The squirrels gnaw
    The frozen fruit;
To their retreat
I track the feet
Of mice that eat
    The apple's root.

The axe resounds,
And bay of hounds,
And tinkling sounds
    Of wintry fame;
The hunter's horn
Awakes the dawn
On field forlorn,
    And frights the game.

The tinkling air
Doth echo bear
To rabbit's lair,
    With dreadful din;
She scents the air,
And far doth fare,
Returning where
    She did begin.

The fox stands still
Upon the hill
Not fearing ill
  From trackless wind.
But to his foes
The still wind shows
In treacherous snows
  His tracks behind.

Now melts the snow
In the warm sun.
The meadows flow,
The streamlets run.
The spring is born,
The wild bees bum,
The insects hum,
And trees drop gum.
And winter's gone,
And summer's come.

The chic-a-dee
Lisps in the tree,
The winter bee
  Not fearing frost;
The small nuthatch
The bark doth scratch
Some worm to catch
  At any cost.

The catkins green
Cast o'er the scene
A summer sheen,
A genial glow.

I melt, I flow,
    And rippling run,
Like melting snow
    In this warm sun.

Why do the seasons change? and why
Does Winter's stormy brow appear?
Is it the word of him on high,
Who rules the changing varied year.

Friends! that parting tear reserve it,
Tho' 'tis doubly dear to me!
Could I think I did deserve it,
How much happier would I be.

In Adams fall
We sinned all.
In the new Adam's rise
We shall all reach the skies.

IN TIMES OF YORE, 'TIS SAID,
THE SWIMMING ALDER

In times of yore, 'tis said, the swimming Alder,
Fashioned rude, with branches lopt, and stript
Of its smooth coat,—
Where fallen tree was not, and rippling stream's
Vast breadth forbade adventurous leap,
The brawny swain did bear secure to farthest shore.

The Book has passed away,
And with the book the lay,
Which in my youthful days I loved to ponder;
Of curious things it told,
How wise Men Three of old,   (Gotham)
In bowl did venture out to sea,—
And darkly hints their future fate.

If men have dared the Main to tempt
In such frail bark, why may not washtub round,
Or bread-trough square? oblong?—suffice to cross
The purling wave? and gain the destined port.

By his good genius prompted or the power
That fills the mind with

APPENDIX A

Two significant manuscripts are transcribed here. Each helps to illuminate Thoreau's method of work; each furnishes a picture of the creative mind in action. The first, in the Huntington Library, *HM 13201*, is perhaps the most interesting of all Thoreau's manuscripts available. It shows how he wrote, blocked out stanzas, expanded themes, and altered lines. Taken in conjunction with the finished manuscripts of some of the poems found there in germ, it shows how Thoreau drew eclectically from the rough verse and worked the best into entire poems. It might be asserted that these leaves are simply an assemblage of verse sheets from among Thoreau's papers, and that consequently they cast no particular light on his manner of composition. It is true that F. B. Sanborn, through whose hands they passed, might so have collected the leaves. But an examination of the pages will show that they are in many ways continuous and that sections within cohere with one another. A theme, for instance, will run over from one sheet to the next. Therefore it is reasonable to believe that *HM 13201* is much as Thoreau left it.

The second manuscript is that of "A Winter and Spring Scene." It is reproduced because of the way it shows Thoreau's minute and particularized attention to the arrangement of his lines. Something of that careful reordering could be judged from *HM 13201*, but here it is concentrated on a single poem. "A Winter and Spring Scene" affords the most detailed example available of Thoreau's full drafting of a poem (in the Huntington Library manuscript, *HM 13182*), of entire rearrangement to produce the refined version first printed in *The First and Last Journeys of Thoreau*, and of selection and rejection to produce the version in *Poems of Nature* called "A Winter Scene." And even at that, the full draft in *HM 13182* is probably not the very earliest, since the stanza pattern is more difficult than usual and *HM 13182* is a fairly clean copy.

In the pages that follow, a picture of Thoreau in the workshop is to be gained. The most graphic picture would have been furnished through an exact reproduction of the manuscripts by, for instance, photostat. However, such reproduction would have been nearly impossible and certainly impractical because almost all the writing is in pencil; and the passing of years has faded the pencillings to a point where often they can hardly be seen. The present form of transcription thus represents a compromise.

HM 13201

Folder and envelope containing twelve sheets and parts of sheets of manuscript material.

Description (like that of all the other Huntington Library manuscripts except *HM 924*) by Miss Edythe Backus:

The sheets are written in pencil on the verso of what, in most instances, seem to be waste sheets of paper which had been used for other purposes previously, *e.g.*, a list of books to be read, a geometry problem partly worked out, a list of directions on how to prepare a manuscript, a partially erased excerpt of French prose, two sheets with poems in ink, one with a short, dated essay on *Gratitude,* in ink, etc. The verso of the leaves thus becomes the recto, so far as the pencilled poems are concerned and I shall so describe them below. On the (now) recto of each sheet is a very large Arabic numeral to indicate the order of the sheets. The numbers from 1 to 10 (8 is omitted) are in ink and the numbers from 11 to 13 are in pencil. That is how it happens that the verses appear in the order that they do. I think the numerals are in Thoreau's hand, but I am not quite sure because on the present verso of leaf 5 is a short note in F. B. Sanborn's hand above his signature and it may just possibly be that he arranged these sheets in order and numbered them. In the case of sheets or parts of sheets which have vertical pencil scorings through them, I think such scorings are probably Thoreau's and not Sanborn's.

Where I have given a stanza number opposite a stanza, in either the left or right margin, that number appears there in Thoreau's manuscript, as if he were reminding himself of the order of stanzas he intended to use.

[Dated in upper right hand corner: Monday Sep. 6''])

[Leaf 1—recto]

["The Fall of the Leaf"]

[17] The evening of the year draws on a «pace»
[18] «And all» the fields a later aspect wear
      Since summers garishness is gone
[19] «A twilight here creeps oer the landscapes face»
[20] Some grains of night tincture the noontide air.

N.B.: All editorial description of the leaves is in ordinary brackets. Moreover, because many of the verses became parts of poems now to be found in the present edition, the bracketed titles of those poems are inserted for easier reference, as are the necessary line numbers, which are cited in the left margin. *HM 13201* furnishes the basic text for two quatrains (pp. 194, 195); consequently, only their bracketed titles appear in the present transcription. Here—and here alone—broken brackets are used to enclose material that Thoreau himself cancelled in the manuscript.

behold
[21] «In every weed» the shadows of the trees
                now   circle wider
[22] «Describe a wider» circuit round their stem
[23] Like «silent» sentries which by slow degrees
[24] Perform their rounds in peace protecting them.

x

From many a crevice banishing the light
[27] Until behind each needle of the pine
[28] There lurks a small auxiliar to the night

Behind each bush and straggling fence   Sep. 6''
Amid the meadows pensive green
And shroud the meadows opulence
Evenings insidious frost at noon is seen

[Below this are some prose notes, some of which are the other way
on the paper.]

[Leaf 1—verso]

[List of books read, with dates, in ink. In lower margin the following
short list of ideas in pencil, some scored through, as if being suggestions
for various sections of the poems.]

            «Night shades»
            «Migration of birds»
            Fall of the leaf
            Harvest & its effect
            «cricket»
            Appearance of the wood
            «Mellow air»

[Leaf 2—recto]

September rides upon the gale
And booms along the creaking roof
Then stoops afar into the vale
Spurning the brake and sumack with his hoof

251

The small birds follow in his wake
Who threads the forest at a rustling pace
Ruffling the surface of the lake
He strews the affrighted leaves upon its face.

«Small birds in fleets migrate on high»
«Or beat across some meadow's bay»

[37] Small birds in fleets migrating by
[38] Beat now across some meadow's bay
[39] And as they tack and veer on high
[40] With faint and hurried click beguile the way.

[49] The loneliest birch is brown and sere
[50] The furthest [*farthest*?] pool is strewed with leaves
    Which
[51] «That» float upon their watry bier
[52] Where is no eye that sees, no heart that grieves

Venice preserved is in each bark
That still restrains [?] the ripples force
But soon [*now*?] to lie deluged and dark
Like sunken isles beneath the sailors course

[Leaf 2—verso]

[Verse in ink at top of page, scored out with pencil.]

["The Bluebirds"]

[45] Meanwhile old earth jogged steadily on
[46] In her mantle of purest white,
[47] And anon another spring was born
[48] When winter had vanished quite.

[Rest of the page in pencil.]

             first   grew rude
I marked «how» when ∧ the wind «first blew»

4 Each leaf curled like a living thing
As with the teeming air it would
Secure some faint memorial of spring

Then for its sake it turned about
5 And dared strange elements to brave [Pencilled figure 5 in left margin.]
Like painted palaces that float
A «patient» summer's hoarded wealth to save.

Grown tired   [Stanza cancelled.]
«I tire» of this rank summer's wealth

Its rare and superficial show
I fain would
«And when I» hie away by stealth
                   but still [it]   [*It* partly erased.]
Where no —rf meet «it still» doth trivial [?] grow

Methinks by dalliance it hath caught   [Stanza cancelled.]
The shallow habits of the town
It self infected most which ought
With «a» stern face upon our tameness frown

["The Fall of the Leaf"]

[9] A sober mind will walk alone   [Stanza cancelled.]
     apart
[10] «Aside» from nature if need be
[11] And only its own seasons own
[12] For nature pulling its humanity

[Leaf 3—recto]

[1] Thank God who seasons thus the year
               kindly
[2] And sometimes ∧ slants his rays
     for   hes
[3] Who in his winter is most near
     «easiest»   «during»
[4] And plainest seen upon the shortest days

[5] Who gently tempers now his heats
[6] An[d] then this [*his* underneath?] harsher cold, lest we
[7] Should surfeit on the Summer's sweets
[8] Or pine upon the winter's crudity.

[13] Sometimes a late autumnal thought
      crossed my mind   rustled mid the leaves of June
[14] Has come to me in green July
[15] And to its early freshness brought
                harvest moon
    «Late ripened fruits and an autumn sky»
[16] Ripe fruits of harvest and an autumn sky.

So in mid summer I have seen
          «birches»

[*Vide* refers to the
verso of this leaf;
see below.]

One pensive leaf «upon the birch»——vide
Grown sere when all the rest are green
Like some fair flower to tempt the traveller's
    search [*reach?*]

A dry but golden thought which gleamed
Athwart the greenness of the swail

Oct. tues.

And prematurely wise it seemed
Too ripe amid the bowers of June to fail.

[Leaf 3—verso]

[At top of verso, in ink and dated, three stanzas of poem, "Friendship." Then follow, in pencil, two versions of the verse above, beginning
"So in mid summer I have seen":]

So in mid summer I have seen
Among the glossy leaves of June
One yellow leaf when all were green

So have I seen one yellow leaf
Amid the glossy leaves of June
Which pensive hung, but not with grief
Like some «f»rare flower, it had changed so soon

[Leaf 4—recto]
[33] The cricket chirps beneath the sod
                further under

[*Further under*
written slantingly
in the right mar-
gin.]

[34] Already in his winter bed
    Where he has made
    His creek grown fainter but more broad
[35] And slowed [*seemed?*] his creaking without fraud
[36] A film of autumn oer [?] the summer spread

254

I   my

«My mind doth» scent «the» med'cine from afar
Where the rude simples of the year
October leads the swelling war [?]
And strews his trophies on the summer's bier
And strews the summer's glory far and near
And with shrill trumpet pierceth now my ear

       [53] The jay screams through the chestnut wood
2   [54] The crisped and yellow leaves around
       [55] Are hue and texture of my mood
       [56] And these rough burrs my heir loom [on] the ground.

       [57] The thread-bare trees, so poor and thin
3   [58] They are no wealthier than I
       [59] But with as brave a core within
       [60] They rear their boughs to the october sky

       [61] Poor knights they are, that bravely wait
                        Aimless
4   [62] The charge of winter's cavalry
       [63] Keeping a simple Roman state
       [64] Discumbered of their Persian luxury.

[Pencilled figure 2 in left margin.]

[Paper smeared and *on* not visible.]

[Pencilled figure 3 in left margin.]

[Pencilled figure 4 in left margin.]

[Leaf 4—verso]

[Prose essay on *Gratitude*, in ink and dated Feb. 24"—38.]

[Leaf 5—recto]

And greatness now need walk alone

5   ardor damp

armor shone
bustling of their camp

[The above stanza blocked out thus.]

[Pencilled figure 5 in left margin.]

The harvest rustles in the wind

3 Red apples over hang the way

The cereal flavor of my mind
Howe'er, tells me I am as ripe as they

[Pencilled figure 3 in left margin.]

255

The moon is ripe fruit in the sky
1 And over hangs her harvest noon
The sun doth break his stem well nigh
From summer's height he has declined so low

The greedy earth doth pluck his fruit
And cast it in Night's lap
2 The stars more brightly glisten mute
Though their tears be, to see their Lord's mishap

The sharp wind searcheth every vein
4 And dries up humors crude,
I spring into my place again
With unwarped strength, like staunch and seasoned wood.

[Leaf 5—verso]

[Half page of prose quotations from various sources in Thoreau's hand; a note, signed by F. B. Sanborn, at bottom of page.]

[Leaf 6 (less than half a sheet)—recto]

[41] Far in the woods these golden days
1 [42] Some leaf obeys its maker's call
[43] And through their hollow aisles it plays
[44] With del'cate touch the prelude of the Fall

[45] Gently withdrawing from its stem
                        lightly
2 [46] It bravely lays itself along,
[47] Where the same hand hath pillowed them
[48] Resigned to sleep upon the old year's throng

Where [*There?*] upon came [?] a mellow air
Floods all the region
As if there were some tincture there
Of ripeness caught from the long summer sun.

[Leaf 6—verso]

[Two prose sentences from which Thoreau evidently worked out the three stanzas above.]

256

["Upon the bank at early dawn"]

[1] When in my bed at early dawn
[2] I've heard the cocks proclaim the day
[3] Though the moon shone securely on
[4] As if here queenly course they could not stay

Or pull her down with their faint din
From riding at that lofty height
Who in her shining knew no sin
As if unconscious of a nobler light

Their 'larum rung the world around   [Stanza cancelled.
Which seemed but lately made
And this its falt'ring infant sound
When the horizon in its cradle laid

[Leaf 7—verso]

[Six pencilled rules for the preparation of a proper manuscript.]

[Leaf 9—recto]

The tidy night with cooler feet
I'm sure, has lately passed this way
And with her trim dispatch so neat
She has arranged the fountains of the day.

In yon thin sheet of mist spread oer
These lowland trees of leaves bereft   [This line erased
Which round her head at eve she wore   and written over.]
Methinks I see the housewife's duster left.

The fragrant priest exhales the scent
Of aromatic herbs, so you
Would say she blest, whereer she went
And through the fields had sprinkled perfumed dew.

257

[Prose notations and excerpts from articles in ink and also the following partial working out of the stanza immediately above:]

the Fragrant mist exhales the scent
Of aromatic herbs, so you
whereer she went
And sunny fields sprinkled with

[This leaf is creased heavily. The recto is written three ways; the verso has three lines of prose in ink, beneath which, also in ink, is the following: The Cliffs. July 8"—38 Monday. Below this are these verses:]

["The Fall of the Leaf"]

[29] I hear the crickets slumbrous lay
beneath
[30] Around «below» me and on high
[31] It rocks the night it lulls the day
[32] And everywhere 'tis natures lullaby

["Inspiration"]

[17] Always the general show of things
[18] Floats in review before my mind
[19] And such true love and wonder brings
[20] That sometimes I forget that I am blind

["Upon the bank at early dawn"]

[Stanza cancelled.]

[5] The stars withheld their shining not
[6] or singly or in crowds
[7] They seemed like Parthian arrows shot
[8] By the retreating night and the advancing dawn

The crickets dream will soon be oer
Beneath the cold and withered sod
or vanished to some distant shore
He'll bring his murm'rings [*musings?*] to a period.

[Two prose sentences.]

258

["Inspiration"]

[21] But soon there comes unsought unseen   [Stanza cancelled.]
[22] Some clear divine electuary   2   [Pencilled figure *2*
[23] And I who had but sensual been   in right margin.]
[24] Do sensuous grow and as God is am weary

[37] More swift its bolt than lightning is   [First two lines
                                    cancelled.]
[38] Its voice than thunder is more loud   5   [Pencilled figure *5*
[39] It doth expand my privacies   in right margin.]
[40] To all, and leave me single in the crowd
     It shows [t]o me new verities

                                            [Light pencil stroke
                                          thus.]

[45] Then chiefly is my natal hour
[46] And only then my prime of life   6   [Pencilled figure *6*
[47] Of manhood's strength it is the flower   in right margin.]
[48] Tis peace's end and wars beginning strife

[25] I hearing get who had but ears
[26] And sight who had but eyes before   3   [Pencilled figure *3*
[27] I moments live who lived but years   in right margin.]
       ⎧ And filled with life, [why should I ask] for more
[28] ⎨   I do not wish
       ⎩ And wisdom get who knew but learning's lore

[In right margin, crosswise on the paper, the following two lines:]

    And who had lowly crept then proudly soar
              can
    So full of life I do not wish for more

[Leaf 11—recto]

[This leaf is so frequently folded that certain lines, indicated below,
simply cannot be read.]

["Delay"]

     act of duty
[1] No generous action can delay
           loftier
[2] «N»or thwart our high and steadier aims
[3] This [*Tis?*] is we are [*can?*] and true as [*are?*] they
[4]   arouse our sight and nerve our frames

[The beginning of the above line apparently partially erased, but the re-written word or words so faint as to be unreadable; it is possible, further, that there is a word between lines 3 and 4 of this stanza.]

["Inspiration"]

[Pencilled figure 4
in right margin.]

[29] I hear beyond the range of sound
[30] I see beyond the verge of sight   4
                                        surround
[31] New lands—new skies new seas around
[32] And the sun paleth his superfluous light
      And   pales his light

[This fifth line is across the heaviest crease and the only other thing noticeable, besides what is recorded above, is that the third word of the line seems to end in *ing*; the dotted *i* and the extension of the *g* below the crease can be seen.]

[Pencilled figure 7
in right margin.]

[65] I will not doubt forever more
[66] Nor falter from an iron faith   7
[67] For though the system be turned oer
[68] God takes not back the word which once he saith

[Leaf 11—verso—in ink]

"The Mountains in the Horizon"

["With frontier strength ye stand your ground"]

      The confines of the sky and ground—
[2] With grand content ye stand around,
[3] Tumultous silence for all sound—
[4] A springing nursery of rills,
[5] Monadnock and the Peterborough hills.
[6] Staid argument that never stirs,
[7] Out-circling the philosophers,
      The sun doth go behind thee not before
      For brief to plenish his diminished store.
      The in's of the sky, ye run
      Round the horizon of its eye
      Whose pupil is the sun.

260

["Inspiration"]

[73] My memory I'll educate
[74] To know the real historic truth   8   [Pencilled figure 8 in right margin.]
      Preserving
[75] Remembering to the latest date
[76] The only true and sole immortal youth.

[69] I will believe the love untold
            worth nor wealth [?] of mine
[70] Which ⌈not my worth nor need has⌉ brought 9   [Pencilled figure 9 in right margin.]
            worth of mine has never
[71] Which wooed me young and woos me old
      And call the stars to witness ⌈now my⌉ thought
                                        the rash

      I will believe the power unseen &c.

                                          sheds
[53] Such fragrance round my sleep it makes
      More rich   are   distills
[54] Richer than this the Arabian drugs
[55] That my soul scents its life and wakes
[56] The body up, which still its slumber hugs

[Top part of sheet taken up with geometry problem in ink; problem, in faint pencil, extends down the page, under the verses.]

[49] 'Thath come in summers broadest noon
[50]   By a grey wall or some chance place
                        insulted
[51] Unseasoned time—undone the [this?] June
[52] And vexed the day with its presuming face

[57] Such is the muse the heavenly maid
[58] That star that guides her [our?] mortal course
[59] Which shows where life's true kernel's laid
[60] On wheat's fine flour, and an undying force.

261

speaks
[41] It «doth detain» with such authority
so
[42] With such serene and lofty tone
[43] That idle Time runs gadding by
[44] And leaves me with eternity alone

["Upon the bank at early dawn"]

[33] There is such health and length of years
[34] In the elixir of that [*this*?] note
[35] That even God more young appears
    And infant worlds through infant spaces float

["Inspiration"]

[33] Whose clear and ancient harmony
                        the worlds
[34] Pierces my «heart» through ⌠all its⌡ din
    &   soul
[35] As through its utmost melody
[36] Further behind than they, further within

[61] Who with one breath attunes two spheres
[62] And also my poor human heart
[63] With one impulse propels the years
[64] Around, and gives my throbbing [*thrilling*?] pulse its
    start

["Who equallest the coward's haste"]

"[Inspiration]"

    Be but the [*thy*?] inspiration
[77] ⌠It is enough if truth be⌡ given
                        trials
[78] No matter through what danger sought
[79] I'll fathom hell or climb to heaven
[80] And yet esteem that⌡ cheap which love hath bought
    For that is always   [*brought*?]

[Leaf 13—verso]

[Upside down is some French prose, partially erased, over which,
the right way of the paper, are the following stanzas:]

["Ive searched my faculties around"]

262

["Inspiration"]

[1] Whate'er we leave to God, God does
[2] And Blesses us
    What we presume [?] to do alone
      He lets be done

    What we presume [?] to do alone
[4]   God lets be done
[1] But what we leave to God, God does
[2]   And blesses us

[1] That which we leave to God, God does
[2]   And blesses us
[3] But what we choose should be our own
[4]   God lets alone

HM 13182

A WINTER AND SPRING SCENE

[57] Now melts the snow
[58]   In this warm sun
[59] The meadows flow
[60]   The streamlets run.

[Page 194, Thoreau's pagination.]

[67] The chic adee «li»
[68]   Lisps in the tree ←
[71] The nuthatch creeps
[10]   The marmot sleeps

[69] The winter bee
[70]   Not fearing frost

[These two lines in margin with arrow thus.]

         peeps
[15] The flag out «creeps»   [13] The rabbit leaps
[16]   Beside the brook
[14] The mouse out-creeps
[12]   «From his snug nook»

[Page 195.]
[This line in margin.]

[25] The apples thaw
[26]   The ravens caw
[27] The squirrels gnaw
[28]   The frozen fruit

263

[29] To their retreat
[30] I track the feet
[31] Of mice that eat
[32]   The apples root.

[61]   The spring is born
[62]   The wild bees bum
[63]   The insects hum
[64]   And trees drop gum
[65] And winter's gone
[66] And summer's come

[9] The ferret weeps
[10] The marmot sleeps
[11] The owlet keeps
[12]   In his snug nook

[71] The small nuthatch
[72] The bark doth scratch
[73] Some worm [?] to catch
[74]   At any cost.

[Page 196.]
[Manuscript thus.]
[79] I melt I flow
[80] And *purring* run   purling—rippling?
[81] Like melting snow
[82]   In this warm sun.

[1] The willows droop
[2] The alders stoop
[3]   The pheasants group
[4]   Beneath the snow

Friday Oct 14" 1842

[17] The snow dust falls
[18] The otter crawls
[19] The partridge calls
[20]   Far in the wood

[21] The traveller dreams
[22] The tree-ice gleams
[23] The blue-jay screams
[24]   In angry mood

264

[5] The fishes glide
[6] From side to side
[7] In the clean tide
[8]   The ice below

[75] The catkins green
[76] Cast o'er the scene
[77] A summer sheen.
[78]   A genial glow

[33] The axe resound   [Page 197.]
[34] And bay of hounds
[35] And tinkling sounds
[36]   Of wintry fame.

[37] The hunters horn
[38]   Awakes the dawn
[39] On fields forlorn
[40]   And frights the game.

           cutting
[41] The tinkling air
[42] Doth echo bear
[43] To rabbit's lair
[44]   With dreadful din

[45] She scents the air
[46] And far doth fare
[47] Returning where «sh»
[48]   She did begin.

[49] The fox stands still ← [50] Upon the hill   [This line in mar-
[51] Not fearing ill   gin, with arrow
[52]   From trackless wind.   thus.]

[53] But to his foes   [55-56 originally
[54] The still wind shows   written in pencil
[55] In treacherous snows   and then traced
[56]   His track behind   in ink.]

265

APPENDIX B

No one can tell just how much verse of Thoreau's exists besides that collected in the present edition. Some pieces are in the hands of private collectors. Others are lost. From time to time the sale of verse manuscripts has been recorded in *American Book-Prices Current*. By far the most important appearance of manuscripts, brought to light by being offered for sale, is registered in the catalogue of the *Stephen H. Wakeman Collection of Books of Nineteenth Century American Writers* ([Arthur Swann] American Art Association: New York, 1924). The dispersal of this rich collection spotlighted a number of Thoreau items.

Of the verse manuscripts whose sale has been chronicled, most can be found collated in the present edition. In some instances, although the poem itself does not appear, a variant version is available. Such is the case of the elegy to, probably, Helen Thoreau. A long version was sold at the Wakeman sale and is not now available; but two shorter versions have been obtained and are here included. In this appendix only the verse which has apparently no cognate in the present edition is described (and the description is based on the sale data alone.) The rest is merely noted. The following pieces are not known to be found in this edition:

"The Fog," manuscript poem written by Thoreau while at Harvard, 12 lines. *American Book-Prices Current*, XII (1906), 763.

"Though my friends are dull and cold I will be quick and warm," autograph manuscript poem, a fragment, two pages, quarto. *Ibid.*, XXI (1915), 906.

"Fair Haven," original unpublished autograph manuscript poem of seven quatrains, written in ink on one side of two quarto sheets, with alterations and emendations in the hand of the author. Is unsigned and dated May 2, 1834. Wakeman catalogue, number 973. The first quatrain runs as follows:

> When little hills like lambs did skip,
> And Joshua ruled in heaven,
> Unmindful rolled Musketaquid,
> Nor budged an inch Fair Haven.

"Delay in Friendship," original autograph manuscript poem, presumably unpublished, of seven quatrains, written in ink on both sides of one quarto sheet, with alterations and emendations in the hand of the author; it is signed "Thoreau" elaborately. It is dated June 16, 1837, but is described as being written "at Concord, in 1841"! *Ibid.*, 977. The first quatrain runs as follows:

The blossoms on the tree
Swell not too fast for me.
God does not want quick work but sure,
Not to be tempted by so cheap a lure.

"Life is a Summer's Day," original autograph manuscript poem, probably unpublished, of eleven stanzas of triplets, written in ink on both sides of quarto sheet, with alterations and emendations in the hand of the author; unsigned. Dated July 2, 1837. *Ibid.*, 978. The first triplet follows:

Life is a summer's day,
When as it were for ay,
We sport and play.

"The Freshet," original incomplete autograph manuscript poem of four six-line stanzas and two lines of a fifth stanza, written in ink on one side of quarto sheet, with alterations and emendations in pencil in the hand of the author. It is unsigned and undated. *Ibid.*, 983. A pencilled memorandum on the back of "The Freshet" concerns Thoreau's board. It begins "Dec. 8 owe Father for board up to Dec. 21st, 41.73" and ends "Settled up to March 22'd 1841," proving Thoreau to have written this poem before he went to live with Ralph Waldo Emerson.

The first stanza of this poem has never been published. It runs as follows:

'Tis now the twenty third of March,
And this warm sun takes out the starch
Of Winter's pinafore. Methinks
The very pasture gladly drinks
Of health to Spring, and while it sips
It quaintly smacks a myriad lips.

The following list is made up of sold manuscripts which have either been incorporated in this edition or else are to be found here in variant versions:

"Independence," *American Book-Prices Current*, XI (1905), 620.
"Godfrey of Boulogne," *ibid.*, XII (1906), 763.
"The Fisher's Son," *ibid.*, XXI (1915), 905; and XXIII (1917), 1062.
"Short Flights," *ibid.*, XXI (1915), 905; and XXIII (1917), 1062, and described in the latter as including "Expectation," "Love's Farewell," and (the quatrain) "Inspiration."
"I knew a man by sight," *ibid.*, XXI (1915), 905.
"Voyager's Song," *ibid.*, XXII (1916), 1053.
"Haze" (see "Woof of the sun, ethereal gauze"), *ibid.*, XXII (1916), 1053.
"Sic Vita" (see "I am a parcel of vain strivings tied"), *ibid.*, XXII (1916), 1053.

"To the Comet," Wakeman catalogue, number 976.
"Cock-crowing" (variant of "Upon the bank at early dawn"), *ibid.*, 1033.
"Inspiration," *ibid.*, 1034.
"The Soul's Season" (part of "The Fall of the Leaf"), *ibid.*, 1035.
"The Fall of the Leaf," *ibid.*, 1036; and a longer version, *ibid.*, 1037.
"I seek the Present Time," *ibid.*, 1038.
"Whether we've far withdrawn" (variant of "Farewell"), *ibid.*, 1039.

It is probable that a few other pieces of verse exist imbedded in the prose manuscripts which have been offered for sale (see, for example, Wakeman catalogue, number 987). In *American Book-Prices Current* no prose manuscript is recorded which has verse mentioned as being a part of it. There is one definite case in the Wakeman catalogue:

Walk to Wachusett, original autograph manuscript; early draft of the essay. "The long verses to the mountain varies [*sic*] materially." Wakeman catalogue, number 986. (The verses are evidently a version of "With frontier strength ye stand your ground." In all probability, the present edition includes the version referred to; see "With frontier strength ye stand your ground," textual note.)

The following pieces of verse are in the hands of Dr. Raymond Adams. He has declined to allow them to be published. In *The Thoreau Library of Raymond Adams; A Catalogue* (Chapel Hill, N. C., 1936), the items are alluded to thus:

1. First pages of 1837 Journal. Page one contains signature in ink of Thoreau, "Henry D. Thoreau-1837" together with penciled poems. Page two contains quotation in ink of six lines from Herbert's "The Church Porch", together with penciled poems.
4. Henry D. Thoreau to Mrs. Lucy Brown, September 8, 1841. A.l. First page of letter in Thoreau's autograph with penciled drafts of poems on reverse side.

An article by Dr. Adams, "Thoreau at Harvard," *New England Quarterly*, XIII (1940), includes a couplet (p. 29), "Pens to mend, and hands to guide," which is apparently by Thoreau. It appears in a letter Thoreau sent to Henry Vose, Concord, October 13, 1837. Dr. Adams quotes the letter as being in the Howe (now part of the Berg) Collection. Permission to use the verse by Thoreau in the Berg Collection has been granted to the present editor by the New York Public Library; but the letter to Vose could not be found before the Berg Collection, because of the exigencies of the war, was boxed and removed for safekeeping.

TEXTUAL PREFACE

SYMBOLS USED IN BOTH THE TEXTUAL AND OTHER NOTES

For comments on the starred volumes see pp. 273-275.

Thoreau's Works
In book form

49W	A week on the Concord and Merrimack Rivers. Boston, etc.: James Munroe and Company, etc., 1849.
68W	A week on the Concord and Merrimack Rivers. Boston: Ticknor and Fields, 1868.
* *06W*	A week on the Concord and Merrimack Rivers. Volume I of The writings of Henry David Thoreau, Walden edition. Boston, etc.: Houghton Mifflin and Company, 1906.
* *FLJ*	The first and last journeys of Thoreau. Edited by Franklin Benjamin Sanborn. Boston: The Bibliophile Society, 1905. 2 v.
54Wa	Walden, or Life in the woods. Boston: Ticknor and Fields, 1854.
06Wa	Walden. Volume II of The writings of Henry David Thoreau, Walden edition. Boston, etc.: Houghton Mifflin and Company, 1906.
* *BSWa*	Walden, or Life in the woods. Edited by F. B. Sanborn, with an introduction by H. H. Harper. Boston: The Bibliophile Society, 1909. 2 v.
06III	The Maine woods. Volume III, Walden edition.
06IV	Cape Cod and miscellanies. Volume IV, Walden edition.
06V	Excursions and poems. Volume V, Walden edition.
* *EL*	Letters to various persons. Edited by R. W. E[merson]. Boston: Ticknor and Fields, 1865.
* *06VI*	Familiar letters. Edited by F. B. Sanborn. Enlarged edition. Volume VI, Walden edition.

* *Jl-JXIV*	Journal. Edited by Bradford Torrey. Volumes VII-XX, Walden edition; but also numbered separately there. (In the present edition of the poems the separate numbering is adopted.)
* *Spr*	Early spring in Massachusetts. Edited by H. G. O. Blake. Volume III of The works of Henry D. Thoreau, The Concord edition. Boston: Houghton Mifflin Company, 1929.
Sum	Summer. Volume III, The Concord edition.
Aut	Autumn. Volume IV, The Concord edition.
Win	Winter. Volume IV, The Concord edition.
* *PN*	Poems of nature. Selected and edited by Henry S. Salt and Frank B. Sanborn. London: John Lane, etc.; Boston, etc.: Houghton, Mifflin and Company, 1895.

In periodicals

* *D*	The Dial. Volumes I-IV. Boston, 1840-1844.
* *C*	The Commonwealth. Boston, 1863.

Biographies of Thoreau

* *17S*	F. B. Sanborn. The life of Henry David Thoreau. Boston, etc.: Houghton Mifflin Company, 1917.
CT	Henry Seidel Canby. Thoreau. Boston: Houghton Mifflin Company, 1939.

Thoreau Manuscripts

For comments on the manuscript sources listed below, see pp. 275-276.

A	Abernethy Library of American Literature, Middlebury College.
B	Berg Collection, New York Public Library.
H	Harvard College Library.
HM	Henry E. Huntington Library and Art Gallery.
L	Collection of Mr. Albert Edgar Lownes.
M1-M31	Pierpont Morgan Library, manuscripts of Thoreau's Journal.
M	Pierpont Morgan Library, manuscripts other than those of the Journal.
T	Collection of Mr. W. Stephen Thomas.
Y	Yale University Library.

Symbols used only in the textual notes

al	Alternative reading by Thoreau.
c	Cancellation by Thoreau (*unc:* uncancelled; no cancellation).
o	Omission by Thoreau.
p	Parenthesizing by Thoreau.
« »	Reading from questionable text not otherwise collated.
E	Emendation by the present editor.

COMMENTS ON THE TEXTS

i

Thoreau's Works
In book form

06W. *06W* and the four volumes of the Walden Edition that follow it were edited anonymously. F. H. Allen, though, did whatever special editing was required.[1] Thoreau's text is adhered to with general fidelity, and Allen's divergence from *68W* is slight and confined almost entirely to a few matters of punctuation.

The Walden Edition, of which *06W* is a part, has been chosen as the basic reference because it is the latest reasonably complete set of Thoreau's writings. It was printed from the plates of the Manuscript Edition, and its introductions were those which Horace E. Scudder had prepared for the Riverside Edition.

FLJ. Where F. H. Allen dealt with materials already in print, F. B. Sanborn—in *FLJ* and elsewhere—did most of his work from Thoreau's manuscripts. Sanborn's editing of the text of the verse conforms to a method no longer fashionable. It is a method that needs discussion in the present edition because of the fact that by far the largest proportion of the posthumous verse to see print (except for that in the Journal) has done so under his supervision. His handling of Thoreau's text has been severely criticized.[2] The best that can be said for it is contained in a paragraph the publishers added to his last life of Thoreau. The paragraph deals with Sanborn's general method, but every word holds true for his treatment of the poetry too:

---

[1] Letter to the editor from the Houghton Mifflin Company, publishers of the Walden Edition, March 27, 1941.

[2] Among the various items Sanborn edited, his edition of the early draft of *Walden* (*BSWa*) has received the most criticism. Dr. Raymond Adams sums up the charges in the edition of *Walden* that he himself prepared (Chicago, 1930). A detailed and analytical indictment is to be found in M. E. Cryder, *An Examination of the Bibliophile Edition of Thoreau's* Walden (University of Chicago master's thesis, unpublished, 1920).

Mr. Sanborn was not a slavish quoter, and in dealing with Thoreau's Journals and those other of his writings which Thoreau himself had not prepared for publication, he used the privilege of an editor who is thoroughly familiar with his author's subjects and habits of thought to rearrange paragraphs, to omit here, to make slight interpolations there, and otherwise to treat the rough and unpolished sentences of the Journals, letters, etc., much as it may be supposed the author himself would have treated them had he prepared them for the press. If, therefore, the reader finds occasional discrepancies . . . , he is not to set them down to carelessness, but is rather to thank Mr. Sanborn for making these passages more orderly and more readable.[3]

BSWa. Sanborn's treatment of the text here is in line with that of the text in *FLJ.*[4]

EL. Emerson felt free to make at least slight alterations in the texts that he printed. In addition he condensed some of the poems by omitting stanzas. However, the authenticity of his texts has been given the benefit of the doubt; and their variations have been recorded in the same manner as those of Thoreau's proven texts.

06VI. See comment on *FLJ,* above.

JI-JXIV. Bradford Torrey, as he explains in his introduction, punctuated and emended the text of the Journal in order to regularize its grammar and style. Where Thoreau had revised a passage in some work already printed, Torrey now printed the unrevised original. In cases of emended passages never published before, he stated that he would print the emendation. The result, though satisfactory enough for the general reader, is an eclectic and insecure text.

Spr. H. G. O. Blake was the first editor to print extensive selections from Thoreau's Journal. In *Spr,* as well as in *Sum, Aut,* and *Win,*[5] he altered Thoreau's text somewhat; but he did not try to regularize it to the extent that Torrey did. (References to *Spr,* etc., in the present edition of the poems are based on the latest reprint.)

PN. Salt edited *PN* in England from manuscripts sent to him by Sanborn and others.[6] The verse was handled fairly freely. The punctuation and spelling were partly altered to follow English, rather than American, usage. A few more changes, additional to those that Sanborn had already

---

[3] *17S xiv.*

[4] Harper himself, in the verse he quoted in his introduction, did not follow Thoreau's text exactly; but the main responsibility for the way the text was treated was Sanborn's.

[5] The present edition of *Spr* contains a little material omitted from the first edition, 1881. The dates of publication for the first edition of Blake's other volumes follow: *Sum,* 1884; *Aut,* 1892; *Win,* 1888.

[6] See *Unpublished Poems by Bryant and Thoreau* (Boston, 1907), introduction to Thoreau's poem by F. B. Sanborn, p. xxiv.

PN was printed, as well as edited, in England. The Houghton Mifflin Company imported its part of the sheets in November, 1895.

made in earlier printings of some poems, were made in wording and stanza form.

In periodicals

D. Editors Emerson and Margaret Fuller gave the verse Thoreau submitted to them a vigorous but mainly sympathetic reception. They rejected some of his poems and sent back others for revision. Yet, on the whole, what they did print was set up as Thoreau wanted it. As Emerson ruefully confessed in yielding to Thoreau's judgment, "Our tough Yankee must have his tough verse."[1] Such discrepancies in the readings as Thoreau later corrected in his personal copy of *D* were the result of his own poor handwriting or his own change of intention.

C. The *Commonwealth* was a Boston weekly newspaper edited by Sanborn. There he printed eight pieces of Thoreau's verse, noting that they were from what he termed unpublished manuscripts. He kept more closely to Thoreau's own readings in *C* than he did anywhere else or at any other time.

Biography of Thoreau

17S. See comment on *FLJ*, above.

Thoreau Manuscripts

A. The text of the verse marked *A* is based on transcriptions made by Dr. Viola C. White, Curator of the Abernethy Library of American Literature.

B. The text is based on photostatic copies or actual examination of the manuscripts themselves.

H. The text is based on examination of the manuscripts.

HM. The text, except that of the verse in *HM 924*, is based on transcriptions by Miss Edythe Backus. A microfilm of *HM 924* was used.
    The manuscript holdings here collated include the originals of both *FLJ* and *BSWa*.

L. The text is based on photostatic copies of the manuscripts.

---

[1] *The Letters of Ralph Waldo Emerson,* ed. Ralph L. Rusk (New York, 1939), II, 322.

M1-M31. The text is based on examination of the manuscripts.

The numbering, in the present edition, of the various volumes of the manuscript Journal requires a word of explanation. The latest numbering of the volumes is by the Morgan Library staff; and it is not ideal for use here since it marks two volumes with the same number and another volume with no number. Consequently, for the purposes of the present edition, these changes in designation are made:

Numbering, Morgan Library	Date	Numbering, this edition
1	October 22, 1837—December 2, 1839	*M1*
— (no number)		
	August 31, 1839—March 13, 1846	*M1a*
1	July 5, 1845—March 26, 1846	*M1b*

For the remainder of the volumes the Morgan Library designation is followed.

The pagination of the volumes of the Journal, though not always Thoreau's own, is followed here. In *M1* alone, each leaf, but not each page, is clearly numbered. The page is then indicated in the present edition by *r* (*recto*) and *v* (*verso*), thus: *M1 23r.*

M. The text is based on examination of the manuscripts. The verse, with two indicated exceptions, is found in M. A. 920, a bound volume of Thoreau's autograph poems, letters, and essays.

T. The text, except that of two epitaphs, is based on photostatic copies of the manuscripts. The text of the epitaphs was transcribed by Mr. Thomas.

Y. The text is based on photostatic copies of the manuscripts.

ii

Selection of basic texts. To present the poetry as it finally left Thoreau's hand is the general textual aim of the present edition. But the practice of using the latest text as the basic one has not been strictly adhered to. The reason for the exceptions, though, lies in Thoreau's method of composition. In terms of it, one can be quite sure that Thoreau wrote the longer drafts of, for example, "Poverty" first, and then took from them the quatrain and couplet he inserted in the *Week.* This would mean, by strict interpretation, that the final version of the poem to receive Thoreau's touch would have been those six lines out of the whole poem's thirty-one. To use the six lines as the basic text, or texts, and to reduce the body of the poem to a textual note, would not seem, to the present editor, to be common sense. Consequently, the longer poem is used as the basic text. As a rule, when there is an apparently complete version and another that is merely excerpted, the long version is chosen as basic even though the other might have been written later. It is true that a practice like this could be carried to extremes, but an attempt has been made to draw the line conservatively.

Fidelity to text. Errors in spelling, too little or too much capitalization, fragmentary sentences, etc., are to be found at times in the verse Thoreau did not prepare for publication. Such flaws have been preserved in this edition, since it was not the purpose of the editor to present "Thoreau Improved."

Order of textual variations. One of the aims of the textual notes is to picture the growth and development of the poem under the poet's hand. It is often impossible to find out the precise order in which Thoreau composed the variant versions. However, the variants at each specific point are ranked according to the assured or probable time of composition, thus: led]leads *H HM D 68W*. The earliest manuscript is put first, and the printed versions are arranged in order of publication. The references are given in the same order, except for the references for small parts of longer poems, which are as a rule recorded at the end of the list of references.

Absence of symbols. When no symbol follows a variation described in the textual notes, the variation is to be found in the basic text, thus: let] leave *c*. This would show that Thoreau had first written *leave* in the basic text and then cancelled it in favor of *let*.

Order of lines. In variant versions (and texts otherwise abandoned; see below), the order and number of the lines are given only, of course, when they differ from those of the basic text. In such cases the phrase *in this order* will appear in the textual notes.

Abandoned collations. To arrive at the best texts, numerous versions of some of the poems had to be compared. Thereafter, since many of the versions, particularly of the posthumously published pieces, were found to represent merely editors' refinishings of manuscripts already available for the present edition, such versions were rejected. They had already been collated, but there was no special gain in weighing down the textual notes with the now useless collations. On the other hand, it did seem worth-while—for the sake of the reader's reference—to note the titles of those versions, as well as the order of their lines when they

277

departed from the order of the basic text. Those items are, as a consequence, recorded in the textual notes; and the page references to the jettisoned versions are found in the textual notes, following the page references to the sound texts.

Word endings. The haste with which Thoreau wrote down much of his verse resulted in his slurring the endings of many words. He often reduced final letters to mere trails or jogs. The problem presented to the editor has been that of drawing the line between the slurrings and absolute eliminations. Where Thoreau really omitted final letters, that has been indicated. There, and elsewhere in the words, such letters have been supplied in brackets. As far as the trailed letters go, they have been read as Thoreau intended them.

Word divisions. Thoreau's haste in writing has created another editorial problem. At times he separated parts of words in order, clearly, to make the physical act of writing easier. On the other hand, he frequently joined two different words together; but for the same reason. Judgment as to whether Thoreau's word division was intentional or simply fortuitous has been based mainly on a study of his practice in words that saw print during his life and in related manuscripts.

Capitalization. An additional difficulty emerges in connection with Thoreau's handwriting. When he used, for instance, a capital *S* and when he used a lower-case *s,* it is at times hard to decide. Judgment has been based, in the present edition, on the meaning of the passage. However, in clear-cut cases—where, say, a lower-case letter plainly begins a line of verse—that letter has been recorded as such.

Carets. Cases where Thoreau used carets are not indicated in the textual notes.

Parentheses. Cases where Thoreau used parentheses are not indicated in the text itself but are recorded in the textual notes.

Cancellations. In the manuscript Journal, particularly, many pages have vertical lines drawn through them. Such cancellations must have been used by Thoreau (and perhaps such an early editor as H. G. O. Blake) to block out material for publication. On the other hand, when Thoreau wanted to cancel a version of some specific poem, he did not as a rule use the single vertical stroke. Nevertheless, when poetry is among the material cancelled by the vertical line or otherwise, the fact is recorded in the textual notes. Thus certain poems will have even their basic text marked *c*. When some lines of a poem are noted as being cancelled after the whole version has already been designated as cancelled, that means a double cancellation for the lines in question.

Titles. Varying styles of titles have been made uniform in the textual notes, as well as throughout the rest of the present edition. Any punctuation at the end of titles, notably in the lifted first lines, has been omitted.

Dates of poems. Dates in parentheses following the source citations, given in the textual notes, are of two kinds: dates of composition and dates of publication during Thoreau's lifetime (posthumous dates are not included). Dates of publication are italicized. Dates of composition are set in roman type.[8]

Additional dates for the *HM* versions which might have been deduced from a study of the manuscripts are not at present available. Dates of composition for almost all the verse that Thoreau entered in his Journal (*M1-M31*) have been ascertained, including dates previously fixed in the printed Journal only within the limits of, say, ten years. Among those dates tentatively assigned there, one is less reliable than the others. The ascription of the year 1842 as the probable date of composition for some of the verse in *M1a* is based on evidence less dependable than the average.

Dates of publication when already implied in the symbols are omitted; it seemed unnecessary to follow the symbol *49W*, for instance, with the date *1849*.

Annotation of variant versions. When lines whose content is to be annotated appear in a variant version but not in the basic text, those extra lines will be referred to (if confusion might otherwise result) as if numbered alphabetically. The first extra line in a poem would be noted as *a*, and so on. If the poem runs to more than a single page of content notations, the numbering will begin anew at the top of each succeeding page. If a note is self-explanatory, it will simply be headed *Textual note*.

N.B.: The first reference listed in the textual note for each poem is that for the basic text. Under the heading *Cf.* the references for the versions once collated but now abandoned are, with a view to the reader's convenience, also provided.

[8] A few dates that are not dates of composition are also set in roman type. These exceptions, however, are pointed out in the notes on the content of the poems.

3. "Within the circuit of this plodding life"

References: "*Natural History of Massachusetts,*" *D III (July, 1842),
19; M6 32 (Dec. 30, 1841).* Cf.: *Win 62; PN 84; 06V 103 (reprint of D);
Jl 304. Entire poem c M6   M6 includes these lines in this order: 1-9,
14-15, 16-18 set up as prose, 29-30 set up as prose, one extra line, 10-13,
three extra lines, a version of l. 18, 19-28 set up as prose. Jl includes these
lines in this order: 1-9, 14-18, 29-30, one extra line, 10-13, three extra lines,
18-20; and 21-24 printed as prose, then an extra prose sentence, and finally
25-28 also printed as prose. The prose is not collated. Win includes only
these lines: 1-9, 14-18, 29-30. no title]* Winter Memories *PN   Variants
all in M6*   2 enter]are   ,]-   3 Untarnished]And as unspotted   4 ,]-
5 meandering rivulet,]south woodside-   which]Which   make]make
untrue   6 untrue that aims]which has so poor an aim   7 grievances]
grievance here   8 ,]o   9 ,]o   10 still]cold   the cheerful moon,]the
moon   11 ,]o   12 were adding to]are doubling   13 the arrows]the
glancing arrows   coming]o   ,]. *These lines follow l. 13:*

> And the shrunk wheels creak along the way—
> Some summer accident long past
> of lakelet gleaming in the July beams—

14 shimmering noon of]o   past]past some   15 beam]beam-   *Another
version of l. 18 reads:*

> Or hum of bee under the blue flag

This line follows l. 30:

> In the still cheerful cold of winter nights

4. "His steady sails he never furls"

References: "*Natural History of Massachusetts,*" *D III (July, 1842),
24; M1 v61 (Feb. 25, 1839).* Cf.: *06V 109 (reprint of D); Jl 74. Entire
poem c M1   M1 Jl include these lines: four extra lines, 1-4. no title]*
The Shrike *M1 Jl   M1 opens with these extra lines:*

> Hark—hark—from out the thickest fog
> Warbles with might and main
> The fearless shrike, as all agog
> To find in fog his gain.

3 perching]perched *M1*   Winter's]winter's *M1*

5. "Sometimes I hear the veery's clarion"

Reference: "Natural History of Massachusetts," D III (July, 1842), 26.
Cf.: 06V 112 (reprint of D).

6. "Upon the lofty elm tree sprays"

Reference: "Natural History of Massachusetts," D III (July, 1842),
26. Cf.: Critic, March 26, 1881; PN 72; 06V 112 (reprint of D). no title]
The Vireo *Critic PN* «2 sweet]meet *Critic* 3 the]these *Critic*»

7. "Thou dusky spirit of the wood"

Reference: "Natural History of Massachusetts," D III (July, 1842),
*27. Cf.: PN 93; 06V 113 (reprint of D). no title]*The Crow *PN*

8, 9. "The river swelleth more and more"

References: "Natural History of Massachusetts," D III (July, 1842),
32; M2 39 (Feb. 24, 1840); M1a 197 (1842[?]). Cf.: PN 46; 06V 120
(reprint of D); JI 122. Entire poem c M2   M2 JI include these lines:
fourteen extra lines (then two dotted lines), 1-14, two extra lines, 15-32.
M1a includes only six lines, the first six of the opening extra fourteen
*lines in M2. no title]*The Freshet *M2 JI;* A River Scene *PN   M2 opens*
with these extra lines:

A stir is on the Worc'ter hills,	Worc'ter]Wooster *M1a*
And Nobscott too the valley fills—	Nobscott]Nobscot *M1a*
Where scarce you'd fill an acorn cup	fill]dip *M1a* -], *M1a*
In summer when the sun was up,	was]is *M1a*
No more you'll find a cup at all,	
But in its place a waterfall.	
Oh that the moon were in conjunction	
To the dry land's extremest unction,	
Till every dyke and pier were flooded,	
And all the land with islands studded,	
For once to teach all human kind,	
Both those that plough and those that grind,	
There is no fixture in the land,	
But all unstable is as sand.	

6 water-rat]water rat *M2*   9 ,]o *M2*   10 ,]; *M2*   13 Nahshawtuck]
Nawshawtuct *M2*   Cliff]cliff *M2*   14 .]; *M2*   *These lines follow l. 14*
M2:

So like a deep and placid mind
Whose currents underneath it wind—

15 But]For *M2*   19 swifter]faster *M2*   faster]swifter *M2*   ,]o *M2*
22 lagoons]lagunes *M2*   ;], *M2*   23 As lovely as]Far lovelier than *M2*
24 ;], *M2*

` 10. "Great God, I ask thee for no meaner pelf"

Reference: D III (July, 1842), 79. Cf.: Critic, *March 26, 1881;*
PN 121; 06V 418; 17Sa 271; 17Sb 502. Critic *includes only these lines:*
*1-4, 9-14. no title]*Prayer Critic *06V;* My Prayer *PN   1 "]o* E   «3
action]conduct *Critic»   14 "]o* E

11. "The Moon"

Reference: D III (Oct., 1842), 222. Cf.: PN 71; 06V 406.

12. "To a Stray Fowl"

References: D III (April, 1843), 505; M (probably in Sophia Tho-
reau's hand); HM 924. Cf.: PN 94; 06V 411; BSWa II, 23; 17S 88.
17S includes only these lines: 1-4, 7-12, 17-24. (The text in HM 924, the
long, early draft of Walden, *is certainly later than the D version, which*
is here used as the basic text. But HM 924 is evidently a hasty copying
of D, with ampersands in place of and's *and three slight changes in*
punctuation). To a Stray Fowl]*o M HM BSWa 17S   5 -],- M HM*
7 heaven]Heaven *M HM   13* look'st]lookst *HM   «16* insidious]invidious
BSWa»   19 -],- M HM   20 and]& *M HM   21* «race]voice *17S»*
o'er]oer *M   22* «its]thy *17S»   ,]; HM   23* ,]o *M   24* Indus']Indu's
M «Indian *17S»   *and]& *M HM* «or *BSWa; of 17S»*

13. "The sluggish smoke curls up from some deep dell"

References: "A Winter Walk," D IV (Oct., 1843), 212; EL 226.
*Cf.: PN 82; 06V 165 (reprint of D). no title]*Smoke in Winter *EL PN*
Variants all in EL   8 mind]mind,   slumbering]slumbering,   12 swing]
wield   *13 no stanza]new stanza   15* the]his   17 And]And,   21 tree
tops]tree-tops

14, 15. "When Winter fringes every bough"

References: "A Winter Walk," D IV (Oct., 1843), 220; M1 v52
(Dec. 15, 1838). Cf.: PN 86; 06V 176 (reprint of D); J1 62. Entire poem
*c M1. no title]*Fair Haven *M1 J1;* Stanzas Written at Walden *PN*
Variants all in M1   1 Winter]winter   4 ;].   5 pent-house]pent

283

house   8   ;].-   10 underneath]there below   12 in the last year's
heath]underneath the snow   13 chicadee]chic-a-dee   15 in]is   17
Fair]Rare   20 ,]-   21 ,]-   22 The while]While that   24 Which]
That   28 deafening]deaf'ning   29 hasten]press me   ,]o   30 if I]
I had   33 gambol]crack me   35 crack]rent   38 faggot]fuel   *This
stanza follows l. 40:*

> Fair Haven is my huge tea-urn,
> That seethes and sings to me,
> And eke the crackling faggots burn—
> A homebred minstrelsy.

16. "Not unconcerned Wachusett rears his head"

References: "A Walk to Wachusett," Boston Miscellany of Literature,
*III (Jan., 1843; July 19, 1842), 34; B (early draft of "A Walk to
Wachusett"). Cf.: 06V 144 (reprint of "A Walk to Wachusett").*   2
field,]fields *B*   won,]won *B*   3 reserved,]unmoved *B*

17-19. "The Old Marlborough Road"

References: "Walking," Atlantic Monthly, *IX (June, 1862), 661;
M3a 139 (July 16[?], 1850); H (only lines 1-6 written in Thoreau's
hand; rest written in "copperplate hand" apparently over Thoreau's own
scribbling). Cf.: 06V 214 (reprint of "Walking"); JII 54. Entire poem
c M3a   H includes these lines: 1-53; three extra lines, c; 54-65. M3a
includes only these lines in this order: five extra lines, 25-26, two extra
lines, 26-28; some prose; 9-16; 1-2; two extra lines; 17-20; 63, 62, 64-65;
21-24, 29-34, 37-38, 46-47, three extra lines, 35-36, one extra line, 42-43,
39-41, 44-45, 48-54, two extra lines, 56-61 (semicolons here mark stanza
divisions). JII includes only these lines in this order: five extra lines,
25-28; some prose; 9-16; 1-2; two extra lines, 17-20; 63, 62, 64-65; 21-24,
29-34, 37-38, 46-47, three extra lines, 39-41, 35-36, one extra line, 42-45,
48-54, two extra lines, 56-61 (semicolons here mark stanza divisions).*
The Old Marlborough Road]The Old Marlboro Road *H; o M3a JII*
1 money]mony *M3a*   ,]o *M3a H*   2 any]"ony" *M3a;* any *H*   ;]o
M3a H   *These c lines follow l. 2 M3a:*

> To market fares
> With early apples & pears.

6 :], *H*   7 ,]o *H*   8 ,-]o *H*   9 0]The *M3a*   ,]o *M3a H*   10 and
rabbits,]& Rabbits *M3a*   11 hast]has *M3a*   12 ,]o *M3a H*   13 ,]o
M3a H   14 ,]- *M3a;* ; *H*   15 And](and *M3a*   16 Constantly](There
constantly; There *c M3a;* Continually *altered to* Constantly H   18
With the instinct to travel]If you are ever disturbed with a desire to

travel *a1 M3a*   20 On]on *M3a*   Marlborough]Marlboro' *M3a;* Marlboro *H*   21 ,]o *M3a H*   22 ;]- *M3a;* . *H*   23 ,]o *M3a H*   24 Chris-
tians]christians *H*   .]- *M3a;* , *H*   *These lines precede l. 25 M3a:*

> O whither doest thou go?
> Which way doset thou flow
> Thou art the way—
> Thou art a rode
> Which Dante never trode

25 there]they *M3a*   26 ,]o *M3a*   *These c lines follow l. 26 M3a:*

> For thou leadest nowhere
> But to the Irishman Quin:

28 .]o *M3a;* , *H*   29 it, what is it,]it- what is it- *M3a;* it what is it?
H   30 ,]o *M3a H*   32 ?]- *M3a;* , *H*   33 guide-boards]guide *boards
M3a;* guid boards *H*   ,]o *M3a H*   34 ;]. *M3a;* o *H*   36 .]o *M3a H*
This line follows l. 36 M3a:

> Huge as Stonehenge

37 going]going there *M3a*   38 *might*]might *M3a*   .]o *M3a H*   40
Did]did *(part of l. 39 but indicated as beginning of a separate line) M3a*
,]o *M3a H*   41 ;]-*M3a;* o *H*   42 ,]o *M3a*   43 selectmen]select men
M3a H   ,]? *M3a;* o *H*   44 ,]o *M3a*   45 ?]! *H*   46 endeavor]
endeavor to; to *c M3a*   47 ;]. *M3a;* o *H*   *These lines follow l. 47
M3a:*

> They are a monument to somebody
> To some select man
> Who thought of the plan

*Lines 39-41 follow "plan" but are indicated for transposition to their
present order M3a.*   48 ,]o *M3a H*   49 ,]o *M3a H*   51 Grave]
Engrave; En *c M3a*   ;]o *M3a H*   52 ,]o *M3a H*   *These c lines
follow l. 53 H:*

> I know two or three
>   Sentences, ie.
> That might there be

54 one or two]two or three *M3a;* one or 2 *H*   *These lines follow
l. 54 M3a:*

> Sentences i. e.
> That might there be.

56 Literature]That Literature; That *c M3a*   57 ,]. *M3a*   58 a man]
a man *al for* men *M3a*   could]might *c for* could *M3a*   59 next]After
c for Next *M3a*   ,]. *M3a;* o *H*   60 ,]o *M3a H*   62 If with]With your
M3a   fancy]fancy *al for* spirits *M3a*   63 ,]o *M3a*   65 Old Marl-
borough]old Marlboro *M3a;* Old Marlboro *H*   .]o *H*

20. "In two years' time 't had thus"

References: "Wild Apples," Atlantic Monthly, X *(Nov., 1862), 518; M24 227 (Oct. 28, 1857). Cf.: 06V 303 (reprint of "Wild Apples"); JX 139. M24 JX include these lines: six extra lines, a sentence of rhymed prose, 1-8 (c in M24), two extra lines. Variants all in M24 M24 opens with these extra lines:*

> 'Twas 30 years ago
> In a rocky pasture field
> Sprang an infant apple grove
> Unplanted & concealed—
> I sing the wild apple theme enough for me.
> I love the racy fruit & I reverence the tree—
> In that small family there was one that loved the sun—
> which sent its root down deep & took fast hold on
> life—while the others went to sleep

1 *two years']*2 years   2 *,]-*   3 *Admired]*& Admired; & (?) *c   ,]o* 4 *flocks]*ox *c for* flocks   *.]-*   5 *new stanza]no*   6 *:]-*   There]Then *These lines follow l. 8:*

> Its heart did bleed all day
> & when the birds were hushed—

21. "Carpe Diem"

Reference: Boatswain's Whistle, *Nov. 16, 1864. (The first and only volume of this periodical is made up of numbers running from Nov. 9 to Nov. 19, 1864. One such volume was sold at the Wakeman sale [Wakeman catalogue, number 1017]. There it is described as including an article by Thoreau, "Looming of the Sun," and a poem. The article appeared shortly thereafter in the* Atlantic Monthly, *according to the Wakeman entry; and the entry concludes with a description of two letters from Francis H. Allen relative to the priority of the article in the* Boatswain's Whistle.

The article referred to appears as part of "The Highland Light" in the Atlantic Monthly *for Dec., 1864. The poem does not. In the* Boatswain's Whistle, *there is a poem—not in the article—entitled "Carpe Diem" and signed "H. T." The authenticity of the poem is thus reasonably established. Thoreau's fragment of an article appears in the* Boatswain's Whistle *for Nov. 18 and is signed "H. D. Thoreau." He probably intended the piece of verse to follow its second, and last, paragraph, which concludes with this admonition:*

> But it behooves us old stagers to keep our lamps
> trimmed and burning to the last, and not trust
> to the sun's looming [ibid., p. 70].

The trite and moralizing jingle of "Carpe Diem" is not too much out of key with that final sentence.)

22. "Each summer sound"

References: "Natural History of Massachusetts," D III (July, 1842), 26; M1 r26 (Feb. 27, 1838); M1 r79 (Feb. 19, 1838). Cf.: 06V 112 (reprint of D). Couplet c M1 (both versions) No variations M1 (both versions)

22. "The needles of the pine"

References: "A Walk to Wachusett," Boston Miscellany of Literature, III (Jan., 1843; July 19, 1842), 31; M5 30 (May 9, 1841); B (early draft of "A Walk to Wachusett"). Cf.: 06V 133 (reprint of "A Walk to Wachusett"); Jl 259. Couplet c M5   no title]Westward-ho M5   1 ,]o M5 B

22. "In the East fames are won"

Reference: "Thomas Carlyle and his Works," Graham's Magazine, XXX (April, 1847), 241. Cf.: 06IV 346 (reprint of "Thomas Carlyle and his Works").

23. "Love equals swift and slow"

References: 49W 285; HM 13182. Cf.: FLJ I, 136. No variations HM

24. "Men say they know many things"

References: 54Wa 46; HM (a and b) 924. Cf.: 06Wa 46; BSWa I, 14. 1 ;]o HMa; , HMb   2 -]o HMa HMb   3 and]& HMa   4 ;]- HMa HMb   6 any body]anybody HMa

25. "What's the railroad to me"

References: 54Wa 133; M3a 151 (Aug., 1850); HM 924. Cf.: 06Wa 135; Jll 58; BSWa l, 164. Entire poem c M3a   1 railroad]rail-road M3a   2 see]see where it ends; where it ends c M3a   3 .]o M3a 4 ,]o M3a   5 ,]o M3a   6 a-blowing]a flowing M3a; a blowing HM ,]o M3a   7 the]o M3a   a-growing]a growing M3a HM   ,]o M3a; -HM

26. "It is no dream of mine"

References: 54Wa 209; HM 924; M3a, torn half page between pp. 142-151, which here touch one another (1850). Cf.: "Is consigned to the nine"; 06Wa 215; JII 58; BSWaa II, 57; BSWab I, xiv. HM BSWaa include these lines: two extra lines, c in HM; 1-4; six extra lines, c in HM; 5-10. BSWab includes only the six extra lines (with l. 1 broken down into two lines) of HM. M3a JII include only lines 5-6, c in M3a. (BSWab contains only the six extra c lines of HM 924, "It is . . . consign." They differ slightly from the same lines in BSWaa, which differ in turn from the manuscript, HM 924.) HM opens with these c lines:

> It is a real place,
> Boston, I tell it to your face.

These c lines follow l. 4 HM:

> It is a part of me which I have not prophaned
> I live by the shore of me detained.
> Laden with my dregs
> I stand on my legs,
> While all my pure wine
> I to nature consign.

1 It is]And c for It is HM   2 ;]o HM   3 cannot]can not HM   and]& HM   5 ,]o HM   stony]stoney HM   6 And]& M3a   breeze]breeze al for gale M3a   o'er]oer M3a   ;]o M3a HM   8 ,]; HM   9 And Its]Its; & Its HM

27. "Light-winged Smoke, Icarian bird"

References: 54Wa 271; D III (April, 1843), 505 (Thoreau calls this poem and another poem there, titled "Haze," Orphics); HM (a and b) 924; EL 225. Cf.: PN 69; 06Wa 279; BSWa II, 146. HMa includes only lines 1-3. HMb, on the following page, is preceded by some lines of c prose and then includes these lines: 1-3, c; 4-10. no title]Smoke D EL PN   1 Smoke,]smoke, D; Smoke! EL   2 ,]; EL   9 thou]thou, EL   incense]incense, EL   10 gods]Gods D   No variations HMa HMb

28. "Die and be buried who will"

Reference: The Maine Woods (Boston: Ticknor and Fields, 1864), p. 82. Cf.: 06III 90 (reprint of "Ktaadn and the Maine Woods").
(The quatrain is part of the material omitted from the first printing of Thoreau's Maine travelogue. See "Ktaadn, and the Maine Woods," Union Magazine, III [July-Dec., 1848], 220. The lines did not appear

until the full version of the travelogue was published, after Thoreau's death, in book form.)

29. "Where'er thou sail'st who sailed with me"

References: 68W 5; M1a 1 (Aug. 31, 1839[*?*]); *49W 3. Cf.: 06W 2.* 2 ,]o *M1a* 3 ,]o *M1a* 4 Muse]muse *M1a* -]o *M1a* *No variations 49W*

30. "I am bound, I am bound, for a distant shore"

References: 68W 6; M1a 217 (1839[*?*]); *49W 4. Cf.: 06W 2. M1a includes only lines 2-4, but the preceding page is cut out.* 2 isle, by]isle *M1a* Azore,]azore *M1a* 3 seek,]seek *M1a* 4 sands]sand *M1a* .] o *M1a* *No variations 49W*

31. "I sailed up a river with a pleasant wind"

References: 68W 7; 49W 5. Cf.: 06W 2. 2 lands,]lands *49W* people,]people *49W*

32. "The respectable folks"

References: 68W 13; HM 13182; 49W 11. Cf.: PN 103; FLJ I, 139; 06W 7; 17S 265. HM FLJ 17S include only these lines: 1-6; four extra lines, c in HM; 7-8; one extra line; 11-22. no title]The Respectable Folks *PN;* Our Neighbors *FLJ;* Our Country Neighbors *17S* 1 ,-], *HM* 4 ;], *HM* *These c lines follow l. 6 HM:*

> They drink at the brooks and the pilgrim's cup,   «and]with *17S*»
> And with the owl and the nighthawk sup;   «sup]they sup *17S*»
> They suck the breath of the morning wind,
>   And they make their own all the good they find.

8 snivel,]snivel *HM* *This line follows l. 8 HM:*

> For they have a lease of immortality.   «a lease of immortality]
>   leased Immortality *17S*»

11 they ever]forever they *HM* 12 ;], *HM* 17 light,]light *HM* 20 ;], *HM* 22 ,]o *HM* *No variations 49W*

33, 34. "Ah, 'tis in vain the peaceful din"

References: 68W 23; 49W 20. Cf.: 06W 15. 19 free-born]free born *49W* 29 land]land, *49W*

35. "But since we sailed"

References: 68W 24; 49W 21. Cf.: 06W 16. See also note. No variations 49W

36. "On Ponkawtasset, since, we took our way"

References: 68W 25; 49Wp (lines 1-4 of uncorrected proofs of 49W also collated here as 49Wp; Allen, Bibliography, *p. 169); 49W 22. Cf.: 06W 16.* 1 since,]since *49Wp*   we took our way]with such delay *49W*   way,]way *49Wp*   2 still]fair *49Wp*   to far Billericay]toward neighboring Billerica *49Wp;* we took our meadowy way *49W*   4 often shine]twinkle oft *49Wp*   often]faintly *49W*   13 paled]pal'd *49W*   15 Ay]Aye *49W*

37. "An early unconverted Saint"

References: 68W 51; HMa 13188; HMb 13195 (Sept. 1, 1839); *49W 47. Cf.: FLJa I, 122; FLJb I, xiv; 06W 42. HMa includes only these lines: 3-6, four extra lines. HMb includes these lines in this order: 1-2, c and indicated for transposition; 3-6; four extra lines. FLJa includes these lines: 1-6, four extra lines. FLJb includes only these lines: 3-6, four extra lines. (Sanborn says that FLJa is an earlier version than FLJb.) no title]Morning HMa FLJa HMb FLJb*   1 An early]Thou *HMb*   ,]o *HMb*   2 Free from noontide or evening]Early Christian without *HMb*   ,]- *HMb*   3 ,]o *HMb*   4 That did]Who dost *HMa HMb*   civil]evil *HMb*   5 And]Who *HMa;* Who *c for* as *HMb*   its] thy *HMa HMb*   birth]birth hast trod; hast trod *c HMb*   6 Had]Hast *HMa HMb*   .], *HMa*   *These lines follow l. 6 HMa:*

>   —The cowards hope the brave man's way,
>   And distant promise of a day—
>   While the late risen world goes west
>   I'll daily bend my steps to east.

These lines follow l. 6 to form an additional stanza HMb:

>   Strict anchorite who dost simply feast
>   On freshest dews—I'll be thy guest,
>   And daily bend my steps to the east
>   While the late risen world goes west.

No variations 49W

38, 39. "Low in the eastern sky"

References: 68W 54; D III (Oct., 1842), *222; 49W 51. Cf.: PN 32; 06W 46; 06V 400. D includes these lines: 1-32, twenty-four extra lines*

(here a-x), 33-48. no title]To the Maiden in the East *D PN 06V*   6
Above]Behind *D*   18 flower-bells]flower bells *D 49W*   26 heave]
heave, *D 49W*   27 low-hung]low hung *49W*   29 ,]o *D*   *These lines*
follow l. 32 D:

> From yonder comes the sun,
> But soon his course is run,
> Rising to trivial day
> Along his dusty way,
> But thy noontide completes
> Only auroral heats,
>   Nor ever sets,
> To hasten vain regrets.

> Direct thy pensive eye
> Into the western sky;
> And when the evening star
> Doth the glimmer from afar   «Doth]Does *PN*»
> Upon the mountain line,
> Accept it for a sign
>   That I am near,
> And thinking of thee here.

> I'll be thy Mercury,
> Thou Cytherea to me,
> Distinguished by thy face
> The earth shall learn my place;
> As near beneath thy light
> Will I outwear the night,
>   With mingled ray
> Leading the westward way.

36 ,]o *D*   40 gentle]slender *D*   42 ,]o *D*   46 water-lilies]water lilies
D 49W

40. "Dong, sounds the brass in the east"

References: 68W 58; M5 31 (May 9, 1841); 49W 54. Cf.: 06W 50;
Jl 259. Entire poem c M5   no title]The Echo of the Sabbath Bell Heard
in the Woods *M5 Jl*   1 Dong,]Dong- *M5*   east,]east- *M5*   2 to a
funeral]for a civic *M5*   5 ringeth]rings *M5*   7 ,]- *M5*   10 air,]air
M5   water,]water *M5*   12 it]o *M5*   .], *M5*   *This line follows l.*
12 M5:

> With a slim silver tongue

13 tolleth]tolls *M5*   ,]o *M5*   15 a far]an *M5*   *No variations 49W*

41. "I make ye an offer"

*References: 68W 76; M1a 162 (1842[?]); 49W 73; H. Cf.: 06W 69. M1a includes only these lines: 1-10, 15-20. H includes only lines 14-20. no title]*The Offer *M1a*   2 gods,]gods *M1a*   4 ,]o *M1a*   .]o *49W*   10 descendants]descendents *M1a*   17 ,]o *M1a H*

42, 43. "Conscience is instinct bred in the house"

*References: 68W 82; 49W 79. Cf.: PN 107; 06W 75. no title]*Conscience *PN*   7 ,]; *49W*

44. "Such water do the gods distil"

References: 68W 92; 49W 88. Cf.: 06W 86. No variations 49W

45. "That Phaeton of our day"

References: 68W 107; 49W 105. Cf.: 06W 103   17 ;]. 49W

46. "Though all the fates should prove unkind"

*References: 68W 155; M; 49W 151. Cf.: Commonwealth, July 24, 1863; Sea and Shore (Boston, 1874), p. 121; PN 41; 06W 151. M and the Commonwealth (hereafter abbreviated to C) include only these lines: two extra lines, 1-6. no title]*Travelling *M C;* Lines on New Hampshire Men Going to Sea *Sea and Shore;* Lines *PN   These lines precede l. 1 M:*

<blockquote>
If e'er our minds be ill at ease   «be]are *C»*
It is in vain to cross the seas
</blockquote>

1 Though all]Or when *M*   should]do *M*   ,]o *M*   2 Leave not your] To leave our *M*   3 ship, becalmed,]ship becalmed *M*   ;]o *M*   4 must]must *c for* will *M*   ;]. *M*   ,5 pace]pace, *49W*   «6 out]rest *C»*

47-50. "With frontier strength ye stand your ground"

References: 68W 173; B (early draft of "A Walk to Wachusett"); HM 13201; M5 26 (May 2, 1841); "A Walk to Wachusett," Boston Miscellany of Literature, III (Jan., 1843; July 19, 1842), 31; 49W 168; EL 221. Cf.: PN 96; 06W 170; 06V 133; Jl 256. See also Appendix A. B includes only these lines in this order: 2-5; 8-12; 18-19; 22-31; four extra lines; 32-35; l. 38, c; 36-43; 51-56; 61-88; 96-99. HM includes only these lines: one extra line, 2-7, five extra lines. M5 Jl include only these lines, c in M5: 73-88, 96-99. Boston Miscellany (hereafter abbreviated to BM) EL 06V include only these lines: 1-5, 8-19, 22-43, 51-56, 61-88,

96-99. (B is apparently a part of the version of the essay described in the Wakeman catalogue, number 986. The draft of the essay in B was written in an old ledger which Thoreau also used as his herbarium.) no title]Wachusett M5 Jl; The Mountains in the Horizon HM; Mountains EL PN   HM opens with this extra line:

The confines of the sky and ground—

2 circle round]stand around *HM*   3 ,]- *HM*   4 Ye distant]A springing *HM*   5 Monadnock]Monadnock, *BM   EL*   Peterborough]Peterboro *BM 49W EL*   Hills]hills *B HM BM EL*   ;-]. *B HM; ; BM EL*   6 Firm]Staid *HM*   7 Outcircling]out-circling *HM*   -]o *HM*   *These lines follow l. 7 HM:*

> The sun doth go behind thee not before
> For brief to plenish his diminished store.
> The in's of the sky, ye run
> Round the horizon of its eye
> Whose pupil is the sun.

8 ,]o *B EL*   10 ;]. *B*   11 on upon]on, upon *BM;* to *EL*   ,]o *B*   14 ,]. *B; ; EL*   16 Sun]sun *BM EL*   18 line,]line *B*   one,]one *B*   19 Ye westward]Ye to the westward *BM EL*   24 ,-], *B; . BM; ; EL*   25 ye]ye, *BM*   here,]here,- *EL*   27 ,]o *B EL*   29 western]Western *EL*   ;], *B*   30 brows]brows, *BM EL*   ,]o *B*   31 Time]time *B EL*   naught]nought *B BM 49W EL*   ;]. *B*   *These lines follow l. 31 B:*

> The wind is blowing on the sea,
> The locust sings in Barbary,
> And from Cape-town to Inverness
> They ply their eastern business;

32 For]But *B*   ,]o *B*   34 primeval]primaeval *EL*   ,]o *EL*   35 ;], *B*   37 *western*]western *BM;* Western *EL*   41 o'ertop]oertop *B*   western]Western *EL*   ,]o *B*   42 yonder]yonder, *BM*   croft]croft, *BM EL*   43 ;]. *B BM EL*   51 silver]silver, *BM*   ,]o *B*   52 o'er]oer *B*   53 such]fresh *EL*   55 ,]o *B*   56 Heaven]heaven *B EL*   59 overnight]over night *49W*   61 ,]o *B BM*   trees]trees, *B 49W*   62 on]in *B*   ,]o *B*   66 ;], *B*   68 ;]. *B*   71 ,]o *B*   73 But special]Especial- *M5*   74 ,]! *EL*   who]who, *EL*   me]me, *EL*   76 ,]- *M5*   77 ,]- *M5*   78 or]of *EL*   79 of]on *EL*   81 true]true, *BM EL;* true but stands *M5*   82 'tween]tween *M5*   84 know'st]knowst *BM*   85 driven]driven, *BM*   86 ;], *M5 B BM EL*   87 canst]can'st *M5 BM 49W EL*   ,]? *(?) M5*   88 ?]; *EL*   97 ;], *M5 B BM EL*   98 one,]one *M5 B*   other,]other *B;* other; *BM*   99 !]. *M5 B*

293

51. "Here lies an honest man"

References: 68W 180; T; HM 13182 ([Oct.] 22, [1843]); *Ha; Hb; 49W 176. Cf.: 06W 178. Hb includes only lines 4-6. no title*]Epitaph *T* 1 honest man]Honest Man *Ha* ,]*o T* 2 Rear-Admiral]Rear Admiral *T HM* .]*o T Horizontal line below l. 2 o T HM; but l. 2 indented HM* 3 ,]*o HM* then]then, *Ha* 4 ,]*o T* 5 For]For, *HM* in his]by your *c for* in his *HM* ,]*o T Ha Hb* 6 Here too] Here, too, *T*; Here too; too *c HM* Engraver]engraver *T HM No variations 49W*

52. "The western wind came lumbering in"

References: 68W 182; M1 r60 (Feb. 3, 1839). *Cf.: 49W 178; 06W 180; Jl 72. Entire poem c M1 M1 Jl include only these lines: 1-2, two extra lines, 5-8. no title*]The Evening Wind *M1 Jl* 1 western wind came]eastern mail comes *M1* ,]*o M1* 2 Bearing a faint Pacific]with outmost waves of Europe's *M1* ,]; *M1 These lines follow l. 2 M1:*

> The western sighs adown the slope,
> Or mid the rustling leaves doth grope,

4 Postmaster]Post-Master *49W* 6 Whate'er]Whateer *M1* 7 brake] brake, *M1* 8 Lake]lake *49W* ;-]. *M1*

53. "Rumors from an Aeolian Harp"

References: 68W 185; D III (Oct., 1842), 200; Thoreau's corrected D (Cooke, Introduction to . . . The Dial, *II, 188); 49W 181. Cf.: PN 39; 06W 184.* 3 ,]*o D* 10 poetry is yet unsung]simple truth on every tongue *D No variations Thoreau's corrected D 49W*

54, 55. "Away! away! away! away"

References: 68W 187; 49W 183. Cf.: PN 43; 06W 186. no title] Stanzas *PN* 22 ;],- *49W*

56. "Low-anchored cloud"

References: 68W 203; M1a 119 (1842 [?]); *HM 956; 49W 201; EL 228. Cf.: PN 68; 06W 201; Jl 457. M1a Jl include these lines in this order: 6-9, one extra line, 1-3, two extra lines, 4-5, 10, three extra lines, 11-12. HM includes these lines in this order: 6-9, 1-3, two extra lines, 4-5, 10, two extra lines, 11-12. See also "Fog," of which lines 2, 8, 9, and 10 are similar in phrasing to lines 1, 4, 5, and 6 of the above poem. no title*]Fog *M1a HM Jl*; Mist *EL PN* 1 Low-anchored]Low anchored

M1a HM   3 Fountain-head]Fountain head *M1a HM*   *These lines follow l. 3 M1a:*

> Ocean branch that flowest to the sun,
> Diluvian spirit, or Deucaleon shroud,   spirit,]spirit- *HM*

4 Dew-cloth]Dew cloth *M1a HM 49W*   cloth,]cloth *M1a;* cloth- *HM* dream]ocean *HM* dream drapery]dream-drapery *EL* drapery,]drapery *M1a*   5 ;]- *M1a;* . *HM*   6 Drifting]Thou drifting *M1a HM* ,]o *M1a*   7 daisied]dasied *M1a* banks]bank *HM* and]& *M1a* ,]o *M1a*   8 labyrinth]labyrinths *M1a*   9 booms]booms, *M1a* heron wades]curlew peeps *M1a* ;]o *M1a*   *This line follows l. 9 M1a:*

> The heron wades and boding rain crow clucks;

10 ,]- *M1a; o HM; ,- EL*   *These lines follow l. 10 M1a:*

> Sea fowl that with the east wind
> Seek'st the shore—groping thy way inland   Seek'st]Seeks't
>   *HM*   -], *HM*   inland]inland, *HM*
> By which ever name I please to call thee   ]o *HM*

12 !]. *M1a HM 49W EL*

---

57. "Man's little acts are grand"

References: 68W 225; 49W 223. Cf.: 06W 224. 5 noontide]noontide *49W*   6 ray]ray, *49W*

---

58. "The waves slowly beat"

References: 68W 229; M1aa 61 (Sept. 3, 1842[?]); M1ab 116 (1842 [?]); HM 956; 49W 227. Cf.: "Where gleaming fields of haze," textual note; 06W 229. M1ab includes only lines 3-6.   1 ,]o *HM M1aa*   2 ,]o *M1aa*   3 And no]Not a *M1ab* o'er]oer *HM M1aa* ,]o *M1aa M1ab*   4 Save]Oer save; Oer *c M1ab* ,]o *M1aa M1ab*   6 a-calking]a caulking *HM M1aa M1ab 49W* .]o *M1aa*

---

59. "Woof of the sun, ethereal gauze"

References: 68W 229; HM 13190 (in Sophia Thoreau's hand); D III (April, 1843), 506; 49W 227; EL 229. Cf.: PN 70; 06W 229. no title] Haze *HM D EL PN*   1 sun]fen *EL* ethereal]etherial *D*   2 Nature's]nature's *HM D*   3 and]& *HM*   7 Ethereal]Etherial *D*   10 transparent-winged]transparent-winged, *HM D 49W EL*   11 noon,]noon *HM*   12 ;],- *EL*

60, 61. "Where gleaming fields of haze"

References: 68W 234; M1a 116 (1842[?]); 49W 231. Cf.: "The waves slowly beat," textual note; 06W 234; Jl 457. M1a includes these lines in this order: four extra lines, 1-20, 23-24, 21-22, six extra lines (the last four, a separate stanza, also being found as part of "The waves slowly beat"; see that poem for collation), 31-42, 25-30. It is hard to discern the stanza breaks in M1a, but lines 25-30, at least, form another stanza. Jl includes only the opening four extra lines of M1a; the editor of the printed Journal notes the lines as preceding the rest of the poem. M1a opens, then, with these extra lines:

> Far oer the bow
> Amid the drowsy noon
> Souhegan creeping slow
> Appeareth soon.

2 voyageur's]voyageurs' *M1a*   3 ,]o *M1a*   4 ,]. *M1a*   9 Are waving o'er]Have accompanied *M1a*   11 ,]o *M1a*   13 ,]o *M1a*   17 With]But with *M1a*   ,]o *M1a*   18 ,]o *M1a*   19 ,]o *M1a*   20 ,]o *M1a*   21 ,]o *M1a*   22 ,]o *M1a*   *These lines follow l. 22 M1a:*

> Which trails in its stream
> The [word] current of its dream [?].

24 .]o *M1a*   26 its]thy *M1a*   ,]o *M1a*   28 ,]o *M1a*   31 ,]o *M1a*   32 flowed]flown *M1a*   33 ,]o *M1a*   34 ,]. *M1a*   35 ,]o *M1a 49W*   36 ,]? *M1a*   38 ,]- *M1a*   39 black]brown *M1a*   40 Thy red forest-floor,]On thy forest floor *M1a*   41 Or]Or the; the *c M1a*   Nature]nature *M1a*   42 ?]. *M1a 49W*

62. "This is my Carnac, whose unmeasured dome"

References: 68W 268; M1b 37 (Aug. 6, 1845); 49W 266. Cf.: 06W 267; Jl 376. M1b Jl omit lines 3-10, although they are approximated in a prose paragraph preceding the verse. The rest of the lines in M1b Jl appear in this order: 11-14, 1-2, two extra lines. 1 Carnac]Carnac neath; neath *c M1b*   ,]o *M1b*   2 Shelters]was born Shelters; was born *c M1b*   and]& *M1b*   .]o *M1b*   *These lines (the last three words of each line are indicated for transposition to their present order) follow l. 2 M1b:*

> Whose propylaeum is the system high [?]
> And sculptured facade the visible sky

8 the]this *49W*   11 Mother]mother *M1b*   sprightly greets us now]with unwrinkled brow *c for* sprightly greets us now *M1b*   ,]o *M1b*   12 Wearing]Wears still *M1b*   radiance]blushes *M1b*   .]o *M1b*   13 If]

And *M1b*   still]why *M1b*   stand]stand they *M1b*   ,]? *M1b*   14 to
enjoy]T'enjoy *M1b*   they remain]they would fain remain *M1b*

63. "True kindness is a pure divine affinity"

*Reference: 68W 275. Cf.: PN 31; 06W 275. N.B.: quatrain o 49W
no title]*True Kindness *PN*

64-66. "Lately, alas, I knew a gentle boy"

References: 68W 276; M1 r68 (June 24, 1839); *D I (July, 1840), 71;
Thoreau's corrected D (Cooke,* Introduction to . . . The Dial, *II, 187);
49W 274; EL 211. Cf.: PN 21; 06W 276. no title]*Sympathy *M1 D EL
PN*   1 Lately, alas,]Lately alas *M1 D;* Lately, alas! *EL*   2 Virtue's]
Virtues' *49W*   4 strong-hold]stronghold *M1 D 49W EL*   6 ,]; *EL*
7 ports]posts *D (but Thoreau's corrected D reads* ports*)*   10 ,]; *D*   12
kingdom]kingdom, *EL*   wheresoe'er]whereso'eer *M1*   17 subtile]sub-
tle *M1 D EL;* subtil *49W*   haze]breeze *D (but Thoreau's corrected D
reads* haze*)*   18 our]the *D*   19 works]worked *D (but Thoreau's corrected D reads* works*)*   24 have loved him]have loved him, *M1 D EL*
25 moment]moment, *D*   26 farther]further *49W*   31 it]it, *EL*   33
,]; *EL*   42 resound]resound, *EL*   *Horizontal line below l. 45 o M1*
46 hath]has *EL*   51 truest]dearest *D (but Thoreau's corrected D reads*
truest*)*

67. "The Atlantides"

References: 68W 278; 49W 276. Cf.: PN 16; 06W 278. 7 Scarcely]
Only *49W*

68. "My love must be as free"

*References: 68W 296; D III (Oct., 1842), 199; 49W 293. Cf.: PN
37; 06W 297. no title]*Free Love *D PN*   4 everything]every thing
D 49W   12 .], *D*

69. "The Good how can we trust"

References: 68W 298; 49W 294. Cf.: 06W 298; 06VI 147 (Dec. 29,
1847). 11 ,]o *49W*

70. "Nature doth have her dawn each day"

References: 68W 301; M1 r72 (July 24, 1839); *D I (Jan., 1841), 314;
49W 298. Cf.: PN 56; 06W 302; Jl 87. no title]*Stanzas *D PN*   3 for
sooth]forsooth *49W*   4 are]are, *M1 D*   10 ,]; *M1 D*   19 sun]Sun *D*

71-73. "Let such pure hate still underprop"

References: 68W 304; H; D II (Oct., 1841), 204; M2 23 (Jan. 19, 1840); *49W 300; EL 214. Cf.: PN 26; 06W 305; Jl 113. H includes only these lines: 1-10, eight extra lines, 11-15, 17-20, thirteen extra lines, 21-54, four extra lines. M2 Jl include only the final four extra lines, c in M2, of H. no title]*Friendship *H D PN;* Romans, Countrymen, and Lovers *EL* "Friends, Romans, Countrymen, and Lovers."]"Friends- Romans- Countrymen- and Lovers" *H; o EL* 3 other's]others *H* 4 our]o *H* 8 ,]o *H These lines follow l. 10 H:*

> False friends and foes I must look after well,
> Whether they'll come or go, how can I tell?
> But the true friend, he is a field well-fenced,
> There's nothing for me there to guard against.

They are preceded by four other lines, for which see "Friendship's Steadfastness." 11 ,-]- *H D 49W* 13 ,]; *EL* 16 ,-]- *D 49W* 17 Love]God *H D* ,]; *EL* 18 it]him *H D* 19 one]our *D* ,]o *H These lines follow l. 20 H:*

> What I can raise
> I will plant thick,
> What I can lose
> I will lose quick.

They are preceded by nine lines, for which see "Friendship's Steadfastness." 21 It]Love *H D* ,]o *H* 22 ,]; *EL* 26 speech]speech, *EL* kind]kind, *EL* ,]o *H;* ; *EL* 28 ,]: *EL* 29 ,]o *H* 34 ,]o *H* 36 ,-]- *H D 49W* ; ; *EL* 37 ,]o *H* 38 Or]Nor *H* ,]o *H* 42 ,]o *H* 43 Or]Nor *H* mine]mine, *EL* 46 warder]warden *D* 47,]; *EL* 48 But,]But *H D* sun,]sun *H D* o'er]oer *H* 49 ,]o *H* 53 ,]o *H* 54 .]o *H These four lines, c in M2, follow l. 54 H:*

> By a strong liking we prevail
> Against the stoutest fort,
> At length the fiercest heart will quail   fiercest]stoutest
> And our alliance court   *c for* fiercest *M2*   quail]quail, *M2*

55 *no stanza]new stanza D*   waits as]waits, as *EL*

74, 75. "The Inward Morning"

References: 68W 311; M6 8 and 11 (written as two separate lyrics under date of Nov. 30, 1841 and Nov. [really Dec.] 12, 1841 respectively); D III (Oct., 1842), 198; 49W 308. Cf.: Aut 351; PN 58; 06W 313; Jl 291 and 292. M6 Jl include these lines (c in M6) in this order: 1-4, four extra lines, 5-8, 13-24; and 9-12, 25-36. Aut includes only these lines: 1-4, four extra lines, 5-8, 13-24. See Appendix A for additions and further

variations. The Inward Morning]*o M6 Aut Jl* 2 ,]*o M6* 3 And in
its fashion's hourly]For as its hourly fashions *M6* 4 .]*o M6 These
lines follow l. 4 M6:*

> My eyes look inward not without
> And I but hear myself—
> And this new wealth which I have got
> Is part of my own pelf.

5 In vain]For while *M6* ,]*o M6* 6 And]I *M6* ,]*o M6* 8 Illumes]
Lumines *M6* .]*o M6* 9 ,]*o M6* 10 ,]*o M6* 11 fast-abiding]fast
abiding *D 49W* 12 ?]. *M6* 13 Lo,]As *M6* wood,]wood *M6 D*
14 ,]*o M6* 15 Where'er]And Where'er; And *c M6* intrude]may
stray *M6* 18 ,]*o M6* 19 humble]simple *M6* 20 ,-]?- *M6; ? D* 21
the]that *M6* 22 ,]*o M6* 24 ?]. *D* 25 heard]felt *M6* 26 ,]*o M6*
28 Have]Ive *M6* orient]morning *M6* ,]*o M6* 29 ,]*o M6* 30 ,]
o M6 31 Are]Is *M6* ,]*o M6* 32 Where]When *M6* ,]. *M6* 33
are]is *M6* ,]*o M6* 34 ,]*o M6* 35 The harbingers of]Foretelling of
the *M6* 36 from afar]far away *M6*

76, 77. "My books I'd fain cast off, I cannot read"

*References: 68W 320; HM 1225; D III (Oct., 1842), 224; Thoreau's
corrected D (Cooke, Introduction to . . . The Dial, II, 188); 49W 318.
Cf.: PN 64; 06W 320. HM includes only lines 17-40. D includes only
these lines: 1-28, 33-40.* no title]The Summer Rain *D PN* 6 Shakespeare's]Shakspeare's *D 49W* were]was *D 49W* 7 read,]read *D*
8 Shakespeare's]Shakspeare's *D 49W* men]men. *D 49W E* 10
Greeks]Greeks, *D* 11 juster]greater *D (but Thoreau's corrected D
reads juster)* 12 ?]. *D* 17 Shakespeare]Shakspeare *D 49W* 20 .]
o HM 21 herd's-grass]herd's grass *HM;* herdsgrass *D* and]& *HM*
24 overtop]over top *HM* .]*o HM* 27 and]& *HM* 28 pool]pond *D*
flower-bell]flower bell *HM;* lily bell *D* 33 Drip]Drip, *D HM* 34
distils]distills *HM* 39 ,-]- *HM D 49W* ,]*o HM D*

78. "The Poet's Delay"

*References: 68W 364; M2 48 (March 8, 1840); D III (Oct., 1842),
200; 49W 362. Cf.: PN 73; 06W 366; Jl 127. Entire poem c M2 M2
Jl include these lines in this order: four extra lines, 5-8, 1-4, four extra
lines (then a dotted line in M2), 9-12.* The Poet's Delay]*o M2 Jl M2
opens with these extra lines:*

> Two years and twenty now have flown—
> Their meanness time away have flung,
> These limbs to man's estate have grown,
> But cannot claim a manly tongue.

These lines follow l. 4 M2:

> The sparrow sings at earliest dawn
> Building her nest without delay;
> All things are ripe to hear her song,
> And now arrives the perfect day.

5 ,]*o M2*   6 ,]; *M2*   9 ,]*o M2*   10 day]ray *M2*   11 curious]empty
M2   12 woods]wood *M2*   *No variations D 49W*

79. "Salmon Brook"

*References: 68W 372; M1a 49 (Sept. 1, 1842[?]); HMa 956; HMb
13182; H; 49W 371. Cf.: 06W 375. Entire poem c HMa* 1 Brook]brook
HMa   ,]*o M1a*   2 Penichook]Pennichook *M1a HMa*   ,]*o M1a*   3
,]*o M1a*   4 ,]*o M1a*   5 ,]*o M1a*   6 your]thy *M1a*   7 ,]*o M1a HMa*
8 ,]*o M1a HMa*   9 ,]*o M1a*   10 dragon-fly]dragon fly *M1a H;* dragon-
fly, *HMa; , c HMa*   11 ,]*o M1a; ,- 49W*   *No variations HMb*

80. "I am the autumnal sun"

*References: 68W 399; M1a 96 (Oct. 7, 1842); 49W 397. Cf.: PN 76;
06W 404. no title]Nature's Child PN* 1 autumnal]Autumnal *M1a*
2 ;]. *M1a T*   3 hazel]hazle *M1a*   4 Or]And *M1a T*   5 or]and *M1a T*
hunter's]hunters *T*   ,]*o M1a T*   6 mid-noon]mid noon *M1a*   7 and]
& *M1a*   9 ,]*o M1a T*   10 winter](word) *c for* winter *T*   ,]*o M1a*
12 .], *M1a T*   *These lines follow l. 12 M1a T:*

> My gay colored grief,
> My autumnal relief.

No variations 49W

81, 82. "I am a parcel of vain strivings tied"

*References: 68W 405; A (probably in Sophia Thoreau's hand); D II
(July, 1841), 81; 49W 403. Cf.: PN 10; 06W 410. A has a line separating
each stanza. no title]Sic Vita A D PN*   3 and]& *A*   4 and]& *A*   12
By]The law by *A*   15 and]& *A*   stems,]stems *A*   16 rout.]rout. *A*
27 ,]*o A D*   29 woe]wo *D 49W*   31 naught]nought *A D*   37 hours]
loss *A*   38 ,]*o A D*   40 and]& *A*

83. "All things are current found"

*References: 68W 410; M1a 126 (1842[?]); A; 49W 408. Cf.: PN 74;
06W 415. no title]Lines PN*   *M1a opens with these c lines:*

300

As oceans ebb and flow
Our spirits go.

2 On earthly]Oer the uneven *p for* on earthly *M1a*   ,]. *M1a*   5 day,]
day- *A M1a*   6 and]& *A*   low,]low- *A;* low *M1a*   7 ,]*o M1a*   9 ,]
o A M1a   11 ,]*o A M1a*   12 ;]. *A M1a*   13 the]your *c for* the *M1a*
14 ;]*o A M1a*   15 ,]*o A M1a*   *No variations 49W*

84. "Who sleeps by day and walks by night"

*References: 68W 48; M1a 33 (1842[?]); A; 49W 44. Cf.: 06W 41.
Couplet c A   On leaf headed "Short Flights" in A   1 ,]o A   No
variations M1a 49W*

84. "We should not mind if on our ear there fell"

*References: 68W 108; 49W 105. Cf.: 06W 104. (It has been tradi-
tional not to consider this couplet an original work because of its resemblance to two lines from Emerson [see 06W 104]. But Thoreau's
method of writing verse included, more than once, only slight trans-
mutation of source material. The most noteworthy case of this is "Sometimes I hear the veery's clarion.") No variations 49W*

84. "Then spend an age in whetting thy desire"

References: 68W 114; 49W 112. Cf.: 06W 111. No variations 49W

84. "Therefore a torrent of sadness deep"

*Reference: 68W 184. Cf.: FLJ 1, xxvi; 06W 183. N.B.: couplet o 49W
«1 torrent]current FLJ»*

85. "Such near aspects had we"

*References: 68W 254; HM 13195; Ha; Hb; 49W 252. Cf.: 06W
253. No variations HM Ha Hb 49W*

85. "My life has been the poem I would have writ"

*References: 68W 364; M5 81 (Aug. 28, 1841); A; 49W 362. Cf.:
06W 365; J1 275. Couplet c M5   Couplet underlined M5   On leaf
headed "Short Flights" in A   1 has]hath M5   2 and]and live to M5;
live to c A   No variations 49W*

85. "We see the *planet* fall"

*References: 68W 386; 49W 384. Cf.: 06W 390. (It is just possible
that this couplet is an instance where Thoreau has simply quoted some-*

one else's verse, except for one word which he has altered and then italicized.) No variations 49W

86. "Voyagers Song"

Heretofore unpublished. References: HM 13190 (June, 1837; *in Sophia Thoreau's hand*); *49W 245; 68W 247. Cf.: PN 51; 06W 247. 49W 68W PN 06W include only these lines: 5-11, one extra line. HM has a horizontal line below every stanza.* Voyagers Song]Boat Song *PN; o 49W 68W 06W* 5 Thus of old our valiant fathers]Thus, perchance, the Indian hunter *49W 68W* 6 agone]agone, *49W 68W* 7 oer]o'er *49W 68W* the]thy *68W* 8 Taught to banish care in]Lowly hummed a natural *49W 68W* 10 lake]waves *49W 68W* 11 Hark across] Faintly o'er *49W 68W* bounding]wearied *49W 68W This line follows l. 11 49W 68W:*

> Come the spirits of the braves.

87. "I love a careless streamlet"

Reference: B (July 11, 1837). *Cf.: Elsie F. Brickett,* Studies in the Poets and Poetry of New England Transcendentalism *(Yale University doctoral dissertation, unpublished, 1937), p. 175.*

88. "To the Comet"

Heretofore unpublished. Reference: L (1837[?]). 6 And]From *c* from]to *c* 14 By]From *c*

(Because "To the Comet" offers so fine an example of the minute care with which Thoreau could compose and of the peculiar extent to which he carried rearrangement, this additional textual note is given in a fuller explanatory form than usual.)

Thoreau wrote most of the lines, with nice alterations, twice. Next he indicated the groups of lines to be rejected by scoring through them. He indicated the order of those he wanted to keep by vertical strokes in the left margin, with numbers opposite them. This order resulted: opposite lines 1 and 2 there is a vertical stroke taking them in, as well as the preceding couplet, which is scored out. This vertical stroke he numbered 1. To show that lines 3 and 4 are to precede lines 5 and 6, Thoreau put a 1 before 3 and 4 (which really come last as he wrote the draft) and a 2 before 5 and 6; then he joined the four lines with a vertical stroke and the number 2. Opposite lines 7-10 there is a vertical stroke and the number 3. Opposite lines 11-14 there is a vertical stroke and the number 4. *Opposite lines 15-24 there is a vertical stroke and the number* 5.

The actual order of the lines in the manuscript follows. Only the cancelled lines are reproduced below:

> Reserved traveller what thy race?
> Tell it to my naked face,   it to my naked]my honest looking *c*
> [*lines 1-2 follow*]
> Distinguished stranger, system ranger,
> Plenipotentiary from on high,
> Special envoy, foreign minister,
> From the empire of the sky.
> [*lines 5-6, 3-4, and 15-24 follow, in that order*]
> Thou runner of the firmament,
> On what errand wast thou sent?
> Art thou some great general's scout,
> Come to spy our weakness out?
> Or celestial privateer,
> Scouring heaven far and near?
> Sculling without mast or sail
> Mid the stars and constellations,
> The pioneer*er* of a tail
> Through the starry nations.
> [*lines 7-14 follow*]
> Reserved traveller, what thy race?
> Tell my honest naked face,
> My sincerity doth surpass
>   The pretence of optic glass.

[*Lines m-p have a vertical pencil stroke (but no numeral) in the left margin.*]

89-91. "Friendship"

References: M1 r35 (April 8, 1838); HM 13201 (same date). Cf.: JI 40. M1 has ll. 21-55 c. HM includes only these c lines: five extra lines, 46-55. Variants all in HM   Friendship]o   HM opens with these extra lines:

> That Love of which I purposed to sing,
>   (It sings itself I ween)
>   Is quite a different thing,
>   For neither needs to cling
>   When both can stand

46 oaks]oak   which]that   side,]side   47 winter's]wintry   50 strong]
strong.   53 you]we

92. "The Cliffs & Springs"

Reference: B (April 25, 1838). Cf.: Brickett, Studies in the Poets and Poetry of New England Transcendentalism, p. 217.

93-96. "The Bluebirds"

Reference: M1 r37 (April 26, 1838). Cf.: Jl 43. See Appendix A for further variations and, perhaps, additions.

97. "May Morning"

Reference: M1 v41 (May 21, 1838). Cf.: FLJ 1, n52; Jl 49. FLJ includes only lines 9-12. M1 has lines 3-4 and 1-2 indicated for transposition to their present order. M1 has dotted lines below every stanza but the last. «10 ,]; *FLJ*»

98, 99. "Walden"

References: M1 r42 (June 3, 1838); H. Cf.: Jl 50; Sum 29. Entire poem c M1 H   H includes only these lines in this order: 17-20, 24-27, two extra lines, 2-7. Sum includes only lines 1-7. M1 has a dotted line below l. 7. Walden]o *H Sum*   2 Only the]The *H*   the surging]thy surging *H*   3 and]& *H*   .]; *H*   4 of thy own waters,]o *H   This line follows l. 4 H:*

> Of thy own waters, wafted as is

5 Wafted as is]o *H*   the]The *H*   6 Soul]soul *H*   it]them *c M1; thee H*   9 stooped]stoopèd *H*   12 -]; *H*   17 O!]O River *H*   the winds]The winds *(starts new line) H*   writ]writ| *H*   within these] for the last *H; al M1*   ,]o *H*   18 vault]vault| *H*   -], *H*   19 Or sun transferred]or sun *(last two words of previous line)* Transferred, H and]& *H*   reprinted]reprinted for thy; for thy *c H*   20 Somewhat] o *H*   23 not]not. *H*   24 I would give much]Much would I give *c* that]the *c*   ,]o *H*   25 a]thy *c*   when Eurus- Boreas-]when Boreas *H*   26 And]Eurus and *H*   host]whole host; whole *p and c H* drivers]o *H*   27 First]Drivers First *H   These lines follow l. 27 H:*

> But thou dost render back thy pure original thought
> Alone as print [?] often [?] converse. Only

100. "Truth—Goodness—Beauty—those celestial thrins"

Reference: M1 v42 (June 14, 1838). Cf.: Jl 51. Entire poem c M1 has a space of two lines separating this quatrain and its succeeding couplet, "Strange that so many fickle gods, as fickle as the weather."

101. "In the busy streets, domains of trade"

Reference: M1 v42 (June 16, 1838). Cf.: Jl 51. Entire poem c

102, 103. "I knew a man by sight"

Heretofore unpublished. Reference: A (June 17, 1838).

104. "Cliffs"

Reference: M1 r43 (July 8, 1838). *Cf.: Sum 348; Jl 51. Entire poem c*

105. "My Boots"

Reference: M1 r79 (Oct. 16, 1838). *Cf.: Jl 60.*

106. "Noon"

Reference: M1 r79 (Oct. 16, 1838). *Cf.: Jl 96. M1 has a 1 in the left margin opposite lines 1-5, a 2 opposite the first four c lines, a 2 opposite the last two c lines. M1 has a dotted line below l. f. M1 opens with these extra c lines:*

> Stretched I far up the neighboring mountain's sides,
> Adown the valley—through the nether air,
> Bathing with fond expansiveness of soul,
> The tiniest blade as the sublimest cloud.
>
> —Straightway dissolved,
> Like to the morning mists—or rather like the
> subtler mists of noon—

107. "The Thaw"

References: M1 v58 (Jan. 11, 1839); *M1a 197* (1842[?]); *(the following is for lines 1-2 only) D III* (July, 1842), *31. Cf.: Jla 71; Jlb 477; (for lines 1-6 only) Win 156; PN 89; 06Vb 409; (for lines 1-2 only) 06Va 120. Entire poem c M1 D 06Va include only lines 1-2. M1a Jlb include only these lines: 3-6, four extra lines. Win PN 06Vb include only lines 1-6. M1 has dotted lines below each stanza but the last. The Thaw]o M1a D 06Va Jlb 1 saw]see D -], D 2 joy that]joy, which D flowed,]flow. D 3 Fain would I]I fain would M1a nig(h)way side]highway side M1a 5 and]& M1a tide,]tide M1a 5 may]might M1a nature]Nature M1a These lines follow l. 6 M1a:*

> Might help to forward the new spring along,
>   If it were mine to choose my toil or day,
> Scouring the roads with yonder sluice-way throng,
>   And so work out my tax on *Her* highway.

108. "Last night as I lay gazing with shut eyes"

References: M1 r59 (Jan. 20, 1839); *49W 379; 68W 380. Cf.: 06W 384; J1 71. Entire poem c M1   49W 68W 06W include only lines 8-11.*
1 gazing]peering *c*   3 I thought]Methought *c   These c lines follow l. 7:*

> 'Twas *there* [*these?*] the world, whatever good or ill,
> Nor [?] needed thought, with rude officiousness.
> Go plant another vale behind the hill.

8 And]Oft, *49W 68W*   turned]turn *49W 68W*   9 heard]hear *49W 68W*   10 it had been]if it were *49W 68W*   noonday]noon-day *49W This c line follows l. 10:*

> And still they lapse, and will lapse evermore.

11 Wandering at Rockaway]drifting down from Nashua *49W 68W*

109. "Love"

Reference: M1 v59 (Jan. 20, 1839). *Cf.: J1 72. Entire poem c*

110. " 'Twill soon appear if we but look"

Reference: M1 r60 (Feb. 3, 1839). *Cf.: J1 72. Entire poem c*

111. "The Peal of the Bells"

References: M1 v60 (Feb. 10, 1839); *M; HM (a, b, c) 924. Cf.: PN 119; 06V 417; J1 73; BSWa I, 165. Entire poem c HMa HMc   M includes only lines 7-22. HMa includes only lines 5 (broken down into two lines) and half of 6 ("And . . . swing"). HMb includes only these lines: 5-6 (broken down into four lines), 7-14. HMc includes only lines 5-14. PN 06V include only lines 1-18. BSWa includes only these lines in this order: 5-6 (broken down into four lines), 11-14, 7-10. M has a line below l. 14 and l. 15.* The Peal of the Bells]o *M HMa HMb HMc BSWa;* Ding Dong *PN 06V*   «2 rocks]nooks *PN»*   5 go]go, *HMa HMb HMc*   then]Then *HMa HMb HMc*   again]again, *HMa HMb HMc* «they go *BSWa»*   6 «swing]ring *PN»*   to]To *HMb HMc* to the same old song,]o *HMa*   7 *no stanza]new stanza HMb*   «And] For *PN»*   8 A-lulling]A lulling *HMb* «A-cutting *PN»*   i(t)s]its *M HMb HMc*   -], *HMb*   «9 Till]While *PN»*   10 and]& *HMc*   11 *no stanza]new stanza M HMb*   14 ding-dong]ding dong *HMb HMc* «15 has]hath *PN»*   19 Thing]thing *M*   20 W(h)ich]Which *M*

112. "The 'Book of Gems'"

Reference: M1 v66 (July 4, 1839). *Cf.: Jl 82. Entire poem c* 9
Where]And *c* I]you'd *c* slaked]slake; d *added* my]your *c* 10
Like a tired traveller at]By the wayside from out *c* *This c line fol-*
lows l. 10:

> Aye, after you had many paces ta'en,

13 you might]might you *indicated for transposition* *This c line fol-*
lows l. 13:

> Until fresh murmurings had drowned that strain

14 Till]And *c*

113-115. "The Assabet"

References: M1 v69 (July 18, 1839); *HMa 13186; HMb 13195; HMc*
13195 (Sept. 1, 1839); *(the following are for lines 5 and 49-55 only)*
49W 189; 68W 191; (the following are for lines 56-60 only) 49W 201;
68W 202; (the following are for lines 36-40 and 31-35 only) 49W 66;
68W 69. Cf.: Jl 84; (for lines 5 and 49-55 only) 06W 188; (for lines
56-60 only) 06W 200; (for lines 5 and 49-60 only) PN 49; (for lines
36-40 and 31-35 only) PN 50; 06W 62. Entire poem c M1 49W
68W 06W include only these lines as one poem: 5, 49-55. 49W
68W 06W include only these lines as one poem: 56-50. PN in-
cludes only these lines as one poem, titled "River Song": 5, 49-60. 49W
68W 06W PN include only these lines, in this order, as one poem: 36-40,
31-35; PN alone is titled: "Some Tumultuous Little Rill." HMa includes
only these lines, in this order, as one poem: 51-55, 46-50. HMb includes
only these lines: 5, 49-50. HMc includes only lines 49-50. The Assabet]
o HMa HMb HMc 49W 68W PN 06W 5 oars,]oars! *HMb 49W*
68W 32 below]below, *49W 68W* 35 still]still, *49W 68W* 36 But
this gleeful]Some tumultuous *49W 68W* 38 Tinkles]Tinkling *49W*
68W selfsame]self-same *49W* tune]tune, *49W 68W* 39 December]
September *49W 68W* 40 Nor doth any drought]Which no drought
doth e'er *49W 68W* 46 ,]o *HMa* 47 For]Where *HMa* 48 and]&
HMa twilight]evening *al HMa* scorning,]nearing *HMa* 49 In]
c HMa dew drop]dewdrop *HMa*; dew-drop *HMb 68W* 50 a]the
HMa .]o *HMa HMc* 51 sun do]sunrise *HMa* [?] *49W 68W* ,]o
HMa 52 ,]o *HMa*; ;*49W 68W* 53 'gainst]gainst *HMa* 54 ,]o *HMa*
55 .]o *HMa* 56 away! away!]"away! away" *49W*; "Away! away!"
68W 57 league]reach *49W 68W* 58 ,]o *49W 68W*

307

116, 117. "The Breeze's Invitation"

Reference: M1 r71 (July 20, 1839). *Cf.: FLJ 1, 51; Jl 86; 17S 230. FLJ 17S include only lines 11-30.* «26 will]shall *FLJ»*

118. "Loves Farewell"

References: A; M1 r77 (Nov. 19, 1839). *Cf.: Aut 297; Jl 95. Entire poem c M1* Loves Farewell]Farewell *M1 Jl; o Aut* 1 Light] —Light *M1* careless]thoughtless *c A;* thoughtless *M1* 4 usurer's] us'rer's *M1* -]o *M1*

119. "Each more melodious note I hear"

References: M (in manuscript of The Service*); M2 7* (Dec., 1839). *Cf.:* The Service *11; Jl 102; 17S 232* (Sept. 2, 1839). *Entire poem c M2* 2 this]sad *c M;* sad *M2*

120. "I was born upon thy bank river"

Reference: M1a 5 (1839[?]). *Cf.: Jl 438.*

121-123. "The Fisher's Son"

References: A; M2 19 (Jan. 10, 1840); *49W 255; EL 220; 68W 257. Cf.: PN 14; 06W 255; 06VI xiii; Jl 110. Entire poem c M2 49W 68W EL PN 06W include only these stanzas: 8, 10, 11, 11a. M2 Jl include these stanzas: 1-11, 11a, 12-15, two extra stanzas, 16. 06VI includes only these stanzas: 2-5, 9, 12.* The Fisher's Son]The Fisher's Boy *EL PN; o 49W 68W 06W 06VI* 7 haven's]havens *M2* «10 credit]credence *06VI»* 13 opened]opend *M2* Sea]sea *M2* «14 Which]That *06VI»* 15 ,]- *M2* 16 «But introduced]While introducing *06VI»* godmother] god mother *M2* Sand]Land *M2* 18 o'er]oer *M2* 20 shore]shore. *M2* 28 the earth once more with tott'ring]once more the earth with infant *M2* 29 years are]life is *49W 68W EL* 30 ;], *49W 68W* 31 sometimes]do oft *c A;* do oft *M2* 35 tempest scours]storm doth scour *c A;* storm doth scour *M2* «deep]sea *06VI»* 37 'tis]'tis, *49W 68W;* is, *EL* 39 pebble]pebble, *49W 68W EL* rare]rare, *M2 49W 68W EL* 40 ocean]Ocean *EL* 41 but few companions]no fellow laborer *c A;* no fellow laborer *M2* ,]: *EL* 42 ,]; *EL* 43 Yet oft]Sometimes *c A;* Sometimes *M2* oer]o'er *M2 49W 68W EL These c lines, stanza 11a, follow l. 44:*

The middle sea can show no crimson dulse,	can show]contains *49W 68W EL*
Its deeper waves cast up no pearls to view,	pearls]pearles *M2*
Along the shore my hand is on its pulse,	,]o *M2* ,]; *EL*

And I converse with many a shipwrecked crew.
                And I converse with many a shipwrecked crew]
                Whose feeble beat elsewhere is known to few
                c A; Whose feeble beat is elsewhere felt by few *M2*
45 sometimes come]come sometimes *c A;* come sometimes *M2*   46 if
they wished]it would seem, *c A;* it would seem, *M2*   47 «straightway]
straight they *06VI»*   go again]take their loads *c A;* take their loads
M2   marts]marts, *M2*   50 storms]storms, *M2*   *These lines follow*
l. 60 M2:

> Far from the shore the swelling billows rise,
> And gathering strength come rolling to the land,
> And as each wave retires, and murmur dies,
> I straight pursue upon the streaming sand.
>
> Till the returning surge with gathered strength
> Compels once more the backward way to take,
> And creeping up the beach a cable's length,
> In many a thirsty hollow leaves a lake.

61 at]as *M2*   ,]o *M2*

124. "I'm guided in the darkest night"

No manuscript authority. References: CT 119 (Nov. 7, 1840); *Aut*
223 (same date). Aut includes only these lines: 1-8, 11-12, 15-28. Vari-
ants all in Aut   3 over dart]overdart   home]home,   7 sunrise]sun-
rise,   11 laugh]laugh,   12 cry]cry,   ,].   15 blame]blame,   16 conscience stricken]conscience-stricken   .],   18 busy body]busybody
20 .],   23 spent]spent,   24 Where]When   25 beside]beside,   27
above]above,

125. "Friendship"

Reference: M5 1 (March 30, 1841). *Cf.: Spr 274; Jl 242.*

126. "On the Sun Coming out in the Afternoon"

Reference: M5 2 (April 1, 1841). *Cf.: Spr 294; Jl 243. Entire*
poem c

127. "They who prepare my evening meal below"

Reference: M5 3 (April 4, 1841). *Cf.: Jl 243.*   «11 Spending]
Speeding *Jl»*

128. "My ground is high"

References: M5 6 (April 7, 1841); *HM 13182. Cf.: FLJ I, 140; Jl*
245. Entire poem c M5   HM FLJ include only lines 1-4. See also note.
2 ,]; *HM*   4 ;]o *HM*

129. "If from your price ye will not swerve"

References: HM 13182; MS 6 (April 7, 1841). *Cf.: Jl 245; FLJ I, 140. Entire poem c MS See also note.* 4 ,]o *MS* 7 pattern,]pattern-*MS* same,]same- *MS* 10 Certain]Full sure *c for* Certain *MS*

130. "Friendship's Steadfastness"

References: MS 11 (April 11, 1841); *H. Cf.: Jl 248. Entire poem c MS Lines 5-16 are found as stanzas 7, 8, and 3 of a long version of "Let such pure hate still underprop" H. Variants all in H* 6 ,]- 7 For lo!]Behold ,]- 8 night.]night *This line follows l. 8:*

> And after absence is new made and crescent.

10 we]one 11 Throughout]Through out universe,]universe 15 ,]o 16 ?].

131. "Death cannot come too soon"

Reference: MS 12 (April 11, 1841). *Cf.: Jl 249. Entire poem c*

132, 133. "Independence"

References: Y (July 30, 1841); *HM 13186; H; D III* (*Oct., 1842*), *180. Cf.: Commonwealth, Oct. 30, 1863; PN 116; FLJ I, 141; 06V 415; 17S 284. H D include only lines 16-29. HM FLJ include only these lines in this order: 3-10, eight extra lines. 17S includes only these lines in this order: 3-10, eight different extra lines (the extra lines also being found as lines 21-24 and lines 37-40 of "Wait not till slaves pronounce the word"; see that poem for collation).* Independence]The Black Knight *D; o H 17S These lines follow l. 10 HM:*

> Can ye instruct who have not learned?
> Or can ye learn who will not hear?
> Can ye inflame who have not burned,
> To virtues' cause or Love's career?
>
> Ye are late comers into life,
> Who have not learned your heritage,
> But proved your right with toil and strife
> Unto your thrones, and title war to wage.

17 -], *H D* 18 -], *H D* 19 «nobles of]noblest of *C;* noblest in *PN*» land]land; *H D* 20 *new stanza]no H D* -]o *H D* 21 hold]hold, *H D* 22 .], *H D* 23 .]; *H D* 24 rings-]sings, *H D* 26 *new stanza]* no *H D* 27 -], *H D* 28 No trade upon the street]Only the promise of my heart *H D*

134, 135. "Our Country"

No manuscript authority. Reference: F. B. Sanborn, The Personality of Thoreau *(Boston, 1901), p. 64* (1841[?]). *Cf.: Cooke,* Introduction to . . . The Dial, *1, 131; 17S 278.* «5 (and)]and what *17S* 8 licks]lakes *17S* 10 corn and rice]rice and corn *17S* 46 man]men *17S*»

136. "The moon now rises to her absolute rule"

Basic text heretofore unpublished. Reference: M1a 62 (Sept. 1, 1842[?]). 1 now rises]no longer reflects the day, But rises; no *has* w *added; longer reflects the day, But c (thus telescoping two lines into one)* 4 in the fields]along the t— (?) *al* 16 But]And *al* man] sickle *c*

137. "My friends, why should we live"

References: M1a 84 (1842[?]); *M. Cf.: Jl 447. M (same sheet as "Guido's Aurora") includes only l. 2.* 2 war]war- *M* ;]. *M* 4 One small]A mere *c* 5 Shall]Shall *p for* now 7 yet]yet *p for* still 10 ordnance]ordinance; i *c* nature's]nature's *p for* religions 12 .]? *c*

138. "I mark the summer's swift decline"

References: T; M1a 94 (1842[?]). *Cf.: Jl 449. M1a Jl include only these lines: 1-2, 5-8.* 6 -]o *M1a*

139. "Methinks that by a strict behavior"

References: M1a 117 (1842[?]); *H. Cf.: Jl 457.* 3 lurks]hides *al No variations H*

140. "I have rolled near some other spirits path"

References: M1a 117 (1842[?]); *H. Cf.: Jl 457. H includes only these lines: one extra line, 1, one extra line (apparently a reduction of lines 2-3 in M1a), 4-5. Variants all in H   H opens with this extra line:*

Oft in my passage through this star-lit clime   star-lit clime]
                                                              trackless night *c*

1 rolled]come   spirits path]spirit's path, *This line follows l. 1:*

And felt its purer influence on my mass

4 ,]o   !]o   5 sidireal]siderial   .],

311

141. "Travelling"

References: Y; M1a 122 (1842[?]); HMa 13182 (also facsimile in FLJ I, opp. 128); HMb 13182; (the following are for lines 9-10 only) H; 49W 225; 68W 227. Cf.: FLJ I, 129; (for lines 9-10 only) 06W 227; JI 459. Entire poem c HMb   M1a JI include these lines: 1-20, two extra lines, 21-23, two extra lines. HMa FLJ include these lines: 1-20, two extra lines, 21-23 (FLJ has l. 23 broken down into two lines). HMb includes only these lines: 1-8, two extra lines, 9-11. H 49W 68W 06W include only lines 9-10, c H. Travelling]o M1a HMa HMb H 49W 68W 06W JI; The Battle of Life *FLJ*   1 man]man, *HMa HMb;* man wh; wh c *Y*   2 He]Who *M1a HMa HMb;* c *Y*   has]hath c *for* has *HMb;* hath *M1a HMa*   span]span, *HMa HMb*   3 But]Yet *al*   treasure] treasure, *HMa*   4 .]o *M1a;* ! *HMb*   5 new stanza]no *M1a HMb*   three score]3score *HMa*   and]& *HMa*   6 «fro]from *FLJ»*   men]men, *HMa HMb*   7 O'er]Oer *M1a HMa*   small]firm *p for* small *M1a;* firm c *Y*   land]land, *HMa HMb*   8 And never uses a]His fancy bearing no *M1a HMa HMb;* c *Y*   *These lines follow l. 8 HMb:*

> His head wants but a fathom from the earth,
> Three feet above the scenery of his birth.   some c
>   *(in left margin)*

9 *new stanza*]no *M1a HMb*   10 life's]lifes *M1a*   go]go, *HMa HMb;* go. *H 49W 68W*   11 Our ambitious]Our most ambitious *M1a HMa HMb;* most c *Y*   ne'er climb]ne'er climb c *for* climb not *M1a;* climb not *HMa HMb*   high]high, *HMb*   12 daily]daily c *for* hourly *M1a;* hourly *HMa HMb*   fly]fly. *M1a HMb*   13 *new stanza*]no *M1a HMa* And]o *M1a*   yonder cloud's borne farther in a day]our most vagrant steps c *for* yonder cloud's borne farther in a day; borne c *for* blown *M1a* borne]blown *HMa*   14 steps]steps c *for* feet *M1a;* feet *HMa* 15 has]hath *M1a HMa*   erred,]erred *M1a*   16 has]hath *M1a HMa* threshhold]birth place *M1a HMa;* birthplace c *Y*   17 *new stanza*]no *M1a HMa*   and]& *HMa*   18 loftier]bolder *M1a HMa*   and]& *HMa* ,]o *M1a*   19 ,]o *M1a HMa*   where]which *M1a HMa*   20 Has]Hath *M1a HMa*   *These lines follow l. 20 M1a:*

> Bearing his head just oer some fallow ground   oer]o'er *HMa*
>   ground]ground, *HMa*
> Some cowslip'd meadows where the bitterns sound.
>   cowslip'd]cowslipped *HMa*

21 *new stanza*]no *M1a HMa*   nigh]nigh, *HMa*   22 dye]die; *HMa;* die. *M1a*   23 ,]- *M1a*   *These lines follow l. 23 M1a:*

> His head doth court a fathom from the land
> Six feet from where his grovelling feet do stand.

312

142. "On fields oer which the reaper's hand has pass[e]d"

Reference: M1a 135 (1842[?]). *Cf.: J1 463.*

143. "To a Marsh Hawk in Spring"

Reference: M1a 161 (1842[?]). *Cf.: J1 471; BSWa II, 228. BSWa includes only lines 1-2. See also note.*

144. "Great Friend"

References: H; HM 13182; M1a 161 (1842[?]). *Cf.: J1 472; FLJ I, 134. Entire poem p H Entire poem c HM HM FLJ include only these lines in this order: 1-15, 18, 17, 19-20, 22-25. FLJ erroneously includes a final stanza of nine extra lines, for which see "I was made erect and lone." J1 erroneously begins with eight extra lines, they and the rest of the poem being titled "To a Marsh Hawk in Spring"; see that poem for those lines. M1a J1 include these lines in this order: 1-15, 22-25, 16-21. See also note.* Great Friend]Solitude *FLJ; o HM M1a* 1 I]We *HM;* Man *M1a* walk]knows *c for* walks *M1a* alone]alone, *HM M1a* 2 know] knows *M1a* one]one, *HM M1a* 3 Discern]Discerns *M1a* «Discovers *J1»* 5 *new stanza]no HM* 6 oer]o'er *HM M1a* me]us *HM* 7 I] we *HM* 8 .]*o M1a* 9 *new stanza]no HM* I]We *HM* 10 ,]*o M1a* 12 man]friend *M1a* I]we *HM* .]:*HM* 13 *new stanza]no HM* 15 grown child]grown-child *M1a* weaning]weaning,- *HM;* weaning. *M1a* 16 center]centre *M1a* ,]*o M1a* 17 ,]*o M1a* 20 -]. *HM; ,* *M1a* 21 least]least, *M1a* 22 *new stanza]no HM* 24 ,]*o HM M1a*

145. "Yet let us Thank the purblind race"

Reference: M1a 198 (1842[?]). *Cf.: J1 477.*

146, 147. "Ive seen ye, sisters, on the mountain-side"

Reference: M1a 198 (1842[?]). *Cf.: J1 477. M1a has the present order of the lines indicated thus: between lines 17-18* When did *is pencilled, to show that l. 18 follows. There is a 1 in the left margin opposite l. 18, a 2 opposite lines 19-20. The original order of the lines, then, was as follows: 1-17, 21-31, 19-20, 18.* 3 smooth]still *c* 19 placid] mild *al* 21 Reveal]Reveal but; but *c* not]now *c* 27 have]have I; I *c*

148. "Ye do command me to all virtue ever"

Reference: M1a 201 (1842[?]). *Cf.: J1 479.*

149. "On shoulders whirled in some eccentric orbit"

No manuscript authority. Reference: 06VI 55 (Feb. 10, 1843).

150. "Fog"

Reference: HM 13182 (April 11, 1843). Cf.: FLJ I, 126. Lines 2, 8, 9, and 10 are similar in phrasing to lines 1, 4, 5, and 6 of "Low-anchored cloud." Entire poem c HM   10 wind-blown]drifting *al*

151, 152. "Brother where dost thou dwell"

References: A (May 23, 1843); T. Cf.: PN 52; 06V 403; 06VI 74. T includes these lines in this order: four extra lines, 5-8, 1-4, eight extra lines, 9-24, twelve extra lines, 25-42. no title]To My Brother PN 06V T opens with these extra lines:

> Brother, where dost thou dwell?
>   Art thou far gone?
> Tell me what there befel;
>   What other morn.

3 ?], *T*   4 «wished]wished thee *PN*»   .]? *T*   *These lines follow l. 4 T:*

> Is nature there as fair?
>   And are there friends as kind?
> Dost thou regret e'en there
>   Those thou hast left behind?
>
> I was the strongest here,
>   Of sturdiest pace,
> Say, am I still thy peer
>   In the foot race?

5 dids't]did'st *T*   6 .]; *T*   13 Yet]But *c for* Yet *T*   18 ?], *T*   22 yonder]our fair *c for* yonder *T*   ?], *T*   24 at]by *T*   *These lines follow l. 24 T:*

> When on the pond I whirl
>   In sport, if sport may be,
> Now thou art gone,
>   May I still follow thee?
>
> For then, as now, I trust,
>   I always lagg'd behind,
> While thou wert ever first,
>   Cutting the wind.

> May thy influence prevail
>   O'er this dull scenery,
> To lift the heavy veil
>   Tween me and thee?

28 ,]o *T*   «31 has]o *PN*»   35 -], *T*   37 !], *T*   41 They have]Have
they *T*   42 .]? *T*

153. "Epitaph on Pursy"

*Reference: HM 13182 (Oct. 22, 1843). Cf.: FLJ 1, 81. (Concerning
the poem Sanborn says:*

> *This and the following lines ["Ep(itaph) on the World"]
> appear to be Thoreau's own composition,—suggested, perhaps,
> by some collection of epitaphs he had found in one of the New
> York libraries [FLJ I, 82].*

*Sanborn is not sure, then, that the "Epitaph on Pursy" is Thoreau's own
work. But a study of the manuscript, with its additional couplets and
false starts, should remove any doubt. Furthermore, lines 7-8 are only
slightly different from the concluding lines of another epitaph, in the
Week, that Thoreau prints as his own. It is the poem "Here lies an
honest man.")*

154. "Ep[itaph] on the World"

*Reference: HM 13182 (Oct. 22, 1843). Cf.: FLJ 1, 82. (Although
it is true Sanborn does not claim this poem absolutely for Thoreau, the
manuscript reveals alterations and emendations such as Thoreau would
not have made on the verse of another. See also the epitaph above.)* Ep
on the World]Epitaph on the World *FLJ*   5 at last]as fast *c*   7 several]
various *c*   8 What year it died]Its birth, its death *c*

155. "Epitaph on an Engraver"

*Heretofore unpublished. References: T; HM (a and b) 13182 (Oct.
22, 1843). HMa includes only lines 1-4. HMb includes only lines 5-6.*
Epitaph on an Engraver]o *HMa*   1 death's]Death's *HMa*   2 the en-
graver]th' engraver, *HMa*   3 o't]o't, *HMa*   5 lies]lies, *HMb*   6 ne'er]
never *c for* e'er *HMb*

156, 157. "The Just Made Perfect"

No manuscript authority. Reference: 17S 363 (1843).

158, 159. "Tell me ye wise ones if ye can"

References: M1b 30 (July 14[?], 1845); *49W 401; 68W 403. Cf.: Jl 373; 06W 407. 49W 68W 06W include only these lines in this order: 32-33, 21-22, 34, 36, 41-42.* 21 We]And we titmen *49W 68W* 22 to] To *49W 68W* 33 above]o'er *49W 68W* .], *49W 68W* 34 The tints and]Theirs is the *49W 68W* flowers &]o *49W 68W* fruits] fruits, *49W 68W* 36 roots]roots. *49W 68W* 41 But for]What are *49W 68W* moment]moments *49W 68W* 42 land]land! *49W 68W*

160. "The Earth"

Reference: M1b 73 (Dec.[?], 1845). *Cf.: Jl 390.*

161-163. "The Hero"

References: M3 2nd page (1845-1846[?]); *HM 924. Cf.: PN 110; 06V 413; Jl 403. HM includes only these lines in this order: 1-6, 15-22, 31-32, 23-24, 55-58 (pencilled in left margin opposite lines 23-24 et al.), 35-38, 39-42 (broken down into eight lines), 47-50; entire poem c except for lines 55-58. Jl includes only these lines in this order: 1-46; four c lines of M3, unc; 47-50; twenty-three c lines of M3, unc; 51-62; twelve c lines of M3, unc; 63-82. PN 06V include only these lines in this order: the twelve c lines of M3 that follow l. 62, unc; 63-78. M has vertical lines in the left margin apparently to indicate the retention of those lines which roughly parallel the ones making up the HM version. There is a 1 opposite the present lines 67-70 and a 2 opposite the present lines 71-74, thus indicating that their actual order in the manuscript is to be reversed, resulting in the present line arrangement.* The Hero] Pilgrims *PN 06V; o HM* 1 doth he]do we *HM* 2 .]: *HM* 3 run] run till the; till the *c M3* 5 that]And that; And *c M3*; That *HM* 15 Hea(l)th]Health *HM* 16 &]and *HM* gain]gain, *HM* 17 nerve] nerve to the; to the *c* 18 his slenderness]our slenderness, *HM* 19 Some]some *HM* 20 He]We *HM* .], *HM* 21 preserve]preserve our; our *c HM* 22 His]Our *HM* 23 Not]Yet not *HM* deceived] deceived, *HM* 24 suffring]suff'ring *HM* bereaved]bereaved.- *HM* 27 Nor]Not *c* 32 any]every *HM* -], *HM These c lines follow l. 34:*

> To open his veins
> And increase his gains—

36 human]a few *c* tears]tears, *HM* 37 And]And sometimes; some- times *c* entertain]entertains; s *c HM* 38 divine]demonic *al M3*; demonic *c for* immortal *HM* 39 all, forever,]all Forever *HM* 40

316

Still to]But Still to; to c *HM*   out]Out *HM*   west]east c *M3;* west,
HM   41 his]our *HM*   to]To *HM*   sighs]sighs, *HM*   42 Still]Still
c *for* But *HM*   by]By *HM*   sun rise]sun-rise— *HM*   46 At]Not
c   his birth]our c   *These c lines follow l. 46:*

      Having sold all
      Something would get—
      Furnish his stall
      With better yet—

47 pleasures]pleasures, *HM*   48 pains]pains– *HM*   49 losses]losses,
HM   *These c lines follow l. 50:*

      Still to begin—unheard of sin
      A fallen angel—a risen man
      Never returns to where he began.
      Some child like labor
      Here to perform   Here]Then c
      Some baby house
      To keep out the storm
      & make the sun laugh   &]Which will c
      While he doth warm—
      And the moon cry
      To think of her youth—
      the months gone by—   the]Of the; Of c
      And wintering truth.

      How long to morning?
      Can any tell?
      How long since the warning
      On our ears fell
      The bridegroom cometh
      Know we not well?   Know]We Know; We c
      Are we not ready   well]very well; very c
      Our packet made   made]steady c
      Our hearts steady
      Last words said

55 must we go out]must we go out by the poor; by the poor c   56 gate]
gate, *HM*   59 road]road this; this c   *These c lines follow l. 62:*

      Have you not seen
      In ancient times
      Pilgrims go by here
      toward other climes
      With shining faces
      Youthful and strong   Youthful]Lusty c
      Mounting this hill
      With speech & with song?
      Oh my good sir   sir]sir I; I c
      I know not the ways
      Little my knowledge
      Though many my days.

65 As]As of; of *c* «*66* Over]These *PN*   *70* far]afar *PN*»   *71* I
have; have *c*   *73* But]Though *c*   *These c lines follow l. 74:*

> I did not fear for my pulse or my grain
> What the Lord gave man [?]
> He took again—

«*81* it is]still *Jl*»

164. "At midnight's hour I raised my head"

Reference: M3 23 (1845-1846[?]). Cf.: Jl 407.

165-167. "I seek the Present Time"

*References: HM 924; M3 26 (1845-1846[?]). Cf.: Jl 409; BSWa 1,
18. M3 Jl include these lines: 1-10, four extra lines, 11-14, six extra lines,
15-16, one extra c line (o in Jl), 17-75. BSWa includes only these lines:
1-10, four extra lines, 11-14, six extra lines, 15-42. (HM has its actual
order of the lines differing from that of the present basic text in that
lines 33-60 follow l. 75. But these facts persuaded the editor to present
the order he did: the final two leaves of manuscript of the poem are
apparently interchanged; l. 75 is followed by a paragraph of c prose, as
if Thoreau had ended the poem with that line; the order of lines in the
early draft in M3 is the same, in general, as the present editor's here
for his basic text.) Variants all in M3*   *1* Present Time,]present time
3 to-day,]today-   *4* Not to]Carry it in to *c for* not to   ,]-   *5* ,]*o*
6 .]-   *7* man, whoe'er]man whoeer   is,]is   *8* ,]*o*   *9* life is]spirit's
c for life's   *These c lines, unc in M3, follow l. 10 HM:*

> My feet forever stand
> On Concord fields,   ,]*o*
> And I must live the life
> Which their soil yields.   their]this *c for* their
>   yields]yilds

12 ?]*o*   *14* ?].   *These c lines, unc in M3, follow l. 14 HM:*

> The love of the new,   ,]*o*
> The unfathomed blue,   ,]*o*
> The wind in the wood,   ,]*o*
> All future good,   All]And all; And *c*   ,]*o*
> The sun-lit tree,   sun-lit]sun lit   ,]*o*
> The small chicadee,   The]And the; And *c*   ,]*o*

15 ,]*o*   *16* Scripture]scripture   ,]*o*   *This c line follows l. 16 M3:*

> The vagabonds garb—

18 signs]else   -]*o*   *19* ,]*o*   *20* things,]things   short,]short   *22* deed]
act *c for* deed   .]*o*   *23* ,]*o*   *24* seek Not]Not seek *indicated for*

transposition HM; I would not seek; I would *c M3* South,]south
L. 26 precedes l. 25 but is indicated for transposition M3 25 But]I
would *c for* But the whole](word) *c for* my whole 26 Of]But if
c for In Present Hour.]present hour 27 thou]thou should'st; should'st
c ,]*o* 28 canst]couldst *c for* can'st ?]*o* 30 ,]*o* 32 Upon]On
34 sunset,]sun set- 36 ?]*o* 37 *new stanza*]no 38 ,]*o* 40 .]*o* 41
,]*o* !]*o* *Lines 44-46 precede lines 42-43 but are indicated for transposition M3* 43 ;-]*o* 44 spare,]spare 45 ,]*o* 46 And]& 47 ,]*o* 48 ,-]*o*
49 paid for]paid for *al for* well earned ,]*o* 50 ;-]*o* 51 ,]*o* 52 ,]*o*
53 And,]And all,]all ;-]. 54 ,]*o* 55 , have]Say have failed,]
failed 56 Wherever]However *c for* Wherever 57 Or]& *c for* or
,]*o* or]& *c for* or 58 *no stanza*]new stanza hayed,-]hay'd 59 ,-]*o*
60 ?]*o* 61 stayed,]stay'd 62 ,]*o* 64 "Today",]"today" 65 Here,]
here 66 ,]*o* 69 o'er,]oer 71 ;]- 72 we]I *c for* he 73 ,]*o* 74
We shall]I shall *c for* He'll 75 .]*o*

168. "Loves invalides are not those of common wars"

Heretofore unpublished. Reference: HM 13182 (1849).

169. "And once again"

Reference: M3a 139 (July 16[?], 1850). *Cf.: Jll 54. Entire poem c*

170. "Old meeting-house bell"

Reference: M3a 141 (July 16[?], 1850). *Cf.: Jll 57. See also note.*

171. "Is consigned to the nine"

Reference: M3a (July 16[?], 1850), *torn half page between pp. 142
and 151, which touch one another. Cf.: Jll 57. Entire poem c M3a
has lines 10-11 appearing as lines 5-6 of "It is no dream of mine"; see that
poem for collation. Jll includes only lines 4-11.* 11 gale]breeze *al*

172. "Among the worst of men that ever lived"

Reference: M3a 151 (Aug., 1850). *Cf.: Jll 58. M3a has lines 6-9
p.* 7 the topmost rider]a 5 rail fence with hand on *p for* the topmost
rider 8 But]Soon, Then *als* our Icarian]by a natural law our *p for*
our Icarian thoughts]thoughts were; were *c* 9 heaven]heaven by;
by *c*

173. "Tall Ambrosia"

Reference: M3a 151 (Aug. 31, 1850). *Cf.: JII 59. See also note.* 4 to]
to *p for* by   5 immortal]immortal *underlined twice and then p for* well
named   once(?) as]as is *c*   7 cross]cross *p for* brush through   11
"thus . . . countryfied" *and* "Fast . . . couch" *are indicated for transposition to their present order.*   15 been]gone *al   These c lines follow l. 15:*

> Who never walk—but live on horse instead—
> Who are *translated* to anywhere—but heaven

16 walk]ride *c*   rather]ever *c;* fitly *al   This c line follows l. 16:*

> Translated from one part of earth to another

17 do]can *al*

174. "Th' ambrosia of the Gods 's a weed on earth"

Reference: M3a 152 (Aug. 31, 1850). *Cf.: JII 59. See also note.*
2 on]only our; ly our *c*   5 As]And *c for* as; as *al c*   nectar is]their
nectar *al*   6 with which we wet our shoes]which our shoes brush aside
and which only our shoes taste (taste]drink *al) als*

175. "I saw a delicate flower had grown up 2 feet high"

Reference: M3a 161 (Sept. 6[?], 1850). *Cf.: JII 66. M3a has lines
1-11 c.*

176. "To day I climbed a handsome rounded hill"

Reference: M3a 163 (Sept. 6[?], 1850). *Cf.: JII 67.*

177, 178. "I am the little Irish boy"

References: M4a 162 (Nov. 28, 1850); *M7, loose pages at end of
volume* (1851[?]). *Cf.: JII 117; JIII 243. Entire poem c M4a   M7 JIII
include only these lines: 1-4; eight extra lines, c in M4a; a sentence of
prose; 5-8. JI includes these lines: 1-19; eight extra lines, c in M4a;
20-31.* 1 boy]boy, *M7*   2 shanty]shanty, *M7*   3 four]four *c for*
5 *M7*   today]today, *M7*   4 twenty]twenty. *M7*   5 *no stanza]new
stanza M7*   6 man]man, *M7   These c lines follow l. 19:*

> At recess I play   *no stanza]new stanza M7*
> With little Billy Gray   Gray]Gray, *M7*
> But when school is done   But]But *p for* And *M4a;* And *M7*
> Then away I run.   away]home *al*   done]done, *M7*

```
   And if I meet the cars                    cars]cars, M7
      I get on the other track            track]track, M7
   And then I know whatever comes
      I need'nt look back                    back]back. M7
```

179. "I do not fear my thoughts will die"

Reference: M8 83 (Nov. 13, 1851). *Cf.: JIII 113.*

180. "Cans't thou love with thy mind"

Reference: HM 13196 (Sept., 1852). *Cf.: 06VI 202.*

181. "Indeed indeed, I cannot tell"

Reference: HM 13196 (Sept., 1852). *Cf.: 06VI 202.* «6 dost]doth *06VI*»

182. "The vessel of love, the vessel of state"

Heretofore unpublished. Reference: HM 13196 (Sept., 1852). *See also note.* 4 union]Union(?)

183. "When the toads begin to ring"

Reference: M17 129 (April 26, 1854). *Cf.: JVI 222.*

184. "Forever in my dream & in my morning thought"

Reference: M24 233 (Oct. 29, 1857). *Cf.: JX 144.* 2 ascends]up-rears itself *p* 4 It]It sinks; sinks *c* ends]fades away *c* 6 unearthly] untrodden *c* 9 soil]ground *c* 12 must I]I must *indicated for transposition* 15 I have not]nor have I *al* 23 reache(s)]climbs up *al*

185. "Strange that so many fickle gods, as fickle as the weather"

Reference: M1 v42 (June 14, 1838). *Cf.: JI 51.*

185. "The deeds of king and meanest hedger"

Reference: M1 v59 (Feb. 3, 1839). *Cf.: JI 72.*

185. "Wait not till I invite thee, but observe"

References: M4 67 (Feb. 7, 1841); *A. Cf.: JI 205. Couplet c On leaf headed "Short Flights" in A* 2 I'm]I'm *c for* That I am *A* com'st] comst *c for* comest *A*

185. "Greater is the depth of sadness"

Reference: M5 97 (Sept. 5, 1841). Cf.: J1 283. Couplet c

186. "Where I have been"

Reference: M5 112 (Sept. 12, 1841). Cf.: J1 285; BSWa I, 1. Couplet c

186. "Better wait"

Reference: M5 115 (Sept. 30, 1841). Cf.: J1 287.

186. "On a Good Man"

Heretofore unpublished. References: T; HM 13182 (Oct. 22, 1843). HM includes only these lines: 2, two extra lines. On a Good Man] Ep—— on a Good Man HM   2 .]o HM   These lines follow l. 2 HM:

> "Here lies"—but no, the spirit's gone,
> I should have said—"There rises one."

186. "Man Man is the Devil"

Reference: M13 149 (Jan. 3, 1853). Cf.: Win 107; J1V 445. Couplet c

187. "You must not only aim aright"

No manuscript authority. Reference: 06V1 223 (Dec. 19, 1853).

187. "The chicadee"

Reference: M24 270 (Nov. 8, 1857). Cf.: JX 172.

187. "Any fool can make a rule"

Reference: M30 (under date of Feb. 3, 1860; page not numbered). Cf.: JXIII 125. (It is just possible that this maxim was ready-made for Thoreau.) Couplet c

187. "All things decay"

Reference: M31 (under date of March 25, 1860; page not numbered). Cf.: JXIII 220.

188. "Expectation"

Reference: A (J. S. Wade, A Contribution to a Bibliography from 1909 to 1936 of Henry David Thoreau *[reprinted from* Journal of the New York Entomological Society, *XLVII (1939], p. 167, records "Expectation" as having been published by E. B. Hill, n. d., no place. Mr. Hill in a letter to the present editor [Jan. 18, 1942] states that the version he printed came either from Dr. J. W. Abernethy, Middlebury, Vermont, or from Dr. Raymond Adams. Apparently it was the former; and the present text is from the Abernethy Library of American Literature, Middlebury Colllege. Mr. Hill said that he printed only half a dozen copies of the quatrain.) Entire poem c*

189. "For though the caves were rabitted"

Heretofore unpublished. References: H; HM 13182. HM has a horizontal line, as well as a prose sentence, between the first and second stanzas of this poem. Variants all in HM 1 rabitted]rabbitted ,]o 2 And]& sweeps were slanted]sweep was slanted(?) 3 seemed] seemed *al for* was inhabited]inhabited, 5 held his]kept the *c H;* kept the ,]o 6 ,]o 7 ideot]idiot ,]o 8 And]&

190. "My friends, my noble friends, know ye"

Heretofore unpublished. Reference: H.

191. "No earnest work that will expand the frame"

Heretofore unpublished. References: H; HM 13187. HM includes only these lines: 9-10, four extra lines, 11-12. Variants all in HM 8 By] by 9 bear]face 10 one]we *c for* one *These lines follow l. 10 (phrases in lines b-c indicated for transposition to present order):*

> For where her fires are seen to gild
>   the [?] horizon like the setting sun
> and livid flames Up to the candle dart in red demons [?]
>   and]her *c* Up]Will *c*
> They will requite the pain—re-   pain]flame (?)
> minding us of pleasant sights on earth.

11 Hell]hell 12 By]by

192, 193. "Godfrey of Boulogne"

References: HM 13197; H. Cf.: Unpublished Poems by Bryant and Thoreau *(Boston, 1907), p. xxvii (and facsimile, evidently, of HM, p.*

xxi); 17S 250. Entire poem c H   H includes only these lines: two extra lines, 1-40. Godfrey of Boulogne]*o H   H opens with these extra lines:*

> Oh ye proud days of Europes middle age
> Transfer your pomp to this my humble page

1 o'er]in *c for* o'er *H*   ,]*o H*   2 'Twas]Twas Lig; Lig *c H*   sea] (midland) sea *H*   ,]*o H*   3 Fair]Sweet *c for* Fair *H*   woo'd]wooed *H*   4 paid]paid her *H*   in]in her *H*   5 «then]there *17S»*   ,]*o H* 6 in]to *c HM*; to *p and c H*   floating to *p H*   ,]*o H*   7 ,]*o H*   9 The herdsman]Therdsman gui; gui *c H*   10 ,]*o H*   11 ,-]*o H*   12 'T]T *H*   Boulogne]Boulogne. *H*   14 lay]rested *c for* lay *H*   shade,]the shade; the *c H*   15 with]their *c HM*; al *H*   ,]*o H*   16 .]*o H*   17 ,]*o H*   18 showed]whispered *c for* told *c for* showed *H*   the]Europes *c for* the; the *c H*   ;]. *H*   19,]*o H*   21 goatherd]goat herd *H*   ,]*o* 22 of battles]of peace *c for* of battles *H*   23 ,-]*o H*   24 'Twas]Twas *H*   25 Night hung upon]Along *c for* Night hung upon *H*   Danube's] Danube's dusky; dusky *c H*   ,]*o H*   26 ,]*o H*   27 ,]*o H*   28 .]*o H* 29 Lord]Lord *H*   30 sleeps]sleeps a sleep; a sleep *c H*   ,]*o H*   32 Moslem]Turkish *c*   Upon the Moslem ground]Upon the Moslem ground *al for* As if she heard a waking sound *H*   .]*o*   33 ,]*o H* *This line follows l. 33 and is rather heavily c H:*

> Scattered only a thunder tone *(reading of whole line questionable)*

34 «glancing]flaring *Unpublished Poems of Bryant and Thoreau»*   ,]*o H*   35 ,]*o H*   36 'Twas]Twas *H*   37 'Twas]Twas *H*   ,]*o H*   38 ,]*o H*   39 Europe's]Europes *H*   40 gathered]Western (?) *c for* gathered *H*; gathering *c HM*   «43 their]the *17S»*   47 their]Upon their; Upon *c*   had acquired]was *c*

194. "Who equallest the coward's haste"

References: HM 13201; Critic, *March 26, 1881. Cf.: 06V 417. no title*]Omnipresence *Critic 06V*   1 equallest]equalleth *Critic*   haste] haste, *Critic*   2 heart]heart; *Critic*   3 lofty]ancient *al HM*   disgraced] disgraced, *Critic*   4 part]part. *Critic*

195. "Ive searched my faculties around"

References: HM 13201; Critic, *March 26, 1881. Cf.: 06V 418. no title*]Mission *Critic 06V*   1 Ive]I've *Critic*   around]around, *Critic* 2 lent]lent: *Critic*   3 sound]sound, *Critic*   4 meant]meant. *Critic*

196. "Until at length the north winds blow"

*References: HM 13182; H. Cf.: FLJ 1, 132; 17S 323. Entire poem
c H   2 and]& H*

197. "I was made erect and lone"

*Reference: HM 13182. Cf.: FLJ 1, 135. FLJ includes ll. 1-9 as
second stanza of "Solitude." See also "I was made erect and lone," note.*
1 I was made]They made me *al*

198, 199. "Wait not till slaves pronounce the word"

*Reference: HM 13182 (also facsimile in FLJ 1, opp. 136). Cf.: FLJ 1,
137; 17S 284. 17S includes only these lines: 21-24, 37-40 (as the last two
stanzas of a version of "Independence"). no title]*True Freedom *FLJ*
«5 are all]all are *FLJ*»

200. "To the Mountains"

*References: HM 13183 (also facsimile in FLJ 1, opp. 122); B. Cf.:
FLJ 1, 123. B includes only lines 3-8. HM has two horizontal lines sep-
arating lines 11-12 from the rest of the poem. Variants all in B*   3 his]
His   4 oer]above   yonder]the   8 melancholy]inharmonious   .-].

201, 202. "The Friend"

*References: HM 13188; 49W 277; 68W 279. Cf.: PN 17; FLJ 1,
126; 06W 279. 49W 68W PN 06W include only these lines (under "The
Atlantides") in this order: four extra lines, 13-16, 25-26, 17-18, 23-24,
21, 19, 22, 20. 49W 68W open with these extra lines:*

> Sea and land are but his neighbors,
> And companions in his labors,
> Who on the ocean's verge and firm land's end
> Doth long and truly seek his Friend.

3 he]he next to; next to *c*   14 ,]. *49W 68W*   15 books]books, *49W
68W*   16 Ever]Always *49W 68W*   17 sea-breeze]sea breeze *49W
68W*   ,]o *49W*   18 ;]. *49W 68W*   *These c lines follow l. 18:*

> In every beholder's eye
> A sailing vessel doth descry

19 hears]hears, *68W*   20 Of]And *49W 68W*   years]years. *49W
68W*   21 In this the]In the *49W 68W*   sullen ocean's]ocean's sullen
68W   22 ;], *49W 68W*   23 companions]companion's *49W 68W*; be-
holder's *c*   25 reads]reads, *49W 68W*   26 .], *49W 68W*

203, 204. "Upon the bank at early dawn"

References: HM 13195; M. Cf.: FLJ I, xvi. M includes only these lines in this order: 5-8; four extra lines, c; 17-20, c; 9-16. See Appendix A for additions and further variations. Variants all in M   6 Or]or scattered]clustered ,]o 7 seem]seemed 8 Night.]night   clouds.] clouds   *These c lines follow l. 8:*

> Some wakeful steed [?] exalts his tramp [?]
> Afar oer the sonorous ground
> And with a sounding eastern pomp
> It barely maketh the horizon sound

9 «their]the *FLJ»* ,]o 10 wakeful]watchful   were there,]there thronged   11 And]Where   its]their   12 To warn us sluggard knights beware.]So is their martial note heroically prolonged   13 on more] from a ,]o 14 fainter,]fainter   still,]still?   15 ah,]ah!   promises, I fear,]promises I fear   16 her]his   .]o 17 The sound invades each silent]Invades each recess of the ,]o 18 Awakes]but awakes *c for* And wakes ,]o 19 Till]Then ,]o 20 «on]in *FLJ»*   .]o

205. "Between the traveller and the setting sun"

References: HM 13195; H. Cf.: FLJ I, xxii. No variations H

206. "Must we still eat"

Reference: HM 924. Cf.: BSWa I, 182. Entire poem c

207. "I'm contented you should stay"

Reference: HM 924. Cf.: BSWa I, 203.

208. "He knows no change who knows the true"

Reference: HM 924. Cf.: BSWa II, 240. Entire poem c but with the direction "copy" in the left margin   8 Forever]While ever *al*

209, 210. "The Departure"

Reference: HM 13184. Cf.: Commonwealth, Aug. 28, 1863; PN 112; 06V 414; 17S 500. The Departure]Departure; The Departure «6 housed]house *17S»*   12 strengthening]rosy *c*   «13 at]by *C*   did] *o C»*   17 their]this *al and then c*   21 bark]ship *c* «barque *PN»* 22 this]that *c* «that *C*   28 to]toward *PN»*   29 And]But *c*   «31 stayed]staid *C»*   *This c line follows l. 32:*

So—Alas! and alas!

33 his]his shrouded; shrouded *c and p; p c* «his shrouded *C*   35 same]
sane *06V»*   *This c line follows l. 35:*

It was that filled his sail

211. "The Funeral Bell"

*References: HMa 13185; HMb 13190 (in Sophia Thoreau's hand);
H. Cf.: Commonwealth, July 3, 1863; PN 62; 06V 405. HMb includes
these lines: 1-12, six extra lines, 13-24. H includes only lines 1-8.* The
Funeral Bell]*o HMb H*   2 throng]throng, *HMb*   3 That]Which
HMb   tread]treads *HMb H*   ;]*o H*   4 ,]*o H*   5 Its sad]Sadly its
HMb H   6 hearths]hearts *HMb*   .]*o H*   7 Flower]But flowerbells *H*
,]*o H*   8 not]not, *HMb*   9 Unto]Upon *c for* Unto *HMa;* Upon
HMb   ;-]*o HMb*   10 *There*]There *HMb*   ,]*o HMb*   *These lines
follow l. 12 HMb:*

The lilies mourn not,
Their leaves are torn not,
Tis not their loss
They are not worried
Their friend is not burried
Nor slain on the cross

13 ,]*o HMb*   15 ;-]*o HMb*   18 heaven's]heavens *HMb*   20 ,]*o HMb*
21 ;]*o HMb*

212. "The Virgin"

Reference: HM 13187. Cf.: FLJ I, 134. «1 aspiring]inquiring *FLJ»*
4 sky]earth *c*

213, 214. "Speech of a Saxon Ealderman"

Heretofore unpublished. Reference: M. 14 Are merry there]
Do banish care. *c*

215. "Farewell"

*Heretofore unpublished. References: Ma; Mb. Mb includes only
these lines in this order: two extra lines, c in Ma; 11-12; 9-10; 13-20;
two extra lines; 21-26; three extra lines; 27-30; and, on verso of sheet,
twenty-six extra lines. Ma has lines 21-22 and lines 23-26 indicated for
transposition to their present order. (The appearance of the manuscript
should be described since it determines which of the two versions of
"Farewell" becomes the basic text. Both versions are on a double quarto*

327

sheet which has the first three pages written on, and the fourth blank. The first version of the poem fills p. 1 and most of p. 2. The next version occupies p. 3, and—most significantly—it has two quatrains added in pencil at the bottom of p. 2, in the space not filled by the first version. They have a pencilled line connecting them with the [former] beginning of the second version. So the second version becomes the basic text.) Ma opens with these extra c lines, unc in Mb:

> Sister mine where'er thou art   mine]mine, *Mb*   art]art, *Mb*
> I have portion of thy heart   heart]heart; *Mb*

Ma has lines 9-12 c and then the cancellation is erased. 10 .(?)]; *Mb* 14 I]I *c*; I *Mb* ,]o *Mb*   16 low]low. *Mb*   17 pure]*originally modified "eye"* 19 so]so sweet and; sweet and *p*   *These lines are inserted after l. 20 Mb:*

> Time cannot dispart
> The united heart;

These lines follow and are c (and then, slightly changed, are re-written as they appear in the basic text):

> My feet would weary be
> Ere they travelled from thee.

21 And my]And *c* my]My *Mb*   22 .]o *Mb*   23 I]For I; For *c Ma*; For I *Mb*   (discover)]discover *c*; know *al c*; see *Mb*   26 sea]see *Mb* *These lines follow l. 26 Mb:*

> Thou wast not born with me
> Heavens beyond heavens, sea beyond sea,
> Here to be sundered on this rood of earth.

27 (be)]live *c*; be *c Ma*; live *Mb*   28 each part become a whole]each may thrive; each part may thrive; may thrive *c*; each part survive; survive *c* ,]o *Mb*   *These lines follow l. 30 Mb:*

> What are the true delights
>   From which distance debars?
> Was my love ever tired
>   Of mounting to the stars?
> It doth as easily surmount their heights
>   In its elastic flights,
> As stoops to pluck the flower
>   That grows within its bower.

> I have seen thee on some way   way]May (?)
> By the light of our day
> When thy soul was far away—
>   From these scenes; hence do I say   From these scenes;
>   hence do I say]So I say—; So *c for* And
>   hence; *whole line c for present reading*

I will go dwell abroad
From thy public road
Where thy absent thought
Doth resort.
For then thou art at home
And when here thou dost roam;
This place is but some inn
For the harboring of thy sin.
I will sit upon thy hearth
And not meet thee in the path.
I will roam
Toward thy home,
And some reflected thought will tell
Perchance where thou dost dwell.

216. "Nature"

References: M; H. Cf.: PN 1; 06V 395. H includes only these lines: 9-10, four extra lines. PN 06V include these lines in this order: 1-12, 19-20, 13-18. M has lines 13-18 written vertically in the right margin, and an arrow shows that they are to be inserted after l. 12.
9 unpublic]untraversed *H*   10 ,]o *H*   *These lines follow l. 10 H:*

> In my place I still will stand
> A pattern now to that [?] firm [?] land
> Until revolving spheres come round
> To embrace my stable ground.

217. "Guido's Aurora"

Reference: M. Cf.: PN 19; 06V 399. Guido's Aurora]The Aurora of Guido   A Fragment *PN 06V*   3 moon's pale orb]lingering moon *al*
«10 washed(?)]unseen *PN*»

218. "Greece"

References: M; 49W 59; 68W 62. M6a, between pp. 136-137, has the torn half of an early, much revised draft—probably, as a matter of fact, the first draft—of "Greece." But the piece has been torn through the center, and only the opening halves of eight lines remain. Cf.: Commonwealth, *July 24, 1863; PN 61;* The Service *30; 06W 54; 06V 404; 17S 257. 49W 68W 06W include only lines 9-12. 17S and* The Service *include only lines 3-8.* Greece]o *49W 68W 06W Service 17S*
9 Greece]Greece, *49W 68W*   ?], *49W 68W*   10 Thermopylae]Thermopylae? *49W 68W*   11 vulgar]vulgar, *49W 68W*   mean]mean, *49W 68W* 12 such]these *49W 68W*

219, 220. "Poverty"

References: M; (the following are for lines 24-27 only) 49W 369; 68W 371; (the following are for lines 8-9 only) 49W 306; 68W 309. Cf.: PN 105; 06V 412; (for lines 24-27) 06W 373; (for lines 8-9) 06W 311. 49W 68W 06W include only these lines in this order: 24-27, 8-9. PN 06V include only these lines in this order: 1 (broken down into two lines), 2-7, 12-15, 24-27. M has a vertical stroke in the left margin, opposite lines 8-9—Thoreau's way of showing that these lines were to be published. Poverty]Poverty A Fragment PN 06V 8 this]this, *49W 68W* 9 condition]condition, *49W 68W* 20 Ill leave]Is not *c* 24 Man kind may delve]Men dig and dive *c M;* Men dig and dive *49W 68W* 25 If I]Who still *c M;* Who yet *49W 68W* «store]wealth PN» appropriate]appropriate, *49W 68W* 26 no]I no *c;* I *c M;* Who no *49W 68W* ships]ship *49W 68W* «into]unto PN» send]send, *49W 68W* 27 «To rob]None robs PN» estate]estate. *49W 68W*

221. "I'm not alone"

Heretofore unpublished. Reference: M. 4 not(?)]rich(?) 5 understood]understood if my; if my *c*

222. "What sought th[e]y th[u]s afar"

Heretofore unpublished. Reference: M. (There is a 2 at the top of this leaf of manuscript, so the beginning of the poem may have been lost. It might be added that every holographic sign supports the belief that this unfinished poem was written at top speed by Thoreau. Often his pen did not even leave the paper between words. There are no revisions and only a single cancellation. Some of the first lines in the last half of the poem are not even capitalized. And the letters in a number of words are reduced to a curve or two; some letters are omitted, resulting in spellings which are most obviously unintended. This last fact will explain some of the emendations.) 11 Thou speakest]To music *al c* 14 Thy] The *c*

223. "Music"

Heretofore unpublished. Reference: M. (As Thoreau first wrote these verses, lines 1-4 were lines 13-16. However he later pencilled a vertical stroke and a 1 opposite them in the left margin, and a vertical stroke and a 2 in the left margin opposite what had been lines 1-10. The pencil stroke fades out at l. 10, but it is apparent that Thoreau meant

*it to include the remaining two lines, which had been 11-12—thus pro-
viding completely for the rearrangement.)* 2 Bursting]Finding *c;* piercing *al* 3 years]years, *; , c* 9 This]It *c* 17 Lately]Alas *c* 20 so]
such *c* 21 Its]Its low and; low and *p*

224. "I'm thankful that my life doth not deceive"

*Heretofore unpublished. Reference: M. (These verses are on the
same double sheet, on the left-hand half, as the M version of "Life.")*
2 loftiness,]loftiness, a; a *p* 3 dip]dips(?) 5 but]but that; but *p;*
that *p and c* 12 slight]trivial *al* forsooth *p* 23 let]may *c These
c lines follow l. 24:*

> It is a charming day—let us go forth
> And snuff the air before the evening fall.

225. "Manhood"

*Heretofore unpublished. Reference: L (The number 4 has been
pencilled at the top of the manuscript leaf containing these verses, and
there is a 2 at the top of the leaf that contains the following "The moon
moves up her smooth and sheeny path." Still, there is enough similarity
of theme and manner to allow the possibility of all this being one piece
of verse.)* 1 to see the]a natural *c* 2 As yet]Still as *c* 5 better still]
with more profit still do *al* love to]*p* 7 hath]'th; ' *c for* ha on]
upon; up *c* 11 Who]Who *c for* And; And *c for* Who *This c line
follows l. 14:*

> And the repose of inexperience

15 there]then(?) 17 the ripe bloom of a self-wrought content]firm
self wrought contentment of its own *c* 18 do]would *c* 23 can]
doth *c* 24 piercing]darting *c;* guiding *al*

226. "The moon moves up her smooth and sheeny path"

*Heretofore unpublished. Reference: L. (This poem has a pencilled 2
above it, so it may possibly be part of the preceding poem, "Manhood";
but see note on that poem, above.)* 2 and happily]hear how the brook
c (?); and happily the brook; the brook *c* 3 Glides]The brook Glides
hap'ly; hap'ly *c* 5 And rise again]But have their end *c;* yield a night
al c; And to rise again; to *c* 9 and devious]but endless *c* Uncertain
(began line originally) 13 resistless]resistless and determined; and determined *p*

227. "Life"

References: Autograph Leaves of Our Country's Authors *(Baltimore, 1864), p. 193 (facsimile); M. Cf.:* Journal of American History, *III (Oct., 1909), 596 (facsimile evidently of* Autograph Leaves*); Saturday Review of Literature, VII (Feb. 7, 1931), 577. (The* Saturday Review of Literature, *hereafter abbreviated to SRL, states that its text is that of the 1864 facsimile. That is not quite true: there are minor differences in wording and punctuation. Dr. Raymond Adams, of the University of North Carolina, has privately printed a text of the 1864 version. The present editor has not seen his production. In the M version, these verses are on the same double sheet, on the right-hand half, as "I'm thankful that my life doth not deceive.")* Life]o *M* 1 stately warrior]stately warrior; proud & stately warrior; warrior *c M* ,]o *M* 2 ,]o *M* 3 upright]single *c for* upright *M* 4 .-], *M* 5 Alas, when]When; -Alas -When *M* will this]shall my *c for* will this *M* neck]neck, alas,; alas *c M* 6 that]this *altered to* that *M* «the *SRL»* 7 goes proudly forth,]keeps on his way *c for* goes proudly forth *M This c line follows l. 7 M:*

> With high o'erarching neck and sparkling eye

8 stately]dainty *c for* stately *Autograph Leaves M* ;]o *M These c lines follow l. 8 M:*

> As if to the beholder's casual eye
> His back supported not a fairy's weight

9 set,]set *M* rise,]rise *M* 11 say,]say- *M* 12 .]- *M The following c line and a half then occur before "Plants" M:*

> You neer may look upon
> The ocean waves at morn or even but

;]. *M* 13 ,]o *M* 14 eventide,]even tide *M* 15 th']the *M* ,]o *M* 16 ,]- *M* 17 well so my]Well so, forsooth, my *M* far,]far *M* 18 not yet explored]not yet explored; not *c;* un *prefixed to* explored; un *c;* not *written again and then c;* un *written again (resulting finally in "yet unexplored") M* 19 ,]o *M* 20 high]high *c for* far; far *c M* ,]o *M* 22 ,]; *M* .]o *M* 23 Nor doth]Nor doth *p for* No more *M* 24 ,]. *M* 25 But still it plows]But it doth plow; But still it doth plow; doth *c;* s *added to* plow *M* «the]its *SRL»* ,]o *M* 26 Breasting] And breasts; And *c;* s *of* breasts *altered to* ing *M*

228. "Pray to what earth does this sweet cold belong"

Reference: F. B. Sanborn, The Personality of Thoreau *(Boston, 1901), facsimile of the manuscript, opp. p. 32. Cf.:* ibid., *p. 31; Cooke,* Introduction to . . . The Dial, *I, 130.* 12 the]some *c*

229. "When the oaks are in the gray"

Reference: HM 924. Cf.: BSWa II, 239.

230-233. "Inspiration"

No manuscript authority for basic text. References: Commonwealth, *June 19, 1863 (there headed "From an unpublished manuscript"); M (in a volume of autograph verse formerly belonging to Mrs. James T. Fields); EL 218; (the following are for lines 25-28 only) HM 13182; A; 49W 368; 68W 369; (the following are for lines 3-4 only) 49W 346; 68W 348; (the following are for lines 29-30 and 39-40 only) 49W 179; 68W 183; (the following are for lines 43-44 only) 49W 179; 68W 183; (the following are for lines 45-46 and 69-72 only) 49W 180; 68W 184. Cf.: PN 3; 06V 396; 17S 267; (for lines 25-28 only) FLJ 1, 130; 06W 372; (for lines 3-4 only) 06W 351; (for lines 29-30 and 39-40 only) 06W 182; (for lines 43-44 only) 06W 181; (for lines 45-46 and 69-72 only) 06W 182. M includes only these lines: 17-32, 37-60, four extra lines, 61-68, 73-84. EL includes only these lines: 5-16, 25-28, 45-52, 69-72. 49W 68W 06W include only these lines, scattered: 3-4, 25-28, 29-30, 39-40, 43-44, 45-46, 69-72. HM A FLJ include only lines 25-28, c in HM. See Appendix A for additions and further variations. HM FLJ include the collated stanza as part of another poem, titled "The Threadbare Trees" in FLJ, untitled in HM. (Sanborn says of the present basic text that he printed it "just as it was left by the poet" [Critic, March 26, 1881]. As was noted earlier, he headed the version in the Commonwealth, "From an unpublished manuscript." Yet of the slightly different version in 17S, Sanborn also says [17S 267] that he there printed the full poem as Sophia Thoreau gave it to him for this same Commonwealth in the spring of 1863, wholly, he thinks, in Thoreau's handwriting and in Thoreau's own arrangement. The variations in the poem, then, as Emerson published it may be Thoreau's or may be Emerson's, Sanborn concludes.)* Inspiration]o 49W 68W 06W «4 lets]leaves PN» 6 muses]Muses EL 9 ,]o EL 12 ,]; EL 16 hath]has EL 19 reverence]rev'rence M ,]o M 21 now]straight M 22 clear]clear, M 24 is,]is M 25 get]get, HM M 49W EL 68W 26 sight,]sight A before,]before; EL 27 live]live, HM M 49W EL 68W 28 discern] discern, HM M 49W EL 68W 30 range]verge M 49W 68W ,],- 49W 68W 31 earths and skies and]earths- new skies- new M 32 day] noon M «40 leave]leaves 17S» 41 It speaks]Speaking M 43 That] Then 49W 68W runs]ran 49W 68W ,]o 49W 68W 44 leaves]left 49W 68W .]; 49W 68W 45 Then]Now 49W EL 68W 46 then] now 49W EL 68W ,]. 49W 68W 48 end]end, EL 49 'T 'hath

come]'T hath come *M;* It comes *EL* 50 grey]gray *EL* wall]wall, *M EL*
51 Unseasoned]Unseasoning *EL* time]Time *M* insulted]insulting *EL*
June,]June *M* 52 And vexed the day]And vexing day *EL* «Vexing the
day *17S*» 53 couch]sleep *M* 55 life]life, *M* 56 up]up, *M* 57
Muse-]Muse, *M* *These lines follow l. 60 M:*

> Whose clear and ancient harmony
> Pierces my soul through all its din,
> As through its utmost melody,
> Farther behind than they, further within.

61 She]Who *M* 64 pulse]life *M* 65 forever more]forevermore *M*
66 steadfast]iron *M* 67 though]if *M* 69 will then]will, then, *49W;*
will then, *68W* then, trust]not doubt *49W EL 68W* untold]untold,
49W 68W will,]will *49W EL 68W* 70 has]hath *49W EL 68W*
71 young]young, *EL* woos]wooes *EL* 78 danger]dangers *M* «80
love has]Love hath *17S*» *Horizontal line below l. 80 o M* 84 «hath]
has *PN*» Maker's]maker's *M*

234. "Inspiration"

No manuscript authority. Reference: Critic, March 26, 1881. *Cf.:
06V 418.*

235. "Delay"

No manuscript authority for basic text. Reference: Critic, March
26, 1881. *Cf.: 06V 418. HM would normally be the source, but the
writing there is almost illegible; see Appendix A.*

236-238. "The Fall of the Leaf"

*No manuscript authority for basic text. References: PN 77; (the
following is for lines 1-16)* Commonwealth, *Nov. 6, 1863; (the following
is for lines 17-52)* Commonwealth, *Oct. 9, 1863; HM 13182. Cf.: 06V
407; FLJ I, 130. Entire poem c HM* Commonwealth *includes only
lines 1-16 and 17-52 as separate poems. HM FLJ include only
lines 57-64, as the first two stanzas of "The Threadbare Trees." See
Appendix A for additions and further variations. C has a row of stars
below lines 8, 16, 28, 40, 52. (An editors' note, in PN, on this poem
reads:*

> *The first four of these stanzas [unnamed by Thoreau] were
> published in the* Boston Commonwealth *in 1863, under the title
> of 'The Soul's Season,' the remainder as 'The Fall of the Leaf.'
> There can be little doubt that they are parts of one complete
> poem [77].*

The editorial judgment of Sanborn and Salt, as exhibited in PN, is frequently suspect. The present case offers no exception. First of all, Sanborn, by implication, admits having invented a title for the poem. Secondly, he and Salt say in the editors' note that the remainder of the text in PN was published in the Commonwealth *as "The Fall of the Leaf." This is not quite correct. PN has three additional stanzas at the end, besides the stanzas that constituted the* Commonwealth *version of "The Fall of the Leaf."*

In the Commonwealth, *Sanborn heads "The Soul's Season" and "The Fall of the Leaf" with the notation "From an unpublished manuscript." What has become of Sanborn's original the present editor does not know. None of three related manuscripts described in the Wakeman catalogue seems to fill the bill. Number 1035, "The Soul's Season," is described as having nine quatrains; number 1036, "The Fall of the Leaf," is described as having twenty-one quatrains; and number 1037, also entitled "The Fall of the Leaf" is described as having forty-two quatrains. The sample stanzas given for the first two items are included in the version used by Sanborn in the* Commonwealth. *The sample stanza given for number 1037 is not included, but is—incidentally—included in the verse printed in the present edition as HM 13201 [see Appendix A]; pointing out the ultimate repository of this poetry.*

After consideration, however, of the various factors just outlined, the lead of the editors of PN is followed; and the basic text is the one they first offered to the public. Sanborn's evidence is accepted by the present editor not because it is good evidence—the flaws in it have already been noticed—but because it is about the only evidence available. In such a situation it has seemed reasonable to give Sanborn the benefit of the doubt and follow his precedent.) The Fall of the Leaf]
The Soul's Season *al C; o HM;* The Threadbare Trees *FLJ* 1 God]
God, *C* 2 ;], *C* 3 near]near, *C* 10 nature,]nature *C* 11 ;], *C*
16 ,]o *C* 18 ;], *C* 19 ,]o *C* 21 !]o *C* 23 that]which *C* 26 sun
allows]Sun affords *C* 30 ;], *C* 31 soothes]lulls *C* 32 Nature's]
nature's *C* 34 has]hath *C* ;], *C* 37 birds,]birds *C* 41 woods,]
woods *C* days,]days *C* 42 Maker's]maker's *C* 44 Fall]fall *C* 49
sere]sear *C* 50 furthest]farthest *C* 57 threadbare]thread-bare *HM*
,]o *HM* -], *HM* 58 ;], *HM* 59 within]within, *HM* 61 which]
that *HM* 62 Winter's]winter's *HM*

239-242. "A Winter and Spring Scene"

No manuscript authority for basic text. Reference: FLJ I, 144. Cf.: PN 90; 06V 410; 17S 262. PN 06V include only these lines in this order: 13-16, 9-12, 25-32, 17-24, 1-4, 75-78. See Appendix A for additions and further variations. (The HM version is given complete in Appendix A because it furnishes interesting data on Thoreau's way of working. The use of the FLJ text here represents a departure from the practice of the present edition, since almost all of the manuscripts from which Sanborn prepared FLJ are now to be found in the Huntington Library. But, in this case, Sanborn's version differs so markedly from that of HM in Appendix A that he must have had some later, shorter text to base the FLJ version on. If not, he was guilty of far more editorial license than usual. Here he is once again given the benefit of the doubt.) A Winter and Spring Scene]A Winter Scene PN 06V «39 field]fields *17S* 41 air]fair *17S* 77 summer]summer's *PN*»

243. "Why do the seasons change? and why"

No manuscript authority. Reference: The Seasons *(Mesa, Ariz.: E. B. Hill, 1916), p. 1. Cf.: 17S 51. no title]*The Seasons *17S*

244. "Friends! that parting tear reserve it"

Reference: H (Class Book of the Class of 1837; the entry is. in Thoreau's hand). Cf.: CT 460. See also note. 1 "]o E   4 "]o E

245. "In Adams fall"

Reference: M5a 6 (Feb., 1851). Cf.: JII 153. Lines 3-4 are original with Thoreau. See also note.

246. "In times of yore, 'tis said, the swimming Alder"

References: 17Sa 59 (Aug. 5, 1836); 17Sb 119. 17Sb includes only lines 11-13. See also note. 11 Men Three of old,]men three of Gotham, in a bowl *17Sb* 12 In bowl did]Did *17Sb* 13 future]awful *17Sb* .];- *17Sb*

247. "By his good genius prompted or the power"

Reference: M3a, in left margin of torn leaf between pp. 142 and 151, which touch one another. See also note.

NOTES

By means of the notes which follow, the present editor has tried to do several things. First, he has used them to mark especially meaningful or unusual ideas and to explain those ideas. Secondly, he has annotated passages in the poems which help to illuminate leading ideas in Thoreau's prose. Next, he has noted interrelations of ideas within the poems, and he has glossed the poems whenever that has seemed necessary or advisable. He has also pointed out such passages as cast light on Thoreau's spiritual and emotional life ("his biography is in his verses"), and, finally, he has used the facts of Thoreau's own life to explain portions of the poems.

References to persons in Thoreau's poetry have been noted and identified wherever possible. Locale was very important to Thoreau, so the geographical references—of which there are many—have been annotated. Thus the reader can get some additional idea of the Concord which was so vital to Thoreau. Of the maps used as a partial basis for these notes, the main one appears at the end of the last volume of the Journal, Walden Edition; it is by Herbert Gleason. Geographical references by the present editor are given in present day spelling, for example, *Merrimac,* not *Merrimack.* Classical references have been noted, classical quotations identified. After all, Thoreau, with one of the best classical backgrounds for his time in America, assumed a detailed knowledge of the myths and could make part of the understanding of his poems dependent on that knowledge. Classical influences have also been noticed. Thoreau's background in English literature was even broader than his background in the literatures of Greece and Rome. Consequently, the influence of the English poets is noted as far as possible, and quotations are identified. A final portion of the notes is critical. The editor has tried, at significant points, to estimate and analyze Thoreau's performance as a poet.

3. "Within the circuit of this plodding life"

The Wordsworth of "I wandered lonely as a cloud" is here given a bias by the increased stress on the usefulness of a recollection of natural beauty. Note especially the idea summarized in the last two lines.

26. *fieldfare:* a medium-sized European thrush.

4. "His steady sails he never furls"

1. *His:* the shrike's (see also textual note).

5. "Sometimes I hear the veery's clarion"

One of the most interesting aspects of Thoreau's method of writing poetry is its flat contradiction of his theory of organic unity. He asserted that the poem should grow like a plant, developing its form from within (see further Fred W. Lorch, "Thoreau and the Organic Principle in Poetry," *Publications of the Modern Language Association of America*, LIII [1938], 286-302). But "Sometimes I hear the veery's clarion" not only failed to grow like a plant—Thoreau found it ready-made in the prose of someone else—but also had its form imposed patently from without. The manuscript Journal in the Morgan Library contains this cancelled sentence:

> Sometimes I hear the veery's silver clarion, or the brazen note of the impatient jay—or in secluded woods the chicadee doles out her scanty notes which sing the praise of heroes, and set forth the loveliness of virtue evermore.—
>
> Phoebe[?] (*M1 v78*).

The sentence, almost word for word, became the poem. It might be argued that the prose, even though still originally prose, had at any rate belonged to Thoreau and not to another author. The printed Journal would seem to support this view, since the sentence there (*JI 70*) has no quotation marks around it. But in the manuscript on which the published Journal was based the quotation marks are present. Thoreau himself was punctilious in indicating quoted material when he was preparing anything for print; and nothing here indicates that he departed from his conscientious practice.

> 1. *veery's*: This bird, which is so well described by Nuttall, . . . is one of the most common in the woods in this vicinity, and in Cambridge I have heard the college yard ring with its trill. The boys call it '*yorrick*,' from the sound of its querulous and chiding note.
> [Thoreau's note, *D III, 26*.]

One of the titles Nuttall gives the bird is enough to describe it: the tawny thrush.

6. "Upon the lofty elm tree sprays"

One earlier parallel to the content of this quatrain is furnished by Wordsworth's poem, "The Reverie of Poor Susan." However, the theme of the quatrain forms a normal part of Thoreau's general regard for the effect of nature (cf. so specific an instance as *JIV 190-191*).

8, 9. "The river swelleth more and more"

> 5. *Ararat:* Genesis, VIII: 4.

Textual note (p. 282): *extremest unction:* cf. the term for the sacrament.

7. *Musketaquid*: according to Thoreau, the Indian name for the Concord River. It meant the Grass-ground River.

13. *Nahshawtuck*, or Lee's Hill, is at the junction of the Assabet and Sudbury Rivers. The cliff here meant is probably the side of Fair Haven Hill, at the far south end of this reach of the Sudbury.

26. *Golden Horn*: the famous harbor of Istanbul; the fabulous richness of its fisheries is said to have been the reason for its name.

10. "Great God, I ask thee for no meaner pelf"
This prayer is peculiarly characteristic of Thoreau.

11. "The Moon"
The quotation is from "Praisd be Dianas faire and harmles light," which is probably by Ralegh.

12. "To a Stray Fowl"
Preliminary to these verses, Thoreau mentions that he once had a stately rooster with a good deal of the "wild Indian pheasant" in him.

> One night he was by chance shut out of the hen-yard, and, after long reconnoitering, and anxious going and coming,—with brave thoughts exalting him, and fancies rushing thick upon him . . . he flew, bird-like, up into the branches of a tree, and went to roost there. And I, who had witnessed this passage in his private history, forthwith wrote these verses, and inscribed them to him (*BSWa II, 23*).

The poem, especially in its conclusion, is a statement of Thoreau's belief in instinct over tuition. Nature is the best educator.

Writing on *Shelley in America in the Nineteenth Century* (University Studies published by the University of Nebraska, Lincoln, Nebraska, XL, 1940, Number 2, p. 27) Julia Power maintains that the "most conspicuous Shelley influence" in the *Dial*—and, by implication, in Henry Thoreau's poetry there—appears in the third volume, 1843. She selects the outstanding examples. She sees first "a ludicrous application of 'To a Skylark' in the opening lines of the very humanitarian poem, 'To a Stray Fowl'." She continues by calling "Light-winged Smoke, Icarian bird" a "more worthy echo of the same poem" (*ibid.*, p. 28). The similarity in two of the titles is obvious; and Miss Power in earlier parts of her book builds up a strong enough case to make Thoreau's awareness of Shelley logical. However, aside from observing that all three poems speak of birds, the present editor is blind to the influence which she perceives. Nor is there comment on Shelley in the twenty volumes of Thoreau's collected works—and this is especially significant when the general allusiveness of his prose writing is noted.

13. "The sluggish smoke curls up from some deep dell"

The most noteworthy feature of this lyric is its intermingling of two strains: the Simonidian (see "Light-winged Smoke, Icarian bird," note) and the Wordsworthian.

26. *refulgent:* an example of Thoreau's happier use of Latinized expressions. The word here adds to the context a deeper meaning than the ordinary cognates *resplendent* or *radiant.* The Latin lends the idea of *flashing back.* The cloud of smoke appears a lesser reflection, or a flashing back, of the vaporous cloud in the sky above.

14, 15. "When Winter fringes every bough"

Emerson, in a letter to Margaret Fuller, July 27-28, 1840 (*Letters,* II, 320), quotes the last half of l. 11 and all of l. 12 as if they are part of "Nature doth have her dawn each day." If they are, this is another example of Thoreau's combining—and later rejecting—stanzas from two different poems (cf. "Independence"). But it may simply be that Emerson turned from one poem to another without making the transition plain in his letter.

16. "Not unconcerned Wachusett rears his head"

1. *Wachusett:* to Thoreau the most interesting mountain in the state (cf. "With frontier strength ye stand your ground," ll. 73-99 and note).

17-19. "The Old Marlborough Road"

Thoreau's enjoyment of solitude caused him to choose isolated paths. A favorite of his, especially after 1850, was the old Marlboro Road, which runs southwest into Sudbury township but "which does not go to Marlborough now" (*06V 214*).

1-2. Miss Sarah R. Bartlett, Librarian, Concord Free Public Library, writes (letter dated November 19, 1940, to the editor) that she could find nothing definite on the statement contained in these lines.

3. *Martial Miles* is often mentioned in the Journal and his place was the frequent terminus of Thoreau's walks.

5. *Elijah Wood, Sr.,* is the only one mentioned in the Journal. There he usually appears as the village historian of far-past natural events.

8. Other members of the family of Dugan are referred to in the Journal, but the man of wild habits is not.

28. The name of the *Irishman Quin* does not appear elsewhere in Thoreau, but Miss Bartlett says the Quins lived in one of the houses where the Library now stands.

340

35. *cenotaphs:* monuments to persons buried elsewhere. The word well characterizes the slabs of stone, by the roadside, near whose top the town names were cut.

44-45. These *selectmen* were probably F. R. Gourgas, Daniel Clark, and Joseph Darby, according to Miss Bartlett. Lee could not be identified by her.

On Thoreau's attitudes toward his Concord neighbors as a whole, see F. H. Allen, *Men of Concord and Some Others, as Portrayed in the Journal of Henry David Thoreau* (Boston, 1936).

20. "In two years' time 't had thus"

The Journal version breaks off at the end of Thoreau's entry for the day.

1. *'t:* one infant apple tree.

3. *Admired:* in the archaic sense, probably, of looking with wonder and astonishment.

22. "Each summer sound"

2. *round:* as in music.

23. "Love equals swift and slow"

This sentence precedes the quatrain: "Love finds its level and rises to its fountain-head in all breasts, and its slenderest column balances the ocean" (*FLJ I, 136*).

26. "It is no dream of mine"

Like "I am the autumnal sun," this poem is fundamentally an expression of Thoreau's identification with nature, or a part of nature. The relation of the first two lines of the poem to the rest, however, is hard to understand except in that they restate one of Thoreau's most basic beliefs. That is the conviction that the work, in this case, the poem, is of far less consequence than the poet's experience in living. To Thoreau, a man's hours were too crowded and too few to allow time enough for both the uncloistered life and the cloistered production of poetry. As he explained tersely:

My life has been the poem I would have writ,
But I could not both live and utter it.

But see also the variant readings, "It is no dream of mine," textual note.

27. "Light-winged Smoke, Icarian bird"

An intricately Grecian content and form distinguish this, the most praised of Thoreau's lyrics. Emerson gave it what to him was a rich recommendation, saying that the "classic poem on 'Smoke' suggests Simonides, but is better than any poem of Simonides" (*06W xxxiv*). The Greek poet he referred to was Simonides of Ceos, distinguished for lyric and epigram, who lived in the fifth century before Christ. But the precise reason for Emerson's reference cannot be determined from Emerson's own works, since he failed elsewhere to amplify his words. It may be that the statement glances at the way Simonides often caught the transient or fugitive, and delicately embodied it in the significant image of an epigram. Of this, an example might be the four lines on "Man's Luck." More probably Emerson had in mind the type of poem of which "Danaë and Perseus" is representative. This is an ornamental piece of verse that is highly adjectived and ends with an address to Zeus which is similar in form to the conclusion of Thoreau's poem.

It is with the latter connotation that the label "Simonidian" has been attached by the present editor to "Light-winged Smoke, Icarian bird" and a few other similar lyrics.

Julia Power (*Shelley in America*, p. 28) asserts that "Light-winged Smoke, Icarian bird" is an echo of "To a Skylark." Her point of view is not convincing. The differences between the two poems are far too many and too great (see further "To a Stray Fowl," note).

Orphics: this was the heading under which Thoreau first published the present poem and "Woof of the sun, ethereal gauze" (see that poem for note on the term).

28. "Die and be buried who will"

This quatrain comprises one of the most direct and concise statements by Thoreau on his view of nature.

29. "Where'er thou sail'st who sailed with me"

4. The *Brother* is John, who died tragically in January, 1842. He had been very close to Henry, and together they had taken a trip on the Concord and Merrimac Rivers which became the basis for the *Week*. Thoreau's friend and biographer, F. B. Sanborn (*Henry D. Thoreau* [Boston, 1886], p. 175) quotes the above quatrain as ending "my Brother John."

31. "I sailed up a river with a pleasant wind"

7. *THOU:* surely Henry Thoreau's brother John, although—to a person more formally Christian than Henry—the pronoun in its setting would fit the idea of God.

33, 34. "Ah, 'tis in vain the peaceful din"

Elsewhere Thoreau says:

On gala days the town fires its great guns,[1] which echo like pop-guns to these woods, and some waifs of martial music occasionally penetrate thus far. . . . When there were several bands of musicians . . . all the buildings expanded and collapsed alternately with a din (*BSWa II, 7*).

> [1] The gala days of Concord . . . were the 19th of April (anniversary of the Concord fight of 1775) and the 4th of July . . . —F. B. S[anborn] (*BSWa II, n7*).

At the dedication of the battle monument, July 4, 1837, Thoreau . . . was one of the singers of Emerson's well-known hymn . . . —F. B. S. (*BSWa II, n127*).

1. Note the use of a classical figure, oxymoron.

22. *That day* must have been April 19, 1775.

24. Of the two monuments at the Battleground, the stone here referred to is the one on which Thoreau reads that the war " 'gave peace to these United States' " (*06W 14*). Incidentally, Thoreau misquotes; the word *Independence* should be substituted for *peace*.

35. "But since we sailed"

It has been customary to index the quatrain "But since we sailed" and the last two stanzas as two separate poems. However, Thoreau made no such distinction, and he often printed a poem made up of different stanza patterns. So the verses here are not split—nor does the content of ll. 1-4 vs. ll. 5-17 show clearly the need of such a dichotomy.

5. This was Dr. Ezra Ripley, who baptized and catechized Thoreau and to whose sermons Thoreau long listened. Dr. Ripley had been dead for eight years when the *Week* was published. The year after his death, Nathaniel Hawthorne succeeded him in the Old Manse. There Hawthorne lived from 1842 through 1845 and wrote *Mosses from an Old Manse*.

9. *pierless:* perhaps one of Thoreau's puns.

15. *Manse:* the Presbyterian term for the residence of the minister.

36. "On Ponkawtasset, since, we took our way"

1. This was a hill on Thoreau's left as he floated down the Concord River, ultimately toward the town of Billerica.

3. The *poet* is Ellery Channing. Channing lived on Ponkawtasset Hill for a time; his residence there was two or three miles from Thoreau's hut at Walden, and he would visit Thoreau even through snows and tempests (*06Wa 295*).

20. *Cygnus:* the Swan, a northern constellation between Lyra and Pegasus.

37. "An early unconverted Saint"

This sentence prefaces "An early unconverted Saint":
It was a quiet Sunday morning, with more of the auroral rosy and white than of the yellow light in it, as if it dated from earlier than the fall of man, and still preserved a heathenish integrity (*06W 42*).

38. "Low in the eastern sky"

Sanborn quotes Marston Watson, acquaintance of Thoreau and litterateur, as saying in a letter: "I have always heard the 'Maiden in the East' was Mrs. Watson,—Mary Russell Watson,—and I suppose there is no doubt of it" (*06VI n329*). But aside from the fact that she and Thoreau lived in the same house (Miss Russell stayed at R. W. Emerson's too, during the summer of 1841 while tutoring Waldo Emerson), there is little to support Watson's statement. Henry Seidel Canby, Thoreau's latest and most penetrating biographer, says (*CT 112-114*) that these verses are to Ellen Sewall and implies that Thoreau was certainly in love with her when he wrote them.

7. *hill:* "Bare Hill by Walden" (*17S n353*).
Textual note (p. 291, l. j): during the time of Thoreau's warmest affection for Ellen Sewall, she was living in Scituate, which is east and somewhat south of Concord.

42, 43. "Conscience is instinct bred in the house"

No less critically, Thoreau elsewhere adds that conscience "is but the repose of a lethargy" (*JI 334*).

44. "Such water do the gods distil"

1. Thoreau, tracing the course of the Merrimac, describes its fine and classic water.

45. "That Phaeton of our day"

The *Phaeton of our day* is traditionally identified as Ellery Channing (see also "On Ponkawtasset, since, we took our way" and note).
Elsewhere Thoreau summarizes the Phaeton myth in a short, jocular paragraph (*BSWa II, 80*).

8. Phaeton scorched into being "the great desert of Sahara" (*BSWa II, 81*).

344

46. "Though all the fates should prove unkind"

The title in *Sea and Shore*, "Lines on New Hampshire Men Going to Sea," is drawn from the content of the paragraph preceding the poem in the *Week*.

47-50. "With frontier strength ye stand your ground"

"This poem," notes Ellery Channing in the copy of the *Week* that Thoreau inscribed to him, "appears originally in a piece called 'The Wild', but now 'A Walk to Wachusett'" (Channing's *49W 168*).

Textual note: "The Mountains in the Horizon": such would have been the concluding part of Thoreau's poem on Concord (*Jl 282*).

11. *emprise:* enterprise.

42. *croft:* a small enclosed field. Or perhaps the idea of tenantry is intended.

57. *Watatic Hill* (or Mountain), close inside the Massachusetts border, would lie between Thoreau and the Peterboro Hills.

60. *duds:* not only clothing, but also belongings in general (cf. *Jl 169; Jl 242*).

74. Mt. *Wachusett* would lie in the distance almost directly west of Thoreau, as he stood on the Concord Cliffs. Over 2,000 feet in height, it rises alone above the surrounding terrain. Thoreau sketched its outline in his Journal (*JlV 273*; and see further "Not unconcerned Wachusett rears his head" and note).

53. "Rumors from an Aeolian Harp"

Aeolian Harp: a long, narrow sound-box, with cat-gut strings stretched over it; when this instrument is placed across a window, the wind causes the strings to vibrate, with resulting sounds of various degrees of beauty. Oddly enough, it was the telegraph wires vibrating in the wind (Thoreau's "telegraph-harp") that enthralled him most.

16. Cf. "And looks commercing with the skies" ("Il Penseroso," l. 39).

54, 55. "Away! away! away! away"

The quotation is from "Paradise Lost," II, 535-538.

2. *Ye:* Milton, whom Thoreau otherwise regards very respectfully, is probably being addressed here. The indictment against him is based on the Thoreauvian doctrine of Life over Work. "Is not eternity a lease For better deeds than verse?"

56. "Low-anchored cloud"

Mist, haze, and fog: these provoked Thoreau to some of his finest poetry. He often observed them and described their effects.

57. "Man's little acts are grand"

11. Senegal tragacanth (gum tragacanth) comes from a shrub growing near the westernmost coast of Africa.

59. "Woof of the sun, ethereal gauze"

Thoreau labeled this poem and "Light-winged Smoke, Icarian bird" *Orphics* when he first published them in the *Dial*. Exactly what he intended by the word cannot be said. It is, of course, the adjective for *Orpheus*. Thoreau owned a copy of some of the poems ascribed to Orpheus (*17S 506*); and the name appears on a list of classical writers to be read which Thoreau prepared (*17S 520*). In Emerson's works Orpheus is the symbol for the classic, inspired singer of poetry (cf. further Bronson Alcott's "Orphic Sayings," which also appeared in the *Dial*). Thoreau apparently had much the same connotation in mind for *Orphic* as Emerson had.

7. *frith:* a narrow arm of the sea.

60, 61. "Where gleaming fields of haze"

6. The *Souhegan* River empties into the Merrimac in south central New Hampshire.

23. The Souhegan, in the last half of its course, runs down from the hills around Lyndeboro east to the Merrimac, which it joins at the city of Merrimack.

62. "This is my Carnac, whose unmeasured dome"

1. *This:* "our America and to-day," says Thoreau earlier. *Carnac:* the Hall of Columns, now unroofed, is the best-known part of the great temple at Karnak, Egypt.

6. *foil:* an architectural term for the space between two curved lines of material; or a curved ornament. However, it is possible that Thoreau is attempting an esoteric pun, with the architectural meaning lying beneath the meaning of *foil* as fencing weapon.

11. In post-Homeric Greek mythology, Memnon's mother was Eos (the Dawn). After a statue of Memnon near Thebes was partly overthrown, it gave out musical sounds each morning on being first touched by the rays of the sun. The sounds were supposed to be Memnon's greeting to his mother. Thoreau refers to the music of Memnon again in *Walden* (*06Wa 40*).

Textual note: *propylaeum:* in classical architecture, a vestibule or entrance.

63. "True kindness is a pure divine affinity"
1. *kindness:* cf. man*kind.*

64-66. "Lately, alas, I knew a gentle boy"
This is one of the two poems which were singled out by name in the "Biographical Sketch" of Thoreau by Emerson, who had had the poem printed in the *Dial.* Emerson remarked that this elegy "reveals the tenderness under that triple steel of stoicism, and the intellectual subtility it could animate" (*06W xxxiv*). A sentence in the Journal for the autumn of 1839 obliquely defines the meaning of the title in the *Dial,* "sympathy," and—more important—epitomizes the whole poem:

> The more complete our sympathy, the more our senses are struck dumb, and we are repressed by a delicate respect, so that to indifferent eyes we are least his friend, because no vulgar symbols pass between us (*JI 108*).

Of the poem, Sanborn says "His first verse printed (in the 'Dial') was that confession of love for Ellen Sewall"; and that she was the gentle boy is testified by Emerson, Theodore Parker, and "other persons who knew the facts" (*17S 350-351*). But Canby (*CT 110*) says her brother Edmund was the subject, agreeing with those who point out that Ellen did not come to Concord until the next month (July, 1839) after the poem had been written. Edmund had come into Henry's ken at the exactly appropriate time, visiting the Thoreau household in June, 1839. The testimony of Ellery Channing, since he was Thoreau's closest friend, ought to have been valuable on this point; but he observes merely, refuting another hazarded identification, that the lyric was "written to one E. S. not to [Thoreau's] brother John" (Channing's *49W 274*).
10. Cf. the title of Chaucer's poem.

67. "The Atlantides"
The last line of the poem is followed by a paragraph of prose, and that in turn is followed by another piece of verse. There is some similarity of theme in the two pieces, but not enough to ignore the intervening prose paragraph (as is done in *PN 17*). Moreover, the extra stanza is also found as a variant of an actual part of another poem, "The Friend" (see also "The Friend," textual note).
The legendary island of Atlantis was first described in Plato's *Timaeus.* It was supposed to lie just beyond the Pillars of Hercules (the Straits of Gibraltar); and beyond it were smaller islands.

2. *Phlegethon:* the river in Hades, according to Greek mythology, which ran with fire instead of water.

9-10. Some of the maps of the Middle Ages, and even later, indicated the location of Atlantis.

68. "My love must be as free"

The person addressed in this poem, Canby (*CT 263-265*) believes, may have been Margaret Fuller; and he suggests that ll. 5-6 refer to her Conversations.

69. "The Good how can we trust"

These closely reasoned verses spring in part from Thoreau's love of paradox, in part from his iron philosophy of conduct. The prose passage preceding emphasizes the clumsiness of the merely good-hearted: goodness is not enough.

70. "Nature doth have her dawn each day"

Despite its use of the masculine pronoun, this poem, to Canby (*CT 112*), describes a stage in the relationship of Thoreau and Ellen Sewall. But when Thoreau employs the word *mate* (l. 10) he may have a Miltonic usage in mind. Cf. Satan's scornful:

> ye knew me once no mate
> For you, there sitting where ye durst not soare"
> ("Paradise Lost," IV, 828-829).

71-73. "Let such pure hate still underprop"

Thoreau's quotation is an amalgam of two lines from *Julius Caesar*. Brutus begins his oration with "Romans, countrymen, and lovers" whereas Antony says "Friends, Romans, countrymen" (III, ii).

Thoreau's revision of the poem led him to make an interesting remark about long lines of verse as opposed to short ones. He put it into a letter to the first woman for whom he expressed his shy, stiff admiration, Mrs. Lucy Jackson Brown (see also "I am a parcel of vain strivings tied," note):

> My verses on Friendship are already printed in the *Dial;* not expanded, but reduced to completeness by leaving out the long lines, which always have, or should have, a longer or at least another sense than short ones (*06VI 38*).

The long lines referred to must be, in part, those which he later gathered together in his Journal and titled "Friendship's Steadfastness." Further, Marston Watson is quoted by Sanborn as writing that he added six new stanzas of Thoreau's to the poem on friendship in his copy of the *Dial*. He added that he thought they had been given to him by Mrs. Brown (*06VI 329*). The manuscript in *H* has those six stanzas. Five of them are chiefly in pentameter, making their lines longer, on the average, than those Thoreau kept in the later version of the poem. Certainly "Let such pure hate still underprop" benefits by their omission. Two of the stanzas are homelier in imagery and two more a bit maladroit and looser than the ones Thoreau let stay in the poem.

These verses furnish the best illustration of Thoreau's view of friendship. Independent, completely undemonstrative, but completely strong, it was one of his salient concerns. The Love-Hate motif is typical.

1. *still:* always. Thoreau sometimes used that older meaning.

11-16. Cf. Thoreau's poem "Love."

61-65. Thoreau prefixes a sentence to the poem that is equivalent to these lines: "We have nothing to fear from our foes . . . but we have no ally against our Friends, those ruthless Vandals" (*06W 305*).

74, 75. "The Inward Morning"

Canby says:

The growth of this poem has been confused by the tentative dating of this section of the Journal in December, which should be in some warm month, as the reference to the season (p. 295) and the general sequence show (*CT 465*).

But such misdating as was done was the work of Thoreau himself; and that was slight enough, involving merely the confusing of November and December. The Journal entry for the 15th does begin "A mild summer sun shines over forest and lake." But analysis of the rest of the entry and of the whole context helps to show that the quoted sentence could perfectly well refer to winter. The point is that Thoreau was expressing one of the minor, but by no means hidden, tenets of his philosophy. It is a variant of the Wordsworthian recollection in tranquillity, with the emphasis thrown on the comforting effect of the recollection. As Thoreau says in "Within the circuit of this plodding life":

I have remembered when the winter came . . .
How in the shimmering noon of summer past
Some unrecorded beam slanted across
The upland pastures.

Remarkable about this poem is its strong strain of philosophic idealism. Emerson, in the section on "Idealism" in the 1836 *Nature*, expresses a similar notion. *Nature* was, if not Thoreau's Bible, at least the Apocrypha; and the whole theme of "The Inward Morning" has an Emersonian cast to it. The theme also calls to mind, though with less

349

chance of there having been a seminal connection, Coleridge's "Dejection: An Ode."

26. *morning:* Thoreau generally considers morning as the most fertile time for poetic inspiration; but he also uses morning to connote any time of freshness.

76, 77. "My books I'd fain cast off, I cannot read"

The theme of these verses, and its general development, exhibits a parallel to Wordsworth's "Expostulation and Reply" and "The Tables Turned" (cf. *Jl 132*).

7-8. These lines are the key to the poem, developing as they do Thoreau's central idea of Life over Work. And, typically too, it is life in a delightful, natural setting.

11-14. Cf. the famous battle between the red and the black ants, written in the Journal and incorporated in *Walden* along with an added scholarly paragraph on decisive battles of the ant world (*06Wa 253-257*).

15-16. Cf. Pope's "An Essay on Criticism," l. 370: "When Ajax strives some rock's vast weight to throw." But a better source might well be the primary one, Book XII of Homer's "Iliad" (see *The Complete Works of Homer,* translated by Andrew Lang and others [New York, n.d.], p. 221).

78. "The Poet's Delay"

Worth noting are the similarities in thought and basic figure to the octave of Milton's sonnet "How soon hath Time the suttle theef of youth."

79. "Salmon Brook"

In what Sanborn considers the first draft of the *Week,* the paragraph before which this poem would appear contains details repeated in the poem which are not incorporated in the 1849 *Week.* Those details include mention of the silver eel and the creels (*FLJ I, 24*).

1-2. *Penichook* Brook, which Thoreau would reach first on his return trip down the Merrimac, joins that river a few miles north of Nashua, New Hampshire. Salmon Brook joins it a bit further south.

80. "I am the autumnal sun"

Thoreau displays in this poem one of his distinctive uses of nature metaphor. He draws his figure from nature, he applies it directly to himself, and he changes and widens his point of view within the compass of the poem. The poet begins "I am the autumnal sun" by identifying himself with merely a portion of nature; and he is microcosmic, not macrocosmic. At the end of the lyric, though, he has become the macrocosm. The details of nature are now part of him, and he has absorbed within himself the entire autumnal scene.

7. "My way of life Is fall'n into the sear, the yellow leaf" (*Macbeth*, V, iii). Cf. also the first quatrain of Shakespeare's sonnet "That time of year thou mayst in me behold" (lxxiii).

81, 82. "I am a parcel of vain strivings tied"

This poem was written on a sheet of paper wrapped round a bunch of violets, tied loosely with a straw, and thrown into the window of a friend. It was read at Thoreau's funeral by his friend Bronson Alcott (*PN 10*).

The friend was Mrs. Lucy Jackson Brown, a sister of Emerson's second wife. In spring, 1837, Mrs. Brown was boarding at the same house where Henry lived. She was the focus of Thoreau's first noticeable interest in the opposite sex. Later he wrote earnest and ethical letters to her (see further: *06VI 35-49; CT 71-73*).

While Thoreau was writing these lines, and for many years after, the cult of flower symbolism was highly popular. How much of that sort of symbolism the twenty-year old poet intended cannot be said; but the poem has additional meaning in terms of it. The violets, inevitably, stood for modesty. The sorrel stood for "wit ill-timed," which is surprising only until one considers both the situation in which the poem was originally sent and the content of the final stanza. (See, for instance, F. S. Osgood, *The Poetry of Flowers and Flowers of Poetry* [New York, 1841] and [Mrs. E. W. Wirt] *Flora's Dictionary* [Baltimore, 1835]).

The stanza form of this poem, in its sharp and intricate pattern, resembles those of the metaphysical poets, particularly George Herbert's (cf. his lyric "The Flower"). Herbert was an early favorite of Thoreau's.

37-42. Canby (*CT 74*) believes, with reason, that these lines imply that Thoreau sees that he will cast off his natural immaturity—and advance, a mature man.

83. "All things are current found"

Thoreau in this difficult poem implies a platonic duality consisting of the world of the spirit and the world of the senses, to which the elements of the world of spirit sometimes descend. This duality he wants to resolve by being taken himself into the world of the spirit. Yet it

351

must be admitted that the second stanza shows a belief in philosophic idealism, at least as far as the world of the senses is concerned. However, Plato (*e.g.* in the *Phaedo*) reconciles the conflict of duality and monity by indicating that the world of the senses and the world of the spirit are basically two aspects of a single unity. Further, an individual man may see only one of the two worlds. If he is gross, he will apprehend only the world of the senses. If he is climbing toward the higher life, he will apprehend both worlds. If he is completely spiritual, he will know only the world of ideas. Thoreau's position in this poem is that of the man aware of both worlds but wanting to rise to the higher.

It should be added that whatever platonism is here came very probably from no close study of Plato's works. But it might have come, for instance, from Emerson or Bronson Alcott. Emerson, early in his career especially, saw nature as "ancillary" to man. Alcott said that not the forms only but also the materials of natural things are "preconceived in man's mind" and bodied forth as the external natural world. However, neither of these Transcendentalist views hits off "All things are current found" fairly or completely.

85. "We see the *planet* fall"

See also textual note.

Any annotations on the content of couplets in the *Week,* aside from the couplets found on pp. 84-85, are to be found under the title of the longer poems of which they are a part.

86. "Voyagers Song"

The germ of this poem is a Spanish ballad, translated in Percy's *Reliques.* From it Thoreau took the first line, the stanza form, and the suggestion for the theme. Thus, Thoreau gave another example of how suggestible a poet he was, and how different his practice was from his theory of the organic unity and growth of the poem. The ballad is "Rio verde, rio verde." Elsewhere Thoreau copied the first two stanzas of the English translation, "Gentle river, gentle river" (*Reliques of Ancient English Poetry,* edited by H. B. Wheatley [London, 1910], I, 335). He changed a significant word, italicizing it, to make it fit the context of the *Week.* The Moorish chief became an *Indian* chief. In the manuscript of a part of the *Week* (*HM 13195*) he did not put quotation marks around the two stanzas, but in the printed version they are carefully added (*06W 175*).

One other element of possible, but only possible, influence on this lyric is to be found in the title of Thomas Moore's "A Canadian Boat-Song." Thoreau sang that song in the Maine Woods (*06III 42*). It was one of the few poems singled out for praise in this country when it appeared in *Odes and Epistles* (American edition, Philadelphia, 1806). Cf. "The Assabet."

87. "I love a careless streamlet"

Thoreau's poem appears, in his own hand, in an autograph album which also contains verses by various other members of his class at Harvard.

17-20. For a similarly unfortunate image, which Thoreau later removed though, see "When Winter fringes every bough," textual note. But observe that "I love a careless streamlet" may be humorously intended.

88. "To the Comet"

The heavenly bodies, especially meteors, were of marked interest to Thoreau; and his awareness of them is reflected in a number of places in the verse.

The first two lines of "To the Comet" are placed according to a strict following of Thoreau's instructions, but it is true that the form of the poem would improve if they did not appear right here.

1-2. This couplet answers a quatrain of George Herbert's which Thoreau copied into the *Week* (*06W 175*) thus:

A man that looks on glass,
 On it may stay his eye,
Or, if he pleaseth, through it pass,
 And the heavens espy ("The Elixir").

89-91. "Friendship"

A consideration of the content of this poem has led to the inclusion in the basic text, contrary to the usual procedure, of some lines that are cancelled in the manuscript. The final two-thirds of "Friendship" has a line drawn through it. But the fact that this produces so truncated a version and the fact that the cancellation is of the single-line variety (see Textual Preface) have resulted in the decision to print the full poem in the text.

This formal, carefully patterned, somewhat prolix piece of verse is characteristic of the best of Thoreau's early work. Its derivation from the work of such metaphysical poets as George Herbert is clear. It resembles his writing in stanza construction and in idea development. Thoreau's feeling toward Love-Friendship is much less marked than Herbert's toward his religion, and is blurred by paradox and over-intellectuality. Still, the piece has a youthful, stubborn strength of its own.

353

26-30. Such unification of truth, beauty, and goodness suggests platonism; so does Thoreau's general attitude toward friendship, in which there is more than a trace of Socrates' idealism about love between man and man—as exemplified in his concluding speech in the *Symposium*. But, once again, the platonism must have come second-hand. Thoreau said in *Walden* (*06Wa 119*) that he had never read Plato's Dialogues, and his few and indifferent references to Plato do not contradict this. Typically enough, he maintained that the wood thrush was "a more modern philosopher than Plato and Aristotle" (*JI 171*).

92. "The Cliffs & Springs"

Cliffs: probably the south side of Fair Haven Hill (see also "The Bluebirds," below).

93-96. "The Bluebirds"

The colloquial tone and homely details of these stanzas conflict with the obvious attempt at poetry that is regular in rhythm and sometimes formal in diction. In spite of these flaws, "The Bluebirds" is notable for including the most graphic account of a mystical experience in Thoreau's poetry.

37. *blowed:* this is Thoreau's customary usage (cf. *JIV 194; JXIII 119*).

44. Several cliffs roughly south of Thoreau's residence at this time make it hard to single out the one here mentioned. Perhaps it was the one indicated as being near Walden (ll. 10, 13). Then too, in this poem Thoreau uses the singular *cliff*; otherwise the geographical location implied would make "The Cliffs" (the better known name for Fair Haven Hill, says Sanborn [*BSWa II, n29*]) the logical choice. Herbert Gleason, in his map of Concord (*JXIV opp. 346*), however, marks the Cliffs as being only the southern slope of Fair Haven Hill. The answer probably lies in a fact that Miss Sarah R. Bartlett points out: either the singular or plural is used in Concord custom as the name for the side of Fair Haven Hill.

65. *bo-peep:* not the only time Thoreau has mentioned this childhood pastime (*06Wa 250*).

68. *Lima* is of course the Peruvian city, but a search of the atlases and gazeteers of Thoreau's time has failed to produce *Segraddo*. Porto Seguro, directly across the continent and in Brazil, may just possibly be the town Thoreau meant. Or, though it was not his habit, he may have invented the place.

97. "May Morning"

"In a pleasant spring morning all men's sins are forgiven" by one another (*JII 81*).

98, 99. "Walden"

Probably no other poem of Thoreau's bears the impress, in its style and tone, of the Wordsworth he read so attentively. The use of the word *converse* in the very first line affords a glance at the extent of the debt, for Wordsworth employs the same word—in the same general way—some two dozen times. But "Walden" is a Wordsworth made rhetorical to the point of conceits.

100. "Truth—Goodness—Beauty—those celestial thrins"

See also textual note.

1. *thrins:* apparently a coinage of Thoreau's (though others have coined it too) suggested, it may be, by an Old English word for *three*.

101. "In the busy streets, domains of trade"

This strong comment on urban trade typifies, in the simple class distinction that it makes, Thoreau's too plain yet powerful thinking in the field of economics. Both the mass of employees and their employers are struck off with harshness.

104. "Cliffs"

Cliffs: see "The Bluebirds," note.

105. "My Boots"

His boots were of real concern to Thoreau, as they would be to any good walker. So his Journal shows. The mock-Miltonic verse with which he celebrates them here is lumpish and heavy. However, it does show some study of the style in "Paradise Lost."

4. Three of the most famous wines of classical antiquity came from, respectively, the Greek islands of Chios and Lesbos and the Falernian district in southwestern Italy.

6. *sole:* one of the most leaden puns in Thoreau.

8. "No light, but rather darkness visible" ("Paradise Lost," I, 63).

106. "Noon"

1. *what time:* a classical formula.

355

107. "The Thaw"

Another expression of Thoreau's desire for union with nature, this is couched in a bold metaphor waveringly worked out. The image of l. 9 intrudes; l. 10 further disturbs the harmony of the comparison.

Arthur Christy (*The Orient in American Transcendentalism* [New York, 1932], p. 205) points out this poem as suggesting absorption into Brahma. It may be; but on the whole there is little orientalism in Thoreau's verse. Almost all the poems were written too early for it to leave any mark. Similarities between the thought in Thoreau's poems and oriental thought are mainly coincidental. It is Thoreau's own statement that puts the matter most justly:

> Like some other preachers, I have added my texts—derived from the Chinese and Hindoo scriptures—long after my discourse was written (*JIl 192*).

In one of the Journal versions of the poem there is an extra stanza (see textual note) which bears on Thoreau's famous incarceration. In 1838, says Canby (*CT 231*), Thoreau protested a church tax; and it was probably in 1846 that his refusal to pay the poll-tax resulted in his night in jail. The last line of the extra stanza compares with these words of his:

> I have never declined paying the highway tax, because I am as desirous of being a good neighbor as I am of being a bad subject ("Civil Disobedience," *06IV 380*).

108. "Last night as I lay gazing with shut eyes"

l1. The rest of the poem makes the reference to Rockaway fit Rockaway Beach, about ten miles from Staten Island, where Thoreau was to stay in 1843 with the family of William Emerson. But the poem is entered in the Journal under date of 1839.

The last line of the version in the *Week* substitutes *Nashua* for *Rockaway*. This alteration is made in order to fit the context, since Nashua, New Hampshire, is on the Merrimac River.

109. "Love"

Of the poets whom Thoreau read with care, it was Donne who most preferred the cosmological imagery that Thoreau employs here. However, the present editor has been unable to find examples of Donne's influence as tellingly displayed as is the influence of Herbert, Milton, and Wordsworth.

7. Among the varieties of cosmological imagery, the song of the spheres was particularly attractive to Thoreau. This was true not only

in the poetry but also in the prose (see, for instance: *JI 53; The Service, passim*).

110. " 'Twill soon appear if we but look"

2. *day book:* in bookkeeping, a ledger in which are recorded the debits and credits of each day in the order of transaction.

111. "The Peal of the Bells"

Sanborn says:

Thoreau had reason to know what were the gyrations and vibrations of the village bell; for he had often pulled the rope to ring one or another of the four bells in the village,—the Unitarian bell, the Orthodox bell, the bell of the county court house, and the school bell. In August, 1844, he had rung the court bell to call together Emerson's Emancipation audience (*BSWa I, 165*).

Musical sound had a surprisingly martial effect on Thoreau.

112. "The 'Book of Gems' "

The Book of Gems, edited by S. C. Hall and subtitled *The Poets and Artists of Great Britain,* was an elegant anthology. Its covers were rich with gilt and its plates chastely engraved. The first volume (London and Philadelphia, 1836) ran from Chaucer to Prior. The second (1837) began with Pomfret and ended with the now forgotten Bloomfield. There was probably no American edition of the third volume which followed; it ran from Wordsworth to Bayly, surveying the poets then alive.

113-115. "The Assabet"

Cf. the "Voyagers Song."

The Assabet joins with the Sudbury, at Nawshawtuct, to make the Concord River.

24. *naiads:* the water-nymphs, in classic mythology, of brooks and streams.

26. *cunning pack:* probably the naiads.

37. *storied pebble:* "Books in the running brooks, Sermons in stones" (*As You Like It,* II, i). Cf. *JV 28.*

47. Cf. "Guido's Aurora."

53. *voyageurs:* in Canada, traveling boatmen.

116, 117. "The Breeze's Invitation"

Prefacing his quotation of the last four stanzas of this poem (*FLJ I, 51*), Sanborn says it "seems to depict an imaginary voyage through the air with Ellen Sewall." Canby (*CT 112*) also points out that the lyric was copied into the Journal the very day Ellen arrived at the Thoreau's, and he agrees that the verses—if not written for her—at least describe Thoreau's amorous and playful mood.

The gracious and playful verse written in their youth by two of the greatest English poets informs "The Breeze's Invitation." The influence of Milton's "L'Allegro" is especially noticeable. The invitations, Come, etc., resemble one another. Zephyrus is mentioned in both poems. Then, while Milton's poem has the line "So bucksom, blith, and debonair," Thoreau writes of "Winnowing the buxom air." And at the end of his poem Thoreau echoes two lines that are near to the conclusion of Milton's lyric. For ll. 29-30, cf. "Lap me in soft *Lydian* Aires, Married to immortal verse" ("L'Allegro," ll. 136-137). The mark of the other great poet, Shakespeare, is of course not nearly so strong. Yet the fourth and fifth stanzas here are reminiscent of Mercutio's "Queen Mab" speech in *Romeo and Juliet,* (I, iv) and of the whole fairy atmosphere in *A Midsummer-Night's Dream.*

118. "Loves Farewell"

See also Raymond W. Adams, "Thoreau and Immortality," *Studies in Philology,* XXVI (1929), 58-66.

120. "I was born upon thy bank river"

1. This is correct in a metaphorical way; and here that is the most important way. But actually Thoreau's birthplace was almost a mile from the Concord River.

121-123. "The Fisher's Son"

In December, 1839, Henry went with John Thoreau to Scituate to visit the Sewall family; there, at the sea, he began to compose "The Fisher's Son" (*CT 113*).

In the extended and carefully wrought metaphor of this poem Thoreau states his case with dignity. Nowhere else does he so fully characterize his way of life. He explains his isolation from his neighbors without any trace of indifferent aloofness.

21. One of the few really bad conceits in Thoreau.
53. Cf. Thomas Moore's popular "Oft, in the stilly night."

Textual note (p. 308): *dulse:* coarse, red seaweed that is sometimes used for food.

358

124. "I'm guided in the darkest night"

Canby (*CT 120*) reads in this poem a confession of Thoreau's troubled love for Ellen Sewall.

2. *auroral light:* probably the aurora borealis.

3. Ellen's home in Scituate was east (and south) of Concord.

128. "My ground is high"

Only a line divides this poem, in the Journal version, from "If from your price ye will not swerve," which there follows it. But in the other collated version, *HM*, although only the first half of "My ground is high" appears, it is separated from "If from your price ye will not swerve" by the following several sentences of prose:

Buy a farm? Buy a broom! What have I to pay for a farm with that a farmer will take?

129. "If from your price ye will not swerve"

See "My ground is high," note, above.

131. "Death cannot come too soon"

If this quatrain is to be taken at face value, it represents the grim opposite of Thoreau's usual view about life. Probably he penned it during one of the occasional times when he felt, as he expressed it, mean and low. The lines are further seasoned, and complicated, by the dash of paradox.

132, 133. "Independence"

Mannered and rhetorical though it is, this poem summarizes Thoreau's noblest statements about civil independence.

134, 135. "Our Country"

In the present basic text, this subhead is added: "Copied from a Poem of Thoreau's Written about 1841." Sanborn says (*17S 277*) that this poem was submitted to the *Dial* but never printed by it. He adds (*17S 279*) that the manuscript shows slight pencil corrections by Thoreau.

3. *Madawaska:* probably the river close to the northern tip of Maine, and not the town of Upper Madawaska, which is right on the northern borderline of Maine as determined in 1842. *Red River:* the one, running into the Mississippi, which forms part of the present boundary between Oklahoma and Texas; from 1819 to 1845 it formed part of the southwestern boundary of the United States. Incidentally, Thoreau's

choice of these two rivers, at opposite corners of the country as he knew it, furnishes evidence for the independent dating of this poem. The northern boundary was not set till 1842, the southern was changed in 1845; so the composition of the poem very probably took place between those years. Sanborn, then, was not too far off in setting the date that he did.

4. The two places here named complement the location of the two in the line above, thus giving four corners of the country as it was then.

8. *licks:* usually salt springs or deposits, but here obviously referring to fresh water. But note that Sanborn reads the word *lakes* in *17S*.

21-24. It would be hard to realize, from this reference, how much the Indians attracted Thoreau's interest and sympathy. There is no token here of the mass of material, now in the Morgan Library, that he collected on them.

36-47. One of Thoreau's few divergencies into the Fourth-of-July nationalism of his time. These lines include most of the stereotypes, Anglo-Saxon supremacy and the Land of Promise among them. For another appearance of this mood of national eulogy, see "Walking" (*06V 218-223*), which is taken mostly from the Journal of 1850-1852.

46-47. Cf. Bryant, "Thanatopsis," ll. 73-75.

136. "The moon now rises to her absolute rule"

It may be that these verses should not be reckoned unpublished. Thoreau used a version of them later in the *Week* as a prose poem, introducing them there with this confession: "To an unskillful rhymer the Muse thus spoke in prose" (*06W 404*).

138. "I mark the summer's swift decline"

The basic text, *T*, ends with this notation: "Birds v fall of leaf." Its reference is clarified in *M1a*, where Thoreau has written after l. 2: "Vide Fall of the Leaf poem." Yet the lines do not appear either there or in the extensive work-sheets of "The Fall of the Leaf" to be found in Appendix A. The stanza pattern and content, however, show similarities. Furthermore, the stanza beginning with l. 37 in "The Fall of the Leaf" does deal with birds; so do the related lines in Thoreau's draft in Appendix A.

141. "Travelling"

The prose surrounding this poem in the Journal has no relevance; among the manuscripts Sanborn prints, however, there is a prose passage preceding the version of the poem printed there. It briefly pictures the quiet, sedentary lives of the New England farmers (*FLJ I, 128*).

The theme of the verses, unless it is developed with a double irony, flatly contradicts Thoreau's general position. His typical view is that man can do best by staying at home (see, for instance, "I seek the Present Time," textual note, p. 318, ll. a-d). Yet Thoreau himself traveled more than many of his townsmen; in the main, though, he devoted himself to cultivating his Concord neighborhood.

8. *divining wand:* a forked stick which, when held, was supposed to tip down on passing over a spot of earth where something precious was deposited.

15-20. One of the few Calvinistic passages (unless again it is meant as irony) in Thoreau; the view of life it expresses is typified in the general theology of Thomas Shepard, Increase Mather, Jonathan Edwards. The passage presents the critic with a problem similar in many ways to that offered by Emerson's "Grace."

142. "On fields oer which the reaper's hand has pass[e]d"

These lines are clearly the conclusion of a longer poem, as is testified by the fact that the leaf of manuscript preceding the one on which the poem appears has been removed from the ledger.

143. "To a Marsh Hawk in Spring"

The published Journal adds twenty-five lines to this lyric, but there is a sharp difference in content between those lines and the two quatrains of the present poem. More important, an examination of the manuscript Journal shows plainly that Thoreau intended two separate pieces of verse: there is a wide space between the two poems on the page. The extra lines are collated in the "Great Friend" (see also "Great Friend," note, below).

Cf. Bryant, "To a Waterfowl"; nor is the possibility of a connection any less because Thoreau replaces Bryant's God with his own Nature.

144. "Great Friend"

The variant version of these lines as given in the Journal was clearly intended as a separate poem (see also "To a Marsh Hawk in Spring," note, above). The case of the lines which Sanborn prints as the second stanza of "Solitude" (*FLJ I, 134*) is not so clear-cut. Still, "Solitude" remains only a variant of the "Great Friend"; and the additional lines, here called "I was made erect and lone," in the *HM* manuscript are written on an extra sheet of paper that is different in size, color, and make.

Beneath the cryptic irregularity of the "Great Friend" lies the confession of a profound dilemma in Thoreau's life. He felt that the world of nature was not enough. It did not fill all his human needs. On the other hand his standard of human friendship was so high that he could find no one able to rise to it. The ideal friend would, and must, transcend nature; and Thoreau actually, of course, never met a person who could do that.

Great Friend: cf. l. 1 of "The Friend."

145. "Yet let us Thank the purblind race"

3. Of the two monuments at the Battleground, the one here referred to gives 1836 as its date of erection.

146, 147. "Ive seen ye, sisters, on the mountain-side"

27. *sisters:* literally, Thoreau had two. Canby (*CT, passim*) gives an understanding portrait of Helen and Sophia Thoreau.

149. "On shoulders whirled in some eccentric orbit"

Thoreau, writing to Emerson about his little daughter, prefixes these three lines with "And now she studies the heights and depths of nature" (*06VI 55*). There is a bare possibility that they are a quotation, although Thoreau was punctilious about indicating quoted material.

2. *Paestum's temples* are among the most notable ruins in Greece. They include the so-called Basilica, Temple of Ceres, Temple of Neptune, and Temple of Peace.

151, 152. "Brother where dost thou dwell"

Perhaps the most moving poem ever written by Thoreau, this elegy reflects the profoundly felt loss of his brother John. John died at the age of twenty-seven in January, 1842, of lockjaw. The agony he suffered is said to have communicated itself "by sympathy" to Henry (see further Max Cosman, "Apropos of John Thoreau," *American Literature*, XII [1940], 241-243).

One strain, more personal than the rest, is found in the early version, *T*, but was taken out of the final draft by Thoreau. That is the comparison of John's achievement with Henry's. As Henry said, he "always lagg'd behind." Surely he must have meant that of himself metaphorically as well as literally.

154. "Ep[itaph] on the World"

These verses are distinctly unusual in the ornate completeness of their central metaphor. The result could not ordinarily be distinguished as Thoreau's.

155. "Epitaph on an Engraver"

In both *T* and *HMa*, this epitaph follows "Here lies an honest man" and is related to it in thought.

2. *lies:* for the full flavor of this pun of Thoreau's see "Here lies an honest man."

156, 157. "The Just Made Perfect"

This poem Sanborn (*17S 365*) blandly admits having polished, re-punctuated, and broken into stanzas.

The ascription of the date is based on Sanborn's statement that the verses were

sent in as a Rhapsody by Thoreau for the "Dial,"—never published, but endorsed by Emerson, from whom they came to me, "H. D. Thoreau, 1843" (*17S 362*).

However sincere the ethical theme of the poem may be, the preten-tiousness and rhetoric of the blank verse are happily unusual for Tho-reau. Judged formally, the metaphors clash and do not cohere; the gen-eral effect is weak. The number of similes is unusually large. Thoreau admired the similes of both Homer and Ossian; and it is not hard to see whose similes these resemble.

158, 159. "Tell me ye wise ones if ye can"

Thoreau's infrequent pessimism finds an outlet in the metaphor that establishes this poem.

16. *titmans:* cf. *titmice.*

18. "Like pygmies we fight with cranes" (*06Wa 101;* and cf. "Iliad," III, *5*).

161-163. "The Hero"

The form of this poem, which is one of the longest extant among Thoreau's verses, is close to that affected especially by Emerson but also at times by Ellery Channing and other Transcendentalist versifiers. It is marked by short lines, brisk rhythms, and couplet or triplet rhymes. Such a form does not lend itself easily to discipline, and in Thoreau's case, certainly, the poems couched in it do not show a diligent arrange-ment of ideas. But "The Hero" has length; and, though this may be a dubious virtue in the eyes of some critics of poetry, Emerson found it worth praising. He saw in some of Thoreau's pieces a healthy fullness that furnished a welcome contrast to the snatches by other contemporary poets.

Thoreau's most comprehensive ethical statement is to be noted in these lines.

33-34. Exodus, VII: 20.

40, 42. Cf. Ben Jonson, "Still to be neat, still to be dressed," particularly Thoreau's parallel use of *still*.

Textual note (p. 317, l. v): Matthew, XXV: 6.

79. *pulse:* beans, peas, lentils, etc.

165-167. "I seek the Present Time"

"I must live above all in the present" (*JIII 138*).

14. In the *Week* Thoreau quotes from Spenser's rendering of Du Bellay in the "Ruines of Rome" (*06W 264*).

27-40. The most Emersonian passage in this poem (cf. the paragraphs against traveling, near the end of "Self-Reliance").

49. *rent:* probably one of Thoreau's puns.

168. "Loves invalides are not those of common wars"

Perhaps the point of departure for these verses was the famous line in *Romeo and Juliet,* "He jests at scars that never felt a wound" (II, ii).

1. *invalides:* used, with this spelling, particularly in the eighteenth century, to describe disabled soldiers.

169. "And once again"

The two pages in the manuscript Journal before the one on which these verses appear are missing; hence the abrupt opening of the poem.

5. Cf. this statement by Thoreau (although it includes a wide use of the word *poetry*): "I do not mean to underrate Linnaeus's admirable nomenclature, much of which is itself poetry" (*JIII 257*).

170. "Old meeting-house bell"

Both internal evidence and a study of the *M3a* manuscript lead to the conclusion that these verses, although usually not indexed as a separate poem, should be parted from "The Old Marlborough Road," which immediately precedes them in the Journal.

1. The *bell* on the First Parish (Dr. Ripley's) Church, according to Miss Sarah R. Bartlett. Emerson, in 1841 (*Letters,* II, 394, 404), mentions that the original old meeting house was built in 1712 and now was to be torn down, a new building to be erected on the old frame.

171. "Is consigned to the nine"

The preceding part of this poem has been torn away in the manuscript.

1. *nine:* most probably the Muses.

4. *it:* the Transcendental, not the actual, Walden Pond (but see textual note).

172. "Among the worst of men that ever lived"

The pages preceding this poem are missing.

The text of this poem in the printed Journal reveals the most curious example of editorial picking and choosing to be found anywhere in the fourteen volumes of the Walden Edition of the Journal.

1-6. Here may be Thoreau's ironic recollection of a "philosophers' club" that lived briefly five years before "Among the worst of men that ever lived" was written down in the Journal. In 1845 Emerson, Thoreau, Alcott, Channing, and others convened at Emerson's home for the sake of conversation and mutual thought. When their first Monday meeting froze into silence, the philosophers addressed themselves to apples too ("Then to a heap of apples we addressed"). The club munched apples for two more Monday nights, but did little else, and so disbanded (see "Emerson" [by G. W. Curtis], in *Homes of American Authors* [New York, 1883], pp. 250-252).

7. *rider:* one piece (of wood, here) used to cover another. *Sine:* without (*Lat.*).

Note: The practice throughout this edition has been to allow parenthesized (that is, semi-cancelled) material to stand in the basic text, but to record the parenthesizing in a textual note. To let it stand in l. 7 would mean an incomplete reading that Thoreau most probably did not intend. In this case, consequently, the editorial practice is reversed.

8. *Icarian:* cf. "Light-winged Smoke, Icarian bird."

173. "Tall Ambrosia"

A paragraph of prose about blueberry bushes separates these verses from the following ones, "Th' ambrosia of the Gods 's a weed on earth," which are usually indexed as part of it.

4-5. Thoreau's revision here recalls one of the most famous sentences he ever wrote. When the July installment of "Chesuncook" appeared in the *Atlantic Monthly*, II (1858), Thoreau in anger saw that Editor James Russell Lowell had struck from the passage in praise of the pine tree its final sentence. "It is as immortal as I am, and perchance will go to as high a heaven, there to tower above me still" (*06III 135*) was too unorthodox a thought for the cautious Lowell. It was several years before Thoreau allowed anything further of his to go into the magazine, and then only at the solicitation of a new editor. In the fourth line of

"Tall Ambrosia" Thoreau first wrote "For to impartial science the humblest weed Is as immortal once[?] as the proudest flower." Next he firmly underlined *immortal* twice. But then he parenthesized it—his usual sign for a tentative deletion—in favor of *well named!*

10-17. See, for further indications of Thoreau's interest in shoes, "My Boots." Incidentally, Thoreau liked them stout and of cowhide as a rule, with special kinds for extraordinary weather.

16-17. *transported:* the reference is to England's practice of deporting her criminals to the colonies.

174. "Th' ambrosia of the Gods 's a weed on earth"

These lines evidently took their origin from the train of thought in "Tall Ambrosia." The facts that they are an obvious re-draft of the prior poem, rather than a continuation of it, and that a paragraph of irrelevant prose is interposed cause "Th' ambrosia of the Gods 's a weed on earth" to be considered a distinct piece here.

175. "I saw a delicate flower had grown up 2 feet high"

The first half of this poem is cancelled in the manuscript; but the fact that this results in a truncated version and the fact that the cancellation is of the single-line variety (see Textual Preface, p. 278) have combined to make the present editor decide to print the cancelled portion as part of the basic text.

Directly following these verses, but written as prose, this sentence is found in the manuscript Journal:

> And then it appeared that this brave flower—which grew between the wheel & horse—did actually stand farther out of the way than that which stood in the wide prairie where the man of science plucked it.

Here, therefore, is the first outstanding example of Thoreau's sinking from verse into prose. Several of the late pieces which follow also illustrate it; but the tendency is implicit even in Thoreau's early verse, which he sometimes first blocked out as prose.

Even the twenty-five lines printed as a poem in *JII* occupy the border between prose and poetry; they are very free free-verse. They are further notable for a moralistic, rather than a moral, tone—a rare quality in Thoreau.

3. The substantial farm of *J. A. Maynard,* whom Thoreau mentions elsewhere in the Journal, was on the Old Marlboro Road. *L. Dakin's* place was on a road running into the Old Marlboro Road.

176. "To day I climbed a handsome rounded hill"

Like the preceding verses, these lines run off into prose. In the Journal they are both written and printed as verse, but there is neither a break in syntax nor in sense between them and the prose following, which begins: "And the young sumacks enjoying the prospect—."

6. These are three towns southwest of Concord.

177, 178. "I am the little Irish boy"

The little Irish boy was Johnny Riordan, about whose childish stoicism Thoreau exclaimed in two versions (*JIII 149-150* and *nn242-244*) of the same prose passage. The poem is Thoreau's only sinking into the bravely pathetic. It also shows traces of the Wordsworthian bathos as seen in "Alice Fell" or, to a smaller extent, in "Simon Lee" (see further Frank Buckley, "Thoreau and the Irish," *New England Quarterly*, XIII [1940], 389-400).

9. *The deep cut,* made for the Fitchburg Railroad, was just west of Walden Pond.

179. "I do not fear my thoughts will die"

Several paragraphs on mountains precede this poem. The sentences coming just before its first line have both a scattering of rhymes and a non-prosaic rhythm:

Instead that I drive my cattle up in May I turn my eyes that way. My eyes pasture there & straightway the yearling thoughts come back. The grass they feed on never withers—for though they are not evergreen they're ever blue to me. For though not evergreen to you—to me they're ever blue.

5. That is, though all eyes reap the sky's beauty by seeing it, it never gives out.

180. "Cans't thou love with thy mind"

This poem is the first of a group of three kindred poems. The other two, which follow it, are more closely connected with one another. They are "Indeed indeed, I cannot tell" and "The vessel of love, the vessel of state." In *06VI* there are these two sentences of prose between the first two poems:

I need thy hate as much as thy love. Thou wilt not repel me when thou repellest what is evil in me (*06VI 202*).

But in the *HM* manuscript the sentences are replaced by a substantial block of three paragraphs of prose. The theme of "Cans't thou love with thy mind" is the universality implicit in loving some one person; while

367

the theme of "Indeed indeed, I cannot tell" is a variant of the frequent Love-Hate motif. The last poem, the unpublished "The vessel of love, the vessel of state," is a natural product—although not a continuation—of the idea of the poem before it. Furthermore, it is separated in the *HM* manuscript from "Indeed indeed, I cannot tell" only by a space.

7-8. Cf. the conclusion of "Let such pure hate still underprop."

181. "Indeed indeed, I cannot tell"

See "Cans't thou love with thy mind," note, above.

11-14. Cf. the beginning of "Let such pure hate still underprop." Worth noting too is the echoing phrase in l. 1 of that poem and l. 14 of "Indeed indeed, I cannot tell."

182. "The vessel of love, the vessel of state"

See "Cans't thou love with thy mind," note, above.

1. *state:* an echo of the word *hate*, judging especially by the context of the whole group of three poems.

183. "When the toads begin to ring"

1. *ring:* this natural detail attracted enough of Thoreau's attention after this period to make him record it several times (cf. *JIX 349; JIX 354*).

184. "Forever in my dream & in my morning thought"

In this, the last poem in the Journal, Thoreau's latest handwriting is well evidenced by—among other things—the number of words that he did not bother to complete.

2. The rhyme-word in l. 4 shows that Thoreau must have preferred *ascends* more definitely than his parenthesizing usually indicates. *Uprears itself* is parenthesized; but usually that does not mean a definite cancellation. Here, though, it seems to.

7. *staff & cup:* of the pilgrim.

186. "On a Good Man"

Both texts of this epitaph are part of a series that Thoreau composed, a series that includes "Here lies an honest man," "Epitaph on Pursy," "Ep[itaph] on the World," and "Epitaph on an Engraver." They all mock the pious platitudes Thoreau must have read in New England graveyards; and they all reveal his interest in playing with the pun on *lies.*

189. "For though the caves were rabitted"

This fragment of a sentence precedes the first line of the *HM* version: "—walked through a country town deserted streets—now in the ninth year of the plague."

191. "No earnest work that will expand the frame"

The opening of the basic version has not been found. The first line here begins at the very top of the manuscript leaf.

192, 193. "Godfrey of Boulogne"

Few other poems cast as unfavorable a light on Sanborn's manner of editing.

Sanborn prints a passage mentioning Godfrey which he says is from the "Red Book," the early Journal which ran from October, 1837, to June, 1840 (cf. *JI 158*).

This literary ballad is singled out among Thoreau's verses by its subject matter as well as its swashing rhythms and refrain. It is not hard to see that it is youthful work although far from being the earliest, as Sanborn assumes, of Thoreau's poetry. He says:

> What we suppose to be the earliest sample of Thoreau's verse that has been preserved, is a ballad, written in his college period. . . . It savors both of Tasso and of Mrs. Hemans (*17S 249*).

It celebrates Tasso's hero.

According to history, Godfrey of Bouillon (*c.* 1060-1100) led a German contingent along "Charlemagne's Road," through Hungary down to ancient Byzantium, now Istanbul, in 1096 at the onset of the First Crusade. After that, he went on to Jerusalem. In Thoreau's poem the second stanza describes the march through the Alps, the third Godfrey's battling in Hungary, and the fourth his arrival in Byzantium.

194. "Who equallest the coward's haste"

The idea of this quatrain is refined out of paradox into a statement that resembles the theme of Emerson's poem "Brahma."

195. "Ive searched my faculties around"

If this quatrain is to be read literally, it does not fit Thoreau's life. It should probably be taken as a metaphor, however, with God standing for the Thoreauvian inner light.

196. "Until at length the north winds blow"

This quatrain is prefaced by a passage in which Thoreau describes the flight southward of the smaller birds as autumn deepens (*FLJ 1, 132*).

197. "I was made erect and lone"

Sanborn prints these lines as the second stanza of "Solitude" but apparently they merely happen to follow the original leaf of manuscript on which the first stanza (which Thoreau elsewhere considers an entire poem) is written (see also "Great Friend," note). It might be added that a number of the leaves in the Huntington holdings, of which these are a part, are obviously in wrong order.

198, 199. "Wait not till slaves pronounce the word"

The quotation is from Vergil's "Aeneid" (XI, 309). It is also the motto of *The Service*. The translation given is by Thoreau.

Here is Thoreau's most vigorous announcement that genuine freedom must start within the individual. To those who agitate for freeing the slaves he says "physician, heal thyself." Nevertheless, Thoreau's stand in favor of emancipation shows that he also saw the need of external aids to freedom. One sentence from the Journal epitomizes the poem:

I wonder men can be so frivolous almost as to attend to the gross form of negro slavery, there are so many keen and subtle masters who subject us both (*JI 362*).

23. *disparting:* separating, but used in the sense of dividing up, for instance, loot. Thoreau also uses this unusual word in one other poem, "Farewell" (see textual note), with a different connotation.

43. *Empire State:* this term for New York State has been traced back to a speech by Washington in 1783 (Charles F. Horne, *History of the State of New York* [Boston, 1916], p. 417).

200. "To the Mountains"

Sanborn thinks, justly, that these verses are a fragment of a longer work.

3-8. A dependently religious tone is revealed here that is rarely found in Thoreau.

14. *civil demons:* among semi-civilized peoples, demons, or spirits who entered into relations with human beings, were either malevolent or benevolent.

18. *"civil-suited" night:* cf. "Till civil-suited Morn appeer" ("Il Penseroso," l. 122). Incidentally, *Daemons* (cf. l. 14, above) are mentioned earlier in the same poem.

201, 202. "The Friend"

In spite of the fact that a substantial paragraph of prose intervenes, it has been customary to index the lines from the *Week* here collated against part of "The Friend" as the concluding stanza of "The Atlantides." The present editor sees no reason for continuing this practice, the more so because the lines in question form some part of the *HM* manuscript of "The Friend."

1. Cf. the title of another poem of Thoreau's, the "Great Friend."

203, 204. "Upon the bank at early dawn"

7-8. Thoreau also uses this figure in the *Week* (*06W 365*).

208. "He knows no change who knows the true"

These lines, along with one other set, are as close to pure platonism as Thoreau ever comes.

209, 210. "The Departure"

Sanborn believes the poem must refer to Thoreau's first stay (not the second stay, as he thought earlier in his *Henry D. Thoreau*, p. 282) at the R. W. Emerson home and his departure from it before going to reside with William Emerson in the spring of 1843 (*17S 499*). Canby (*CT 171*) agrees. Certainly, if Thoreau's biography is in his verses, here is one of the best examples. Nor does the reticent shift from first to third person, after the opening stanza, make the meaning of the poem any less valid. However, the shift appears to be a flaw, formally.

The whole poem is a thoughtful metaphor and furnishes one of the few examples of deeply communicated emotion to be found in the poetry of Thoreau. Its atmosphere has something almost indefinably Anglo-Saxon in it; the verses here could be a gentler companion to "The Wanderer." The same sort of metaphor appears in the Journal for October 19, 1840 (quoted in *CT 118*).

211. "The Funeral Bell"

Thoreau here achieves what is distinctly one of the lovelier of his lyrics through a disciplined though traditionalized use of stanza form and rhythm. As a rule, his ear, sensitive to the "telegraph harp" and music box, was indifferent to the making of melodious rhythms in his own poetry.

4. If Thoreau intends any local reference in this poem, the church-bell is that of Dr. Ezra Ripley's church. It is still, according to Miss Sarah R. Bartlett, tolled at the death of a well-known townsman of Concord.

212. "The Virgin"

Sanborn refers these verses to a prose passage in which Thoreau says:

My most intimate acquaintance with woman has been a sisterly relation, or at most a catholic virgin-mother relation (*FLJ 1, 106*).

213, 214. "Speech of a Saxon Ealderman"

Thoreau's headnote to the manuscript reads:

"Delivered in (Witena gemot) the assembly of the wise, convened at Godmundingaham (the protection of the Gods) now Godmundham, a little to the east of York, by Edwin king of the province of Northumbria, in 625, to consider the propriety of receiving the Christian faith."

This, the most famous incident in English religious history of that period, had a great deal of interest for Thoreau. Into a college commonplace book now in the Morgan Library he copied, first of all, an Old English version, heading it "King Alfred's translation." Then, next to it and parallel with it on the page, he entered an English translation, probably his own, of the Old English. Thereafter, he quoted Sharon Turner's translation of the incident. Finally, rephrasing Turner's prose, Thoreau composed his own poem on the subject.

Which edition of Turner's *The History of the Anglo-Saxons from the Earliest Period to the Norman Conquest* Thoreau used has not been determined. Only the second edition is listed as being in the Harvard College Library when he was in residence, and there the whole conversion of Edwin is dismissed in a paragraph of only three lines. The earliest of the expanded editions of Turner's popular work that has been available to the present editor is the sixth (London, 1836); and it, along with two editions that follow, includes the incident in a form that differs only minutely from the passage Thoreau copied into his commonplace book.

Additional light on Thoreau's method of composition is cast by the passage from Turner as he copied it (cf. the sixth edition, I, 355-356):

The present life of man, O king, seems to me, if compared with that after-period which is so uncertain to us, to resemble a scene at one of your wintry feasts. As you are sitting with your Ealdormen and thegns about you, the fire blazing in the centre, and the whole hall cheered by its warmth,—and while storms of rain and snow are raging without,—a little sparrow flies in at one door, roams around our festive meeting, and passes out at some other entrance. While it is among us it feels not the wintry tempest. It enjoys the short comfort and serenity of its transient stay; but then, plunging into the winter from which it had flown, it disappears from our eyes. Such is here the life of man. It acts and thinks before us; but, as of what preceded its appearance among us we are ignorant, so are we of all that is destined to come afterwards. If, then, on this momentous future this new doctrine reveals anything more certain or more reasonable, it is in my opinion entitled to our acquiescence.

215. "Farewell"

This elegy is evidently to Thoreau's older sister, Helen, who died in 1849. The same disease, tuberculosis, turned out to be fatal for both of them. Henry's correspondence with her reflects an intellectual intimacy.

Textual note (p. 328): *dispart:* cf. "Wait not till slaves pronounce the word," note.

29-30. There is, perhaps, an echo here of what Ellery Channing called one of Thoreau's favorite quotations:

Unless above himself he can
Erect himself, how poor a thing is man! (Samuel Daniel,
    "To the Lady Margaret, Countess of Cumberland.")

216. "Nature"

Here is the most explicit statement in Thoreau's verse of his relation to nature. That he is sincere, no one with a knowledge of his general position can doubt. But he strikes an attitude throughout the whole poem, and mars his meaning by the pastoral artificiality of his style.

2. *quire:* variant of *choir.*
3-4. Cf. "To the Comet."

217. "Guido's Aurora"

"Suggested by the print of Guido's 'Aurora,' sent by Mrs. Carlyle as a wedding gift to Mrs. Emerson" (*PN 19*).

This fragment exhibits a fairly literal examination of Guido Reni's popular painting, "Phoebus and the Hours Preceded by Aurora." Reproductions of it hung in many a nineteenth century American parlor. Elsewhere Thoreau reflects that

true art is not . . . to be wrought at in parlors . . . but [is] such a master-piece as . . . a human life, wherein you might hope to discover more than the freshness of Guido's Aurora (*JI 167*).

218. "Greece"

"In imagination I hie me to Greece as to enchanted ground" (*JI 29*).
Thoreau's deep admiration for classic Greece is in these verses outstand-

ingly testified. It was its literature, not its philosophy, that left the greatest imprint on him.

219, 220. "Poverty"

The poem gives Thoreau's most particularized poetic statement about one of his central doctrines. *Walden* could begin with these lines.

The abrupt force of the opening, as well as the general style of the poem, is reminiscent of a poet whom Thoreau admired (with qualifications), quoted, and copied into his commonplace books: John Donne.

222. "What sought th[e]y th[u]s afar"

5-10. The quoted verses are by Ellery Channing. It was Channing who identified many of the authors from whom Thoreau quoted in the *Week*. The last two lines of the present passage appear in that work; and opposite them, in the copy of the *Week* that Thoreau gave him, Channing has pencilled his own name (Channing's *49W 104*). The quoted passage, furthermore, is also found in a commonplace book of Thoreau's now in the Library of Congress. In that place, the version, although annotated by an unknown hand as being an original poem by Thoreau, is headed "C———."

223. "Music"

In few other poems does Thoreau exhibit as close affinities with Wordsworth as he does in the first paragraph of this. Yet the notable point of the poem is not its resemblance to the "Ode, Intimations of Immortality," but the music motif. The power of music, even of the "telegraph harp," over him, Thoreau frequently testifies. And the present poem takes the Wordsworthian idea and gives it a striking bias: it is music that will bring Thoreau renovation (see also "Manhood").

6. *boyant:* here apparently is another of Thoreau's puns; and his spelling helps to underline the interplay.

9. *This:* probably music.

224. "I'm thankful that my life doth not deceive"

These lines are on the same double sheet as is one version of "Life"; and the two poems are suffused with the identical creative atmosphere.

Here the dominant tone and form show an influence which is far from new—that of Wordsworth's blank verse. Yet the conclusion of the poem, specifically ll. 19-24, suggests some of the stately and heavy pastoral poetry of the late eighteenth century, something certainly not frequent in Thoreau. The last lines have the calmness, though not the portending solemnity, of the opening of Gray's "Elegy."

It is hard to decide why Thoreau cancelled the last two lines of the poem (see textual note). They round out the lyric and give it finality.

8. *it:* still *my life.*

225. "Manhood"

Of all Thoreau's poems, this is one of the two bearing the strongest stamp of Wordsworth. It is the Wordsworth particularly of the great "Ode, Intimations of Immortality." But it is Wordsworth pondered, weighed, and in good part rejected. The center of the ode's ideas serves merely as a point of departure for Thoreau. He gives his own poem determined independence instead of philosophic acquiescence. He stresses not the infant, but the upstanding man; not the loss of innocence, but the gain of moral strength.

226. "The moon moves up her smooth and sheeny path"

12. *a rod:* Mr. Albert E. Lownes points out in favor of this reading that Thoreau, as a surveyor, would be used to such a term of measurement.

227. "Life"

Marked with bold, ill-chosen metaphors, this poem represents an unusual mingling of the Wordsworthian and the metaphysical strains in Thoreau's poetry.

228. "Pray to what earth does this sweet cold belong"

Sanborn says these verses were included in the manuscript of "A Winter Walk" but were omitted by Emerson when he printed the essay in the *Dial.*

10. *titmice:* chickadees.

230-233. "Inspiration"

In this famous poem is to be found Thoreau's richest mine of self-quotation as well as his most notable utterance about the way poetry begins. The philosophy at the heart of the poem is Transcendental and dualistic—with the dualism stressing, naturally, not the material but the ideal. The Emersonian doctrine of union with the Over-Soul is, furthermore, clearly paralleled; and that union is described in terms so strong that they might be used by a mystic.

The especially interesting thing about the poem in its external relations is the denial of its thesis by Thoreau's actual method of composition. Instead of springing from inspiration, the poem was the result of careful culling from a large stock of poetic stuff (for which see Appendix A), while the poem in turn was culled for quatrains and couplets to fit into the prose of the *Week*. "Inspiration," along with "The Assabet," furnishes the best example of the eclecticism out of which much of the verse came into being.

234. "Inspiration"

Cf. the related idea in the longer "Inspiration."

239-242. "A Winter and Spring Scene"

Sanborn says (*17S 261*) that Emerson excluded this poem from "A Winter Walk" when he printed it in the *Dial*.

This is probably the major attempt at detailed description in Thoreau's verse; and even this is far from minutely particularized.

10. *marmot:* woodchuck.
15. *flag:* the iris.
62. *Bum:* hum (*dial.*).
79-82. Cf. "The Thaw."

243. "Why do the seasons change? and why"

This quatrain of Thoreau's heads what Sanborn calls "a faultless specimen of his composition at about the age of ten" (*17S 51*). It is followed by Thoreau's brief characterization of the four seasons. According to Sanborn, the composition was brought to light by Alfred Hosmer.

244. "Friends! that parting tear reserve it"

Canby (*CT 460*) implies that the quatrain is Thoreau's own work. The doubt about its authenticity is based on the fact that Thoreau put quotation marks around it; and he was, as a rule, careful thus to designate material drawn from other writers. On the other hand, this bit of verse is in precisely the vein that some of his youthful pieces would lead anyone to expect.

245. "In Adams fall"

The opening two lines of this quatrain are from the famous *New-England Primer,* where they adorn the first letter of the alphabet. The last two lines are original.

376

246. "In times of yore, 'tis said, the swimming Alder"

These lines are part of a letter by Thoreau, dated from Concord, to Charles Wyatt Rice (first printed by E. B. Hill, Mesa, Arizona, 1916[?]). Sanborn says that he has restored "the rhythmical passage into what may have been its original form" (*17S 61*). The first stanza Sanborn thinks a rendering of Ovid; the rest he deems Thoreau's own.

The three collated lines are from a college theme on the story-telling faculty.

7-13. Of the editions of Mother Goose, it may be that the one Thoreau refers to was *The Original Mother Goose's Melody*, reprinted by Isaiah Thomas at Worcester, Massachusetts *c*. 1785 (reproduced in facsimile, with introduction by W. H. Whitmore, Albany, 1889). There the quatrain reads:

> Three wise Men of *Gotham*
> They went to Sea in a Bowl,
> And if the Bowl had been stronger
> My Song had been longer (p. 21).

In a Harvard manuscript Thoreau also deigns to quote "Goosey Goosey Gander." Nor is this the only other time he shows a knowledge of Mother Goose.

247. "By his good genius prompted or the power"

The cadence here is nearer to Milton than to Thoreau. But the fragment is not Milton's, however, nor does Thoreau begin it with a quotation mark. If by Thoreau, this bit of verse is heretofore unpublished.

Enlarged Edition:
Added Poems

When little hills like lambs did skip,
And Joshua ruled in heaven,
Unmindful rolled Musketuquid,
    Nor budged an inch Fair Haven.

When principle is like to yield,
To selfish fear, or craven,
And fickle mortals round me fall,
    I'll not forget Fair Haven.

If there's a cliff in this wide world,
'S, a stepping stone to heaven,
A pleasant, craggy, short hand cut,
    It sure must be Fair Haven.

Oft have I climbed thy craggy steep,
Where ceaseless wheels the raven,
And whiled away an hour at e'en,
    For love of thee, Fair Haven.

If e'er my bark be tempest-tossed,
And every hope the wave in,
And this frail hulk shall spring a leak,
    I'll steer for thee, Fair Haven.

When cares press heavy on my soul,
And devils blue are craven,
Or e'er I lay me down to rest,
    I'll think of thee, Fair Haven.

And when I take my last long rest,
And quiet sleep my grave in,
What kindlier covering for my breast,
    Than thy warm turf Fair Haven.

Life is a summer's day
When as it were for aye
    We sport and play.

Anon the night comes on,
The ploughman's work is done,
    And day is gone.

We read in this one page
Both Youth, Manhood, and Age
    That hoary Sage.

The morning is our prime,
That laughs to scorn old Time,
    And knows no crime.

The noon comes on apace,
And then with swel'tring face
    We run our race.

When eve comes stealing o'er
We ponder at our door
    On days of yore.

The patient kine, they say,
At dawn do frisk and play,
    And well they may.

By noon their sports abate,
For then, as bards relate,
    They vegetate.

When eventide hath come,
And grey flies cease their hum,
 And now are dumb,

They leave the tender bud,
That's cooling to the blood,
 And chew the cud.

————

Let's make the most of morn,
Ere grey flies wind their horn,
 And it is gone.

I'VE HEARD MY NEIGHBOR'S
PUMP AT NIGHT

I've heard my neighbor's pump at night,
Long after Lyra sunk her light,
As if it were a natural sound,
And proper utterance of the ground—
Perchance some bittern in a fen—
Or else the squeak of a meadow hen.

Who sleeps by day and walks by night,
Will meet no spirit but some sprite.

WHEN WITH PALE CHEEK
AND SUNKEN EYE I SANG

When with pale cheek and sunken eye I sang
Unto the slumbering world at midnights hour,
How it no more resounded with war's clang,
And virtue was decayed in Peace's bower;

How in these days no hero was abroad,
But puny men, afraid of war's alarms,
Stood forth to fight the battles of their Lord,
Who scarce could stand beneath a hero's arms;

A faint, reproachful, reassuring strain,
From some harp's strings touched by unskilful hands
Brought back the days of chivalry again,
And the surrounding fields made holy lands.

A bustling camp and an embattled host
Extending far on either hand I saw,
For I alone had slumbered at my post,
Dreaming of peace when all around was war.

I arose before light
To work with all my might,
With my arms braced for toil
Which no obstacle could foil,
For it robbed me of my rest
Like an anvil on my breast.

But as a brittle cup
I've held the hammer up,
And no sound from my forge
Has been heard in the gorge.
I look forward into night,
And seem to get some light;
E're long the forge will ring
With its ding-dong-ding,
For the iron will be hot
And my wages will be got.

I WILL OBEY THE
STRICTEST LAW OF LOVE

I will obey the strictest law of love
As if I dealt with cherubim above.
    I will accept no half gift from my friend
    By which he thinks for hate to make amend.
But every friendly thought
Will come to me unbought
    My friend may do whate'er he will
      And I shall love him
        If he doth it from love.
    But let him do whateer he will
    I think that I must hate him still
      If lower motives move.

    I love not all
      I love not one alway
But that I love is one & all
    And lasteth ever and aye.

I will leave him I hate
    And cleave to him I love
I will forsake my earthly mate
    And seek my mate above.

Though my friends are dull and cold
I will be quick and warm.
Though their love groweth old
Mine shall be new born

Though they understand me not
   I shall be understood
Though by them I am forgot
   Not therefore by the good.

   My friend can wound me
   For to him I bare my breast—
   But his wounds save me
   From a foe's embrace
      But these are honorable scars
      And fit the wounded heart for Love's more glori-
      ous wars.

   These wounds are not fatal though inflicted on the
      heart
   For the heart's not less a vital than a mortal part.
      Unlike the inferior part
         The wounded heart
      Is not repaired with wood
      But by fresh currents from above
      Which fit it for a purer love
For all that's true & beautiful & good.

Alas, when will this roving head & breast
Be welded to that firm & brawny beast?
The sun may set the silver moon may rise
But my unresting steed holds on his way
He is far gone ere this, then, you would say.
He is far going.
The eagle sailing high with outspread wings
cleaving the silent air, Resteth him not
An instant in his flight, the air is not his perch
No more my steed slackening his onward pace
Dismounts his rider by the tedious way
my bark neer furls its weatherbeaten sails
And rest[s] its keel upon a friendly shore—
But still it plows the shoreless seas of time—
Breasting the waves with an unsanded prow

Who hears the parson
Will not hear the bell,
But if he deafly pass on
He will hear of hell.

I' faith the people go to church
To leave the devil in the lurch,
But since they've carpeted the pews
To squat with hymn book he doth use.

FRIENDS

Friends—
They cannot help,
They cannot hurt,
Nor in indifference rest,
But when for a host's service girt,
They are a mutual guest.

They are a single power
Plenipotentiary,
No minister of state,
Anxious and wary
Decides their fate.

Where interest's self is
There is no go-between,
But where another reaps,
They do but glean
In scanty heaps.

They have learned well to hate,
And never grant reprieve,
Nor e'er succumb to love,
But sternly grieve,
And look above.

———

If faults arise, my friend will send for me
As some great god,
Who will the matter try,
Holding the scales, even or odd,
Under the sky—

Who will award strict justice
All the while,
Confounding mine and thine,
And share his smile,
When they 'gainst me incline.

When in some cove I lie,
A placid lake at rest,
Scanning the distant hills,
A murmur from the west,
And gleam of thousand rills
Which gently swell my breast,
Announce the friendly thought,
And in one wave sun-lit
I'm softly brought
Seaward with it.

The blossoms on the tree
Swell not too fast for me.
God does not want quick work but sure
Not to be tempted by so cheap a lure.

Owing to slow steps I shall be never
By my friend out run,
More than the tide can land from ocean sever,
Or earth distance the sun.

The friend is patient, he can stay
Some centuries yet,
Though then I may not get
So on my way
As fit to be his mate.

Wilt thou not wait for me my friend,
Or give a longer lease?
Why think I can wait for myself,
If so I please.

Now as ye take one step away
Thinking to leave me here—
The heavens will still beyond ye lay,
And though ye are far they will be near.

Ye will be pilgrims on the road
Whither my heart has single gone,
And never looks back from its abode
On ye thus left forlorn.

Love equals swift and slow
And high & low—
Racer and lame—
The hunter and his game.

Thou little bud of being, Edith named,
With whom I've made acquaintance on this earth,
Who knowest me without impediment,
As flowers know the winds that stir their leaves,
And rid'st upon my shoulders as the sphere,
Turning on me thy sage reserved eye,
Behind whose broad & charitable gaze
Floats the still true & universal soul
With the pure azure of the general day,
Not yet a peopled & a vulgar town,
Rather a pure untarnished country ground;
For thou art whole, not yet begun to die,
While men look on me with their shrivelled rays
Streaming through some small chink of the broad sky;
Pure youthful soul, thou hast begun to be,
To cumulate thy sin & piety.

As often as a martyr dies,
This opes its petals to the skies;
And Nature by this trace alone
Informs us which way he is gone.

APPENDIX TO ADDED POEMS

Under the somewhat ambitious title of "Thoreau's New Poems" (*Emerson Society Quarterly*, 1959, 21-32), Kenneth Cameron prints facsimiles of a group of Thoreau's verses now accessible in the Washington University Library. Most of the poems are not new. They have been printed either by Thoreau himself or, more usually, by his editor F. B. Sanborn, and then reprinted in the *Collected Poems*. In general their usefulness lies in providing manuscript authority and furnishing variants and additional passages. Annotated typescripts of the same texts are printed in "Thoreau Poems in Bixby Washington-University Manuscripts" by Laurence Cummings (*Emerson Society Quarterly*, 1962, 9-28). In both Cameron and Cummings the manuscripts are cited as A, B, C, D, E, and F. Their correlation with verses in the *Collected Poems* is as follows:

MS A: *Collected Poems* 37 ("An early unconverted saint") and 290 for textual additions and variants. In MS A the verses are preceded by nine new but cancelled lines and include in addition three new uncancelled lines.

MS B: *Collected Poems* 137 ("My friends, why should we live") and 311 for textual variants. In MS B four new uncancelled lines follow line 4 and one new uncancelled line follows line 8.

MS C: *Collected Poems* 181 (lines 11-14 of "Indeed indeed, I cannot tell") preceded by five uncancelled and six cancelled lines; 180 (lines 5-8 of "Cans't thou love with thy mind") preceded by twenty-six uncancelled lines and eight cancelled lines; 180 (lines 1-4 of "Cans't thou love with thy mind") preceded by eighteen uncancelled lines and two cancelled lines; 69 ("The Good how can we trust").

MS D: *Collected Poems* 156 ("The Just Made Perfect"). In MS D there are an additional fifteen lines at the end, all but one of which represent simply a recasting of some of the lines above them.

MS E: Called "The Centaur," this is the one new poem in the Bixby manuscripts and is now reprinted in the *Collected Poems* 390.

(However, it should be noted that MS C includes two long new passages, if not a new poem such as "The Centaur.")

MS F: *Collected Poems* 134 ("Our Country") and 311 for textual variants. In MS F there are six new uncancelled lines.

One other group of poems should be mentioned. Among the items sold by an anonymous "New England Private Collector" at the Parke-Bernet Galleries on April 30, 1958, nine were described in the sales catalogue as manuscript poems by Thoreau. According to the catalogue eight of them were, in all probability, largely unpublished. Actually, "in all probability" seven of the eight were not. An analysis of the eight will be found in Carl Bode, "Thoreau's 'Unpublished' Poems," *Thoreau Society Bulletin*, 1959, #66. They are: "Life is a summer's day," "Inspiration," "The Freshet," "The Soul's Season," "Whether we've far withdrawn," "The Fall of the Leaf," another "The Fall of the Leaf," and "Cock-Crowing." The one poem, "Life is a summer's day," which had not been printed in great part has since been published in full and is reprinted in the *Collected Poems* 382.

To the poems not known to be found in this edition (*Collected Poems* 267) but mentioned in auction records should be added:

"The morning in our prime," autograph manuscript poem, complete (running to about 150 words), unpublished; dated July 2, 1837. Two pages, quarto. *American Book-Prices Current 1962*, 767. The first lines run as follows:

> The morning in our prime
> That laughs to scorn old Time
> and knows no crime. . .

Besides additions to the Thoreau canon, two subtractions should be made. Francis Allen, in "Thoreau's Collected Poems" (*American Literature*, XVII [1945], 260-267), established that "Carpe Diem" was not by Thoreau; and Kenneth Cameron, in "Four Uncollected Thoreau Poems, with Notes on the Canon" (*Emerson Society Quarterly*, 1956, 13), did likewise for the couplet "Therefore a current of sadness deep."

TEXTUAL AND EXPLANATORY
NOTES FOR ADDED POEMS

Additional source symbol: *MM*. For texts from Thoreau's manuscript Journal for July 30, 1840–January 22, 1841, now in the Morgan Library and printed in Perry Miller, *Consciousness in Concord* (1958).

381. "Fair Haven"

Heretofore unpublished except for the first stanza. References: manuscript from collection of George Davenport, Jr.; Wakeman catalogue, number 973. (Davenport dated at end "May 27, 1837.") Wakeman includes only lines 25-28 (Collected Poems 267).

"Fair Haven" was one of several poems received by Ellen Sewall from the Thoreau brothers. The Davenport copy of it is in John Thoreau's hand but the author is surely Henry. The original version, with its emendations, may well be the one described in the Wakeman catalogue. However, the date of composition given in the Wakeman catalogue, May 2, 1834, is suspiciously early. The date attached to the Davenport copy is probably the date of composition. It is not the date when Thoreau sent the verses, for he did not meet her till two years later.

The note of youthful ebullience this poem strikes is rare in Thoreau's verse; there is almost a sense of frolic here, perhaps because he was shortly to leave Harvard as a college graduate.

382. "Life is a summer's day"

References: manuscript from collection of Charles Feinberg; William White, "An Unpublished Thoreau Poem," American Literature, XXXIV (1962), 120-121. (At the end of manuscript "July 2d——37.") The title is pretty well erased in the manuscript; it was "Sic Vita" and in a private printing (1962) the Silverado Press so entitles it.   2 as it were for aye | in the month of May   *c*   14 swel'tring | such tiring *White's first reading, which he corrected*   28 bud | mud?; head?; herd? *White's conjectures*

400

The theme of this lyric is not so much "Sic Vita," as White suggests, as "Carpe Diem." That the poem, plainly derivative, is one of Thoreau's earliest is shown by internal as well as external evidence. The rhetoric is neo-classical, the tone sentimental-romantic. As White points out, the second stanza reminds us of Gray's "Elegy" and the last stanza borrows almost verbatim from the line in Milton's "Lycidas," "What time the gray-fly winds her sultry horn."

384. "I've heard my neighbor's pump at night"

References: MM (before July 30, 1840); Consciousness in Concord *(1958); 49W 44. 49W contains only lines 7-8, c in MM.*

These verses and the others from the Morgan Library which follow are all contained in a lost journal of Thoreau's which was acquired from a dealer in 1956 and published two years later in an elaborate edition by Perry Miller. This journal runs from July 30, 1840 to January 22, 1841, but there are several preliminary pages and "I've heard my neighbor's pump at night" is copied out on the final one of these. The term "copied out" is used advisedly because of the even tenor of the handwriting and the lack of emendations in the manuscript. (The only one is the insertion with caret of "else" after "Or.") The other poems likewise have the look of fair copies.

The verses are another reminder of Thoreau's preoccupation with sound and his nice ear for it.

385. "When with pale cheek and sunken eye I sang"

References: MM (Aug. 12, 1840); Consciousness in Concord *(1958). Entire poem c MM; stanzas are separated by horizontal lines MM.*

The heavy, regular measures and the ornate chivalric language betray the young Thoreau, who had not yet found his proper voice.

386. "I arose before light"

References: MM (Oct. 14, 1840); Consciousness in Concord *(1958); A. A includes only lines 9-10 and 7-8 in that order. Entire poem c MM.*

387. "I will obey the strictest law of love"

References: Manuscript Division, New York Public Library and transcript, Emerson Society Quarterly, 1956, 13-16. In printing these verses Kenneth Cameron sees them as not one poem but four and as-

401

signs a title of his own choosing to each ("Four Uncollected Thoreau Poems, with Notes on the Canon"). To the editor of the Collected Poems *the divisions are only stanza breaks and the verses as a group no less coherent than some of Thoreau's other longer efforts. In the printed version lines 1-12 are called by Cameron "The Law of Love," 13-20 "Spiritual Love," 21-28 "Response," and 29-42 "The Course of True Love." Apparently this is the same manuscript, with its two pages in reverse order, that was sold as "Though my friends are dull and cold I will be quick and warm"* (Collected Poems 267 and American Book-Prices Current, XXI [1915], 906). 7 will]may al for will; every day al for may 8 him]still p after him 13 all]one c 14 alway] always; s c 15 that]this c 18 I love]above c 34 the wounded heart]me c 36 For the heart's not less a vital than a mortal part]Its scars are on an honorable part al; and the heart written below scars are

Out of young Thoreau's workshop about 1840 these stanzas came, later perhaps to be improved and culled out. Though their subject is a favorite of his, the present poem is singled out by two things: its marked Platonism and its touch of Old Testament sternness.

389. "The Centaur"

References: Ridgley Library, Washington University; facsimile in Kenneth Cameron, "Thoreau's New Poems," Emerson Society Quarterly, 1959, 30, and transcript, Laurence Cummings, "Thoreau Poems in Bixby Washington-University Manuscripts," Emerson Society Quarterly, 1962, 17-18. In the facsimile lines 10-11 have the figure 1 and a vertical line opposite them on the left and lines 12-15 have the figure 2 and a bracket opposite them. This means that, according to Thoreau's practice elsewhere, these six lines are intended to come in the order now given in the Collected Poems. *The first order in the facsimile is, however, lines: 1-9, 12-15, 10-11. These c lines follow line 6:*

> Plants grow & rivers run.
> You neer may look upon the ocean waves
> At noon or even-tide but you may see
> Far in the horizon with expanded sail
> Some solitary bark stand out to sea,
> Farbound—Well so my life glides on ward still
> To double some far cape, not yet explored.
> A Cloud neer standeth in the summer's sky,

8 cleaving the silent air, Resteth him not]an instant in his flight c after not; cleaving the silent air, prefixed to Resteth 12 my]No more c

before my neer furls its weatherbeaten]doth[?] furls its ragged *c*
13 upon]within *c*   shore]port *c*   15 prow]plow *altered to* prow

If these verses are considered close to being finished, they represent
some of the most metaphysical of Thoreau's work. In three widely different images—the centaur, the eagle, and the ship—he suggests the
restlessness of our animal nature. The humane is still not united with the
inhuman in us, is still not in control. It is uncertain when "The Centaur"
was written, perhaps about 1840.

390. "Who hears the parson"

References: MM (Jan. 10, 1841); Consciousness in Concord (*1958*).
Lines 1-4 c in MM.

Thoreau remarks, just before he writes down the poem, "The church
bell is not a natural sound to the church goer." The lines that follow are
among the most pungent to be found in his poetry.

391. "Friends"

References: MM (Jan. —— 1841); Consciousness in Concord (*1958*).
Entire poem c in MM.

Here again is a fair copy of some verses Thoreau evidently worked
up earlier. The theme and general tone are reasonably unified; the
five-line stanza pattern holds throughout—except for the final stanza
as printed in *Consciousness in Concord*. It may well be that this
stanza actually constitutes a separate lyric. It is inscribed on a separate
page; its stanza is twice as long as the others; its tone is gentle, not
strained as it is in the previous stanzas; and its imagery is drawn from
nature, not from man's affairs as it is in the other stanzas. The horizontal line separating the last two five-line stanzas from the ones before may simply indicate that the two are a coda. In consideration of
these factors "When in some cove I lie" is printed below as a separate
lyric.

393. "When in some cove I lie"

References: MM (Jan. —— 1841); Consciousness in Concord (*1958*).

For the basis for believing this is a separate poem, rather than the
final stanza of "Friends," see the note above to that poem.

394. "Delay in Friendship"

Heretofore unpublished except for the first and last stanzas. References: XX; Wakeman catalogue, number 977; 49W 285. (XX dated at end "Concord 1841.") Wakeman includes only lines 1-4 (Collected Poems 268); 49 W includes only lines 26-29 (Collected Poems 23). 3 ,]o *Wakeman* 9 stay]wait *c* 12 So]So for want; for want *c* 18 Now]When *c* 26 slow]slow, *49W* 27 & low—]and low, *49W* 28 —], *49W*

Deeply concerned with what he means to others and others to him, Thoreau in these rough stanzas further explains his kind of friendship. Elsewhere he has announced that it must be high-minded, hard, austere; here he maintains that it must be slow-ripening.

396. "To Edith"

References: facsimile (from H) and transcript, Kenneth Cameron, "A New Thoreau Poem—To Edith," Emerson Society Quarterly, 1960, 40-41.

Edith Emerson was born on November 22, 1841. She obviously captivated Thoreau, who lived in her father's house during her first seventeen months. "To Edith," Wordsworthian in both tone and style, was doubtless composed during this time. Emerson made a copy, now in Harvard's Houghton Library, which Kenneth Cameron published in the *Emerson Society Quarterly* ("A New Thoreau Poem—To Edith"). There is a reference to it in a letter from Emerson to Thoreau (December 2, 1847), mentioning "Edith who long ago drew from you verses which I carefully preserve."

397. "The Rosa Sanguinea"

Heretofore unpublished. Reference: B (after Dec. 2, 18——). Beneath the title Thoreau has written in parentheses "which opened Dec. 2nd." 3 Nature]wise men *c* 4 Informs us]Can tell you *c*

This quatrain was found by Professor Walter Harding among the manuscript leaves of Thoreau's "Notes on Fruits" and is in Thoreau's hand. Guided by the handwriting, Professor Harding suggests that the date of composition is the mid-1850's.

404

INDEX OF TITLES AND FIRST LINES

Titles are given in roman; lifted first lines when used as titles are italicized and set within quotation marks; first lines are given in quotation marks.*

---

* Since the titles (Thoreau's or otherwise) of variant versions are also listed in this index, each variant title is ascribed to the first page of its related basic text. Thus, the title "Winter Memories" was given, in *Poems of Nature*, to one version of "Within the circuit of this plodding life"; and a reader looking for the poem "Winter Memories" and referred here to p. 3 will find on that page Thoreau's final version of the poem in the form of "Within the circuit of this plodding life"—even though he will not find the title "Winter Memories" there. (In the Critical Edition, however, all titled and untitled variant versions are recorded in the textual notes.)

408

410

412

413